THE VIEW FROM THE BRIDGE

THE VIEW
FROM
THE BRIDGE

Memories of STAR TREK
and a Life in Hollywood

NICHOLAS MEYER

VIKING

VIKING
Published by the Penguin Group
Penguin Group (USA) Inc., 375 Hudson Street,
New York, New York 10014, U.S.A.
Penguin Group (Canada), 90 Eglinton Avenue East, Suite 700,
Toronto, Ontario, Canada M4P 2Y3
(a division of Pearson Penguin Canada Inc.)
Penguin Books Ltd, 80 Strand, London WC2R 0RL, England
Penguin Ireland, 25 St. Stephen's Green, Dublin 2, Ireland
(a division of Penguin Books Ltd)
Penguin Books Australia Ltd, 250 Camberwell Road, Camberwell,
Victoria 3124, Australia
(a division of Pearson Australia Group Pty Ltd)
Penguin Books India Pvt Ltd, 11 Community Centre, Panchsheel Park,
New Delhi – 110 017, India
Penguin Group (NZ), 67 Apollo Drive, Rosedale, North Shore 0632,
New Zealand (a division of Pearson New Zealand Ltd)
Penguin Books (South Africa) (Pty) Ltd, 24 Sturdee Avenue,
Rosebank, Johannesburg 2196, South Africa

Penguin Books Ltd, Registered Offices:
80 Strand, London WC2R 0RL, England

First published in 2009 by Viking Penguin,
a member of Penguin Group (USA) Inc.

1 3 5 7 9 10 8 6 4 2

Photograph credits
*Star Trek: The Motion Picture; Star Trek II: The Wrath of Khan; Star Trek VI: The Undiscovered
Country*: Courtesy of Paramount Pictures. © Paramount Pictures. All rights reserved.
Time After Time: © Warner Bros. Inc. and Orion Picture Company. All rights reserved.
The Seven-Per-Cent Solution: Courtesy of Universal Studios Licensing LLLP. © 1976 Universal City
Studios, Inc.
The Deceivers: Courtesy of Merchant Ivory Productions.
Newsweek cover: Issue of November 21, 1983. © 1983 Newsweek, Inc. All rights reserved.
Courtesy of Newsweek, Inc. and the photographer, Steven-Charles Jaffe.
All other photographs from the collection of the author.

ISBN 978-0-670-02130-7

Printed in the United States of America
Set in ITC Garamond
Designed by Alissa Amell

*Penguin is committed to publishing works of quality and integrity. In that spirit, we are proud to
offer this book to our readers; however, the story, the experiences, and the words are the author's
alone.*

For Stephanie & Roxanne
With Love

AUTHOR´S NOTE

Trial lawyers will tell you that the least reliable witnesses are eyewitnesses. I had difficulty grasping this idea until I saw Akira Kurosawa's film *Rashomon*, which succeeded in persuading me of the evanescent nature of Truth.

Truth—like Beauty—appears to lie in the eye of the beholder.

In writing this book, I have primarily used my memory, with some ancillary research to remind me of certain events and dates, but what follows must surely be taken as an eyewitness account.

In the interest of treading that fine line between tact and truth, some names have been changed.

So here goes my memoir. As the title suggests, it is about my experiences in Hollywood, making and trying to make movies, with a special emphasis on my encounters with the phenomenon known as *Star Trek*. Over the years, I've been asked a lot of questions about the *Star Trek* movies with which I was involved. Sometimes I feel like those guys in noir movies being grilled under the glaring light of a lone gooseneck lamp, while interlocutors hover in the shadows: "All right, let's go over it again" . . . "But I've told you—I've told you a thousand times, told you everything I know!" I wail. "I told you on the DVD! I told you on the Special Edition! I've told you on Blu-ray!" "Tell us again," they insist. The temptation at such times is to embroider, for my sake if not for theirs. To vary the facts as I recall them, throw them a bone, start imagining things instead of remembering them. I will try my best to resist such temptations here.

But this book isn't just about *Star Trek*. I've taught classes in screenwriting and I've found myself reflecting on the unique perspective my background

afforded me as a stranger in a strange land and the adventures I've had trying to make the movies I wanted to watch. When I started out heading for
California to make movies, what I was doing was considered unusual. At best.
There weren't film courses being offered in high schools back then and only a
few were starting to be available in universities. Nowadays my children *study*
Italian neorealism and American film noir; when I was sixteen, I played hooky
watching the stuff on Broadway and 88th Street or caught it on late-night
television.

Everybody got their popcorn?

PART 1

PRE *TREK*

PROLOGUE

A FUNERAL

It was December of 1982 and Verna Fields was dead. The woman known as Mother Cutter, editor of *Jaws*, had died, aged sixty-four, of cancer and a memorial service was being held at the Alfred Hitchcock Theater at Universal Studios. I had known Verna socially and like many other young directors, I had benefitted from her counsel, support, and advice. She would take me to lunch and afterward treat me to an expensive cigar from the humidor of a nearby tobacconist. "Verna," I would protest, "how are you paying for this?" She'd grin merrily behind large glasses. "I'm wooing you, baby, I'm wooing you." She was a brilliant editor so of course after *Jaws* they'd made her an executive and stuck her behind a desk, which you might say was like promoting Captain James T. Kirk to Admiral. What a waste.

Anyway, there we all were, crammed into the intimate Hitchcock Theater, listening to Ned Tanen, head of Universal and a devoted friend of Verna's, deliver the eulogy. Tanen, who had a mercurial temperament and was as prickly as the cacti that he loved to grow, opined that Verna Fields had been the only decent human being in this dirty, rotten stinking town—or words to that effect. The thing about funerals, I find as a rule, is that you don't listen to such speeches critically. People say some outlandish or exaggerated things, carried along in the currents of emotion and the moment, so I don't suppose I blinked at Ned's impassioned words. I just sat there and felt sad thoughts.

It was only later, standing alone outside the theater, surrounded by people chatting together in little knots while waiting to leave for cold cuts at Verna's house, that I became aware of someone else speaking. If this were a film and we were mixing this scene, the voice that impinged on my idling consciousness would be dialed up slowly and would go something like this:

3

". . . biggest crock of shit I ever heard in my life—mind you: I take a backseat to no man where my affection for Verna Fields is concerned but I don't think I would have lasted thirty years in this business if I hadn't found it to be populated by some of the kindest, most loyal, generous, talented, and loving people I could ever hope to meet in this or any other lifetime."

It was as if someone had thrown cold water on my face. The speaker, when I turned to look, was Walter Mirisch, a producer whose list of great movies is probably as long as George W. Bush's war crimes.

Yes, I thought, decisively. This is true. I hadn't been in the business anything like thirty years—it was more like ten—but since my arrival in Los Angeles, a stranger in a very strange land, I had met with as much kindness, generosity, and support as I had found anywhere else. Maybe more. Me and Blanche DuBois.

EARLY DAYS

And in those ten years I had certainly needed (and continue to need) all the help I could get. One group I came to envy as I got to know them were children of those already in the business. Not that all of them were happy or even prospered, but like medieval stonemasons or shipwrights, they seemed to be part of a familial continuity that I didn't possess. There was Steven-Charles Jaffe, for instance, who with his father, Herb, produced the first film I wrote and directed, *Time After Time*. I envied father and son their professional bond. Herb told me, "I am a lucky man; I get to see my son every day." I had no such family anchor in Los Angeles. For years I was always conscious of being on my own in California, the boy who had run away to join the circus that was movies. Nobody from the world in which I grew up was in "show business." The children of my parents' friends followed their footsteps and became doctors or lawyers or went into "business" (whatever that was); I was the only one I knew who wanted to go to Hollywood and make movies. I must have set the fashion, for later everyone did. I don't think movies at that time were even regarded as a profession. The famous stars and directors hadn't studied to become filmmakers; they had sort of fallen into it. Second unit directors had begun as cowboys. Some were in fact Indians.

In the years to come I would meet and become friends with many people in the business whose fathers or mothers had been in it before them. This conferred a kind of tradition on the whole enterprise, or at least to my way of thinking a legitimacy that I sorely lacked and missed. My own family never quite understood what it was that I was doing or attempting to do, even though it was tacitly acknowledged that I wasn't fit for much else. My father always was an astute and subtle critic of anything I wrote, a wonderful editor, but there his involvement ceased. In the years that followed, no matter how successful I became, or even how proud they were of my success, my parents never made it their business to master the nomenclature or glossary of terms that would have enabled them to better understand what I had to tell them about my life.

"Mom, I'm in preproduction."

"Uh huh. What's that?"

And so on.

I was born in Manhattan on Christmas Eve, just after the end of the war. My parents were a rather glamorous pair, a handsome psychoanalyst and his concert pianist wife, and postwar New York, if you were cut of such cloth, was definitely the place to be. I wasn't named Nicholas because of any religious association—my parents were in fact third-generation nonpracticing Jews—but rather in honor of my maternal grandfather, a Russian violinist in the Boston Symphony Orchestra. And when I say, "nonpracticing," I am understating. Neither my father nor I was bar mitzvahed. I never attended temple or religious school and never had the inclination. I was born without the religion gene. I was raised in an atmosphere of undoubted privilege and culture, fell in love with Mozart by age five, and thought Jews were people who read books with hard covers. My father was witty and also an excellent pianist. Once I heard him accompany Leontyne Price in the living room of our brownstone (shrewdly purchased east of yet-to-be gentrified "Thoid" Avenue, which then still had its elevated subway line); another time, in Princeton, after a filling Thanksgiving dinner, he did the same for Einstein, who soloed on a squeaky violin. (Sitting next to the great man at dinner, I complained I had a hair in my turkey. "Not so loud," he counseled me, "everyone else will want one.") Were we rich? I once asked my father. "We're comfortable," he explained, which was precise. Rockefellers we were not, but my father earned what he needed to live in what he might have characterized as a civilized fashion. My father, like his father, thought of himself as a liberal in the Jeffersonian tradition. He twice supported the candidacy of Adlai Stevenson. Years later, in my autobiographical novel, *Confessions of a Homing Pigeon*, I depicted my parents as circus acrobats, performing without a net, which is how they must have appeared to me.

I happily absorbed everything that was thrown at me—theater, music, books—until it was time to go to school. It was there that my difficulties commenced. Today, I would've been diagnosed with some form of ADD, but at the time there seemed merely a mysterious disconnect between an evident intellectual capacity and an ability to translate it into any sort of academic prowess. I had difficulty focusing on anything in which I was not passionately interested. This certainly included math, where the numbers went all fuzzy and refused to stay steady in my head while I tried to add them, but also other issues and subjects that required concentration, organization, or the citing of specific examples to illustrate my point. I could read for hours and did—but only the books that I wanted to read. I loved building model boats and could likewise spend hours at a time on them. Talk about concentration. I was crazy about plays, opera, ballet, art, dinosaurs, movies, and musicals—all of which you could trip over in New York—but my eyes would glaze over when the teachers started to talk. It's not that they were bad teachers, either; I went to a very sophisticated school. They were very good teachers; I was just a very bad pupil. I couldn't keep up. My mind wandered into narratives, some of my own invention, others culled from Jules Verne, Dumas, Arthur Conan Doyle, the Hardy Boys, the Lone Ranger, Rodgers and Hammerstein. I repeated fourth grade, which didn't do wonders for my self-esteem.

Occasionally, I was taken to places or events where my parents thought a necktie was de rigueur. This article of apparel I loathed at first sight, and many red-faced struggles were involved in slamming me into it. I sometimes think I longed to make movies because I was sure you didn't need to wear a necktie. (In fact, old photos of many directors at work reveal them to be wearing neckties, so perhaps the dispensing of neckwear was more a generational transition—my time had, simply, come.)

When I was about ten, my mother was diagnosed with ovarian cancer, though this dreadful fact was kept from both of us by my father. She was told, instead, that she had a cyst removed. My father edited a volume of essays by doctors entitled *Should the Patient Know the Truth?* He contributed an essay of his own to the collection, in which he asked, "What Patient, What Truth?" pointing out that how and what is communicated to the terminally ill patient may ease or increase his distress and ability to cope with his fate. He used the (unidentified) example of my mother, in which, encouraged by her cyst diagnosis, she did not die within the predicted three months but instead lived almost three *years* before succumbing (hideously) at age forty-five. I was in the room with her when she drew her last, gasping breath at around ten in the evening. In trying to prepare me for this moment, my father had explained some months earlier what was going on and said he would need me to be strong. I interpreted this—wrongly, I now suspect—to mean that I must not cry. And so I didn't. I told myself, as I listened to her rasping breaths in the low-lit room, surrounded by sorrowful relatives, that I must remember everything that happened, so one day I could write about it. The result, I think, was not a fortunate one, for in that moment of decision, I converted myself from a participant to an observer. When she was dead—the rasping abruptly ceased—I reached out and placed my hand on my mother so that I would know what it was like to touch a dead person. (It was like touching a dead person.) I did indeed remember everything, though, interestingly, I never did write about it.

Years of psychotherapy followed, paralleling my high school years. My grades were never cause for congratulation, though I gradually attained my own cachet. By the time I was a senior and all that peer conformity had begun to wear off, one or two girls actually began to take an interest in me. If high school had gone on another year, I would have ruled.

My mother and I were never particularly close—I don't think she ever quite knew what to make of me, especially since, while I was crazy about music (where my knowledge was becoming encyclopedic), it was clear that, with my numerical dyslexia, I would never become a musician. But my father and I had much in common. True, I exasperated him with my forgetfulness and academic failures—he was a Harvard man, class of '32—but we loved music and movies and books together. We were dedicated Marxists. He preferred *A Night at the Opera* but I knew *Duck Soup* was funnier. When I was twelve he took me to see the Mike Todd movie of *Around the World in Eighty Days*, and I had my first religious experience. I had always loved movies, even other Jules Verne movies (I was nuts for the Disney *20,000 Leagues Under the Sea*—still am), but this was different. The theater lobby sold a souvenir program book, which I still have, in which can be found an article titled: YOU TOO CAN MAKE A MOTION PICTURE—NO PREVIOUS EXPERIENCE NECESSARY. Rereading the article now, I recognize that it was a sort of sarcastic piece, intended to trumpet the staggering statistics behind Todd's production. All you need is six million dollars and 68,000 people in fourteen different countries . . . etc. But the sarcasm at the time was lost on me.

YOU TOO CAN MAKE A MOTION PICTURE—NO PREVIOUS EXPERIENCE NECESSARY. I showed the article to my dad and told him I wanted to make a movie. As it happened, we had an 8mm wind-up Revere camera that my father used for our home movies. I wanted him to help me make my own film of—what else?—*Around the World in Eighty Days*. I would write the script and play Phileas Fogg, of course; my best friend, Ron Roose, son of a psychoanalyst colleague of my father and oddly born on the same day as me, would play the loyal valet, Passepartout, etc.

I am not sure why my father fell in with this plan. It is certainly true that he was an artist manqué himself, who would later publish two splendid full-length biographies (one of Joseph Conrad, the other of Houdini), and something of my scheme must have stirred promptings he had long ignored. Ultimately, the film took five years to make. It was shot on weekends and over Christmas, Easter, and summer vacations and involved my father driving a host of hyperkinetic kids in costume to various locations—Central Park, Cape Cod, Cowboy City, New Jersey—and somehow pulling the thing together. He told me he would lie awake at night devising shots and silly bits of business, clearly enjoying himself. We shot out of sequence, of course, like a real film, compelled by necessity, so that the cast aged and shrank as we assembled the scenes. I edited the film with my cousin Bob on our kitchen table. The result was an eighty-minute masterpiece that seemed to charm everyone who saw it. Now matter how hard I fought with my father throughout my fraught adolescence, work on the film went on, and I think it held us together as well as setting my feet on the path they would follow for the rest of my life.

My movie schooling was completed when my father remarried. Leonore brought few material possessions with her when she moved into our house, but one of them was choice, and I got custody of it: a large Zenith (black and white, of course) TV found its way into my room. Any chance of academic advancement went right out the window with this part of my stepmother's "dowry." In those far-off times, television stations ran endless late-night movies from all eras, and I sat and watched every one of them, staying up till all hours and learning about . . . what? Damned if I know. Having a good time. Escaping. Memorizing the names of the actors, the cameramen, the composers and directors, whoever they were. With my memory and capacity to absorb what interested me, I shortly became an autodidact of this arcane world. Who cared? Nobody except me.

I could probably write a(nother) book entitled *Everything I Know I Learned from the Movies.* (Or *Everything I Know I Learned from the Backs of Record Jackets.*) Unlikely as it may seem, I was one of those people who actually derived knowledge from the *content* of movies. I did the same thing with comic books. There used to be something called *Classics Illustrated,* a series that was more or less what its name implied, comic book versions of every great book you ever heard of. The optimistic idea of whoever was behind the project was self-evident: if you liked the comic, try going on to read the book, which was exactly what I did every time. To this day—for better or worse— many of the original illustrations in those comics still inform my visualization of *Moby-Dick* or *A Tale of Two Cities.*

IOWA

In the summer of 1964, following my surprising graduation from high school, I sailed to Europe on the *Queen Mary* and backpacked all over the place, alone, as usual. In the fall, I entered the University of Iowa, which may seem a strange choice for a Jew(ish) New Yorker, but with my academic record the possibilities were not limitless. Harvard was not holding its breath and Iowa did boast the Writers' Workshop, the foremost place in the world to study guess what. I did meet New Yorkers in Iowa who didn't care for the place, thought it too remote, too provincial, were put off by the food, etc., but I was not among them.

Iowa was my chance to start over, and I did well there, almost from the beginning. I wasn't always or particularly a great student, but I did find a niche for myself, friends, and a measure of success. In the theater and film departments I met other people who were like me, and, as no one knew of my previous existence, I was approached with no particular prejudice. Since I had few preconceived ideas of my own, I was a blank slate on which there was room to write a great deal.

I don't think I'd been in Iowa City a month when a vacancy for a film reviewer occurred at the *Daily Iowan,* the school paper, and I landed the job. The paper didn't care about such things as film criticism, being preoccupied with sports, student politics, and the war in Vietnam (wherever that was), but I viewed the position as nothing less than a heaven-sent opportunity. I seized hold of that post in an iron grip and never let it go—for the next four years. Before my arrival, reviewers covered one or two movies before irate letters to the editor drove them figuratively out of town. With a thicker skin and a surprising instinct for the long-term possibilities of the post, I stuck it out and gradually the hostility dissipated. In four years I wrote four hundred reviews—averaging three a week—and had what was said to be the most popular column in the Big Ten newspapers. I remained in Iowa City even during the summers for fear of forfeiting the position. It was the beginning of the making of me. I got to air my opinions about film or anything else that was suggested to me by what I was watching. I experimented with my own aesthetic theories and enunciated my philosophical musings as they seemed relevant to whatever Paramount was releasing that week. I had a bully pulpit, and for once there was an audience ready to listen to what I had to say. They didn't always agree, but they got used to the idea of me.

I don't know if this is true for anyone else, but I can dissect my life in terms of conscious and unconscious goals. I seem to have had one of each. My conscious goal was to be an actor, an occupation that made a kind of inevitable sense, given my fragmented identity, lack of self-esteem, and other random personality disorders. If I can't be the King, let me play the King. Writing, on the other hand, was just something I always did; it never occurred to me to become a writer or that a writer was what I wished to become. Without actually denigrating my gifts in that direction (this would come later), I never gave them much thought.

Writing must therefore have been my unconscious goal; later, directing proved to be a bit of both. For starters, until I became an actor, I don't think I actually knew what a director did. It wasn't until I heard one shouting at me while he was comfortably nursing a cup of coffee in one of the orchestra seats that it occurred to me I was in the wrong line of work. Directors got to watch and criticize. And they were brought the coffee. More seriously, I think I had trouble acting because I thought I knew—more than the director—how scenes should be played.

I had a new career goal.

I wrote my first full-length screenplay at Iowa. I had read and been knocked out by a Jack Finney novel called *Assault on a Queen*. It was about a scheme to hijack the *Queen Mary*, of all things, and I was riveted from first page to last. What an amazing film this would make! I didn't have the rights, of course, but this never troubled me, as I knew my script would never be bought or filmed—it was simply the experience, the exercise, and the challenge of adapting the book, which, to my way of thinking, was absurdly simple. I didn't know anything about the format of screenplays (far fewer were published then than now), but I started with page 1 of Finney's novel, boiled it down into what I thought it should read like as a screenplay, and then went on to page 2, and so forth through the entire book. The result, I decided, was not bad. I telescoped here and there, tightened the dialogue a lot, and dispensed with a character or two, but I faithfully followed Finney's ingenious plot and preserved, it seemed to me, the narrative excitement of the book, albeit my Smith Corona had a lot of Wite-Out clinging to the keys by the time it was finished.

Two years later I found myself reviewing Hollywood's version of *Assault on a Queen*, which starred Frank Sinatra and Virna Lisi and had a screenplay credited to Rod Serling.

Everyone agreed it was about the worst film of the year. I sat in the theater, stunned by what seemed to me to be the arbitrary and utterly perverse departures from the novel that the film had made. I was unable to account for why the filmmakers (I had never heard of the director) had taken a perfectly serviceable, not to say ingenious plot and made it all-over dumb. I never did find out for sure but I feel fairly certain that Mr. Sinatra had a lot of ideas that wouldn't go away—unless he did. The six-hundred-pound gorilla sleeps where he wants.

The last thing worth mentioning in this brief account of my Iowa years was my first, glancing encounter with *Star Trek*. I had made friends with two New Yorkers from the Bronx, a husband and wife, both in graduate school. She was in the workshop and he was getting a PhD in American Indian studies. He was, among other things, a terrific pianist and also addicted to the *Star Trek* television series, then being broadcast daily in Iowa City. My friend watched *Star Trek* daily, for fifty-four days, at the end of which time his wife left him. A couple of times I tried to watch along with him. For whatever reason, *Star Trek* flew by me at Warp Speed. I think there is something "earthbound" in my temperament, a kind of flat-footed literalness that made me concentrate on the cheesy sets and silly costumes—to say nothing of the pointy ears—a lack of sympathetic imagination, if you will, the absence of which might have allowed me to dispense with all that literalness and open myself to what was going on underneath all that cardboard.

PARAMOUNT PICTURES

Following Iowa, I faced the the choice of heading east or west to continue my life, and I chose to go back to New York. I had never heard anything good about Los Angeles and knew no one there, so my hometown seemed a more sensible possibility.

I landed a job in the publicity department of Paramount Pictures, then located in picturesque Times Square, i.e., before its Disneyfication, when you had to run the gantlet of unhappy-looking ladies on your way to work. (They were already *at* work.) I didn't actually know what a publicist did but that seemed beside the point; it was a job and it was vaguely connected with the movie business. I had joined the circus at last. Sort of.

The old Paramount Pictures building was a massive stone affair with gorgeous elevators whose gold-paneled doors were crafted in some eerie echo of Ghiberti's *Gates of Paradise* in Florence. There's plenty of irony in Hollywood, but no one ever gets it—which is also ironic, I guess. The older I become, the more I decide that irony is generally a cheap shot, anyway.

In any event, those gorgeous doors didn't open onto Paradise, or anything like it, not if you hit the eleventh-floor button. They opened onto something called the Snake Pit, a huge area with a two-story ceiling subdivided at the floor level by translucent cubicle walls with little desks within each cubicle. There were no windows anywhere and the lighting was atrocious. Why this dismal arrangement should have gained the name Snake Pit I am at a loss to explain, but somehow it fit.

It was here that the publicity department toiled away, doing—what? With my limited powers of observation and even more limited gifts of analysis, it was almost impossible for me to figure out. I knew what my job was (sort of), and I knew my boss.

His name was Bill Schwartz and he kept a pencil over one ear, the tip jutting past his right eye as though it was a permanent feature of his physiognomy. He was cynical but not bitter, or perhaps it was the other way around, but this certainly was not the life he'd planned as a graduate of CCNY. He was a decent man, highly intelligent, and he wrote novels that didn't get published.

On the other hand, he did know how to write a simple declarative sentence, a skill that I had apparently failed to master during four years at the University of Iowa.

My job was a curious one. It was to write "press kits" for each Paramount film, these "kits" to contain a synopsis of the film's plot (in case the viewer couldn't follow it?—actually I discovered this failure was far from uncommon), production "notes," assorted biographies of the stars, writer, director, producer, etc., plus various "human interest" articles, anecdotal items regarding alleged incidents that took place during the production that newspapers might use for column fillers. (These fillers were always lies and were interchangeable: simply substitute the title of the film you wished to promote and keep the anecdote as is. The one that sticks in my mind dealt with a pesky tourist, who insisted on photographing the actors on the set of movie "X"—change title here, ad lib—until an assistant director explained that his color shots would be useless, as this was a black and white picture. Great, huh?)

Actually, writing "press kits" was not my job. In fact, these "kits" had already been written in Hollywood (a place somewhere to the left of me as I faced the Harlem River), but they had been composed in "Hollywoodese," a separate argot, untranslatable to the layman. If you don't believe me, try reading *Variety* sometime and see if you can understand what they are talking about.

My job was essentially that of translator, taking the Hollywoodese version of the press kit and rendering it into normal English. I would take phrases like "The Walter Matthau–Jack Lemmon starrer" and reconfigure it as "The film, which stars Walter Matthau and Jack Lemmon . . ." and so on. There was little room for improvisation, either. Billing was always in contractual order and repeated ad nauseam. When the film's title changed, every piece of paper in the kit had to be retyped and rephotocopied. This was before the days of computers, and we chopped down an awful lot of trees for no good reason. One film—a picture that actually interested me—started out being called *Fräulein Doktor*. Then someone somewhere decided it should be called *Betrayal*. Then they decided to call it *The Betrayal*. Then they called it something else and then they went back to *Fräulein Doktor*. It did no business under any of these titles but we had to change the press kits no one was interested in every time.

One would have thought I could do this stuff with my eyes closed. Hadn't I written those four hundred film reviews, hadn't my column been judged (where I can't remember) the most popular in the Big Ten newspapers? Wasn't I then and therefore about to be a Big Asset to Paramount Pictures?

But my inflated sense of brain got the better of me, as did my stash of cinematic lore and my sense of mission, the certainty that I was about to change forever this mundane job into something that every newspaper editor from here to Omaha would cherish when our press kits crossed his desk.

After I had finished a piece I'd turn it into Bill for his okay. I can still remember the blank astonishment with which I viewed my copy when he first returned it to me. The text, so erudite and witty, so knowledgeable and insightful, was scored all over with heavy black pencil. Where had all my scintillation gone? All the adjectives, adverbs, fun or arcane phrases had bit the dust. There was virtually nothing left.

When I had the temerity to protest this butchery, I was told bluntly, "Look, this isn't film school. Just write a simple declarative sentence, why can't you, and stick to *The New York Times* copy style book."

It was months before I learned how to do this. I am not a fast learner, but I do learn thoroughly, if anyone is still speaking to me by the time the process is concluded.

During this period, Paramount made a number of terrific films, all of them for about two million dollars each. Lindsay Anderson's *If. . . .*, Franco Zeffirelli's version of *Romeo and Juliet*, Haskell Wexler's *Medium Cool*, Richard Attenborough's *Oh! What a Lovely War*, and Larry Peerce's *Goodbye, Columbus* were among them. They were good films or interesting or intelligent and it was fun to work on them. It is hard to imagine a studio making such a varied and ambitious slate of films today when each movie has the budget of a small country.

In my spare time I continued trying to write screenplays and using the Paramount photocopying facilities to assist me.

"Remember," Schwartz would intone, solemnly tapping me on the shoulder when he passed my desk and caught me at it. "Everything you do here belongs to Paramount." I never caught him working on any of his novels, although he had a door to his office, whereas I didn't even have a cubicle but sat in the center of the Snake Pit, my life exposed for all to see.

The Paramount staff were an interesting crew and included old Adolph Zukor himself, the founder of Paramount Pictures, who, at one hundred years of age, was still shuffling along the corridors of the eleventh floor in short white shirtsleeves, carrying bundles of paper that no one but he knew anything about. One intuited the old man must have been a tiger, but now his comings and goings were ignored, or at best viewed with a patronizing tolerance by the young wheeler-dealers who rushed past him in the halls.

"Good morning, Mr. Zukor," Charlie Bluhdorn would say, without pausing for an answer, which was just as well because Zukor turned to me, who happened to be walking next to him at the time and asked who that man was. I told him I didn't know.

One of the folks in our department creatively suggested in a meeting that we have Otto Preminger slugged at Kennedy Airport when he got off the plane by way of promoting his latest turkey, something called *Skidoo*.

That was one of his better ideas, but it made my eyes pop.

Another trick we had was getting books Paramount owned onto the best-seller lists. In those good old days all the people who worked in the building were presented with fifty dollars cash to take with them to various bookstores on their lunch hour. We were to purchase ten copies each of *The Godfather*, or whatever else we were pushing that week, at these emporia. As to what we did with the books themselves, that was our business. Chuck 'em in the garbage, if we wanted. (Paramount was not unique in this activity; later, working at Warner Brothers, I can recall everyone being sent out to purchase copies of *Summer of '42*, with similar results.)

Nowadays, of course, such a dreadful piece of manipulation could never occur.

We had our own Sammy Glick too, a kid from Fordham with insane blue eyes that looked at you but saw something else. He had spent some time in a monastery, and I knew for a certainty he was off his chump. In the Snake Pit it was passed off as Ambition and therefore regarded as harmless.

There was also Winifred Gibbons, the office beauty, an English girl a year or three older than myself with a delicious Oxbridge accent and a lot of jewelry that jangled teasingly whenever she moved. She specialized in organizing our society and charity benefits and was, as you might expect, hotly pursued by a lot of high-powered executives, none of whom ever entered the Snake Pit, but one of them sent her a *dozen roses every day*. I was crazy about her.

There was even a novel about the Snake Pit that was circulated surreptitiously among new inmates. Called *The Wall-to-Wall Trap*, the book fascinated me as the nightmare of all I hoped to avoid and feared I wouldn't. Bill Schwartz pressed a battered copy into my hands with something like glee. I can't say I remember it well, but I seem to recall that it featured a protagonist who wants to write novels, or otherwise distinguish himself, and who winds up instead toiling forever in the Snake Pit, where conditions described in the book spookily paralleled my own (even to the screenplay the hero attempted to work on between times). The cast of characters might have different names or genders, but they were strikingly similar to those around me.

Once in a while a filmmaker in town to promote his movie (we learned never to call them movies, they were always *films* or *motion pictures*) might wander into the Snake Pit by accident, looking for an office in the real world. It might be Martin Ritt or Richard Attenborough or Robert Redford or who knows? My heart would start jumping out of my chest, and I'd be on my way to buttonhole the poor guy with a display of my cinematic erudition when Schwartz would nab me by the collar of my jacket.

"Back to the salt mines, kid."

And I'd watch whoever it was being gently led away, his head twisting back on his neck in surprise, likely as not, getting one last glimpse of our particular circle of Hell.

It began to seem I was destined never to escape that circle except at night when it was time to go home. Home was now a one-room apartment, three flights up, that I had rented at 88th Street and Second Avenue.

Next door to my building was a restaurant called Elaine's. I had no idea of the place's reputation and all unaware went in one night to have a beer. Meet the Invisible Man. After five minutes, even *I* understood. In the midst of Marlon Brando, Woody Allen, and Jackie Kennedy, all of whom happened to be there that evening, they simply weren't about to take my order. I slunk out and climbed my three flights back to *la vie de bohème*.

At home at night, still within earshot of the demi- and haute mondes at Elaine's below, I'd peck away at my screenwriting efforts. The first script I wrote was a life of Heinrich Schliemann, the amateur archeologist who discovered Troy. The world was obviously waiting for this one with bated breath. If I'd been working at Warner Brothers in the late thirties they would have made the picture, no question. Paul Muni would've played Schliemann.

Next.

BABY STEPS

My father had recently introduced me to an essay in a psychoanalytic journal, written by a fellow shrink, Philip Weissman, on why John Wilkes Booth had shot Lincoln. The piece intrigued me, and with Weissman's permission, I set about dramatizing its thesis, namely that the real target of Booth's rage was not the president but Booth's own brother, the highly successful tragedian Edwin Booth. I produced my best piece of work to date, a thriller that informed at the same time as it entertained, a combination that was to become my specialty— also, on occasion, my curse. The structure of the piece was what made it work: I juxtaposed an hour-by-hour account of Booth's movements on the day of the assassination with flashbacks to earlier portions of his life, thereby suggesting psychological connections of which Booth himself was not consciously aware but which seemed to explain the true motives behind each of his actions on the fatal day. I called my movie *The Understudy*.

We never really understand—at least I don't—the progressions we make in life, why one thing leads to something else. About the time I was convinced I was going absolutely nowhere, I managed to escape the Snake Pit by getting Paramount to assign me the role of unit publicist on another of their small movies, this one called *Love Story*, to be shot in Boston and Long Island. A unit publicist is the guy who writes the original press kit and captions the photos taken on location—the stuff that I had previously been hired to translate into English. I leapt at the chance to go on location (a) because it got me out of the Snake Pit and (b) because I could get to watch a movie actually being shot. The director, Arthur Hiller, was extremely encouraging and open and at the conclusion of filming, the producer, Howard Minsky, optioned *The Understudy*. This left me with the vexing question of whether

I should or should not wear my glasses when I appeared on *The Johnny Carson Show*.

These grandiose fantasies died with the option expiration date on my script and in 1971 I took another job, this one in the story department at Warner Brothers, where I discovered that I could synopsize any narrative, including *War & Peace*, in two pages. I also read enough dreck to encourage myself; I had to be better than 90 percent of what I was being asked to read. (Later, I would have occasion to wonder if dreck wasn't exactly what they were looking for. An executive returned a positive reader's report I had submitted on a serious novel with the note, "Nick, did you see what was number one this week? *The Love Bug*!" I.e., Get With the Program.)

But I was starting to realize I couldn't keep this up forever. Yes, I had had a script optioned and even acquired an agent; yes, I had watched a film being shot and learned a good deal about the process; yes, I had figured out my stuff was as good, if not better, than the junk I was reading for Warner—but it all wasn't adding up to anything. I may not have been treading water this whole time but I didn't seem to be getting any nearer shore, either.

My poor agent, Janet Roberts, still couldn't get me arrested. She'd given up, in fact, which I learned in the usual way of agencies: I found myself assigned a new agent, who cared for me about as much as I do for anchovies.

It was problematic—no, embarrassing—when people asked what I did for a living. How could I tell them I was a writer? I wasn't a writer; I was a reader. To call myself a writer, I had to write something that sold.

What the hell could I write that would sell? Not screenplays; not yet, anyway. Not novels, either, obviously; each one of mine was more dreadful than the last.

What books were selling these days?

Nonfiction.

What the hell could I write that was nonfiction?

The answer was staring me in the face. I was six months late with the idea, but it was the only nonfiction subject I knew about firsthand that might find an audience.

I sat down and wrote about the making of *Love Story,* the film based on Erich Segal's surprising bestseller, on which I'd served as the unit publicist. A shrewd updating of *La Dame aux Camélias,* the book—and film—relate the story of a prosperous Harvard undergrad who defies his patrician father to take up with an "ethnic" girl from the wrong side of the tracks, who gets sick and dies, reconciling the estranged father and son. Lest the *La Traviata* of it all be lost on you, the girl's name was Jenny Cavalleri and she was a music major. The famous catchphrase of both book and film was "Love means never having to say you're sorry," which I later found is not the case. I called my book *What Can You Say About a 25-Year-Old Girl Who Died: The Love Story Story.* I worked night and day, bashed it out, and showed it to my family.

My father gave his opinion: "If you publish this book, you'll never work in the movie business again."

I got the book to Juris Jurjevics, an editor working for Avon Paperbacks. He abbreviated the title to *The Love Story Story* and offered me a three-thousand-dollar advance. I took it, converted the money to traveler's checks, and had my car (preserved all this time since college at various sidewalk parking spaces through snow and slush) tuned for a cross-country journey. I finally realized, with some encouragement from my sister Constance's boyfriend, Michael Pressman, that the place I ought to be trying my luck was Los Angeles.

"And don't think you can go out there for two weeks and head home," Michael cautioned. "You can't do the tourist thing and accomplish anything. You've really got to put in the time."

I decided to take his advice.

GO WEST

Driving long distances by yourself produces the illusion of thought: Time passes behind the wheel; the road unfolds before you like an endless typewriter ribbon (anyone remember them?) . . . and you think you are thinking.

But later, lying exhausted in your motel bed, or trying on paper to recall what it was you were pondering, you are at a loss. The thoughts, like caged birds set free, are gone forever. Maybe they weren't ever in the cage to begin with; you just thought they were.

I had put my small stash of clothes (mainly jeans and blue cotton work shirts), my portable electric typewriter, my stereo, and my large record collection into the capacious trunk of my faithful Pontiac Tempest. I had sent my two best screenplays, *The Understudy* and something called *The Frame-Up*, to the West Coast branch of my agency, International Famous, along with a letter stating that I would be in Los Angeles by August "in search of representation" and were they interested?

I hoped they were, for they were my only contact in a city where I had never been before and knew not a soul. If they didn't take me on, the stark fact was that I had no alternative plan for my life. In later years, recalling this dicey approach, I wonder at my chutzpah (or incredible stupidity) when I come to recall how I had staked my entire future on one roll of the dice. I was simply terrified. Terrified, but going forward. I was out of choices.

West of Iowa City, I was into terra incognita. I couldn't believe how flat the road is through Nebraska, then Colorado. You can drive all day and all night (and I did) through endless fields of wheat and corn.

And then, just as you feel sure these grains will go on forever, a wall rises up before you, abruptly ending it all. The Rockies. I had reached Denver.

In Denver I made the discovery that my driver's license was due to expire in two weeks. What to do? I decided to adopt a local address, betook myself to the Denver DMV, and got myself a temporary license.

When I wended my way into the Rockies, I was the proud possessor of a Colorado temporary driver's license. It was my only piece of identification. Certainly my bank account was not the sort that rendered you eligible for credit cards. If anything happened to me, some place in Denver was where they would look. What could possibly happen?

All the way across the country, I made unsuccessful attempts to reach the agent who has been foisted on me by IFA, following the defection (if that is the right word) of Janet Roberts. This fellow had had no use for me and kept ducking my calls. Finally, quite by accident, he picked up his own phone and found me at the other end, haranguing him from a phone booth near the freeway outside Sacramento. The conversation was brief and unpleasant and when I hung up, I was in tears, doubly angry because not only was I getting nowhere in my chosen profession, but I would now be driving into San Francisco, a city about which I've heard all my life, too angry and upset to enjoy it.

Or so I thought. The wonder of San Francisco (when I laid eyes on it two hours later) was so overpowering that by the time I got off the Bay Bridge I'd forgotten the guy's name. I forgot everything except one of the most beautiful cities I'd ever seen.

I spent the latter part of July and the first two weeks of August exploring this enchanting place. After lingering almost a month, I didn't want to leave San Francisco (a) because it was so wonderful and (b) because I was scared to death of where I was heading.

Nevertheless it was time to face the music, and so I turned south along the scenic Pacific Coast Highway. I visited San Simeon, and at the local luncheonette encountered a fellow traveler, a lady of about forty, who struck up a conversation. She was friendly and intelligent—until I told her I was on my way to Los Angeles to make films—at which point she smiled and said, "Oh, my husband is a film producer. You must look us up when you arrive."

Aside from the delusion that her husband was in the movie business (a delusion that, I confess, I expected everyone to harbor, such was my fantasy about Angelenos), Fran Laurence seemed tolerably sane on all other subjects, so I took her address. Who knew? In the end, her husband did turn out to be a genuine film producer (he'd worked with everyone from Judy Garland to Elvis), and the whole family sponsored me with a generosity unparalleled in my experience, greatly changing my perception of Los Angeles, when I reached it. Walter Mirisch was right.

Meantime I motored uneasily south, only half-registering the fabled wonders of Highway One as my anxiety increased. In Santa Barbara, I checked into a cheap motel. I was now a mere ninety miles from my goal, the dreaded Big Orange, where I didn't know anyone nor had I any particular prospects. (Unless you counted Fran Laurence's husband, and I wasn't.)

I turned on the motel TV. I watched Tyrone Power and Dean Jagger in *Brigham Young*. Vincent Price plays John Smith. The Mormons have always interested me, courtesy of Sherlock Holmes in *A Study in Scarlet*. (I had made it a point, going cross-country, of visiting Salt Lake City.)

But I was restless. The film exerted an almost nightmarish fascination, the Mormon odyssey mirroring my own uncertain transcontinental meanderings. The movie was making me more uptight, not less.

Then an odd idea struck me. All the way west I had been reading paperback editions of Ross Macdonald's Lew Archer novels. On the back of each book it was unaccountably explained that "Ross Macdonald" is the nom de plume of one Kenneth Millar, who lived in—wait for it—Santa Barbara!

What is the point of having a nom de plume if you're going to tell everyone your true name and town of residence? The logic, I confess, is beyond me. But just for the hell of it, in my restless humor, I got out the Santa Barbara telephone directory, stashed near the Gideon bible next to my bed, and looked up Kenneth Millar. Lo and behold, there he was, big as life. I dialed the number.

"Hello?"

"Is this Kenneth Millar?"

"Yes?"

Wow. Now what?

"Well, uh, you don't know me, but I've been driving across the country, reading your books."

"Oh?" He was definitely wary now. No surprise. With the kind of books he wrote, the notion of some wacko picking up the phone (or worse) must have occurred to him, or even happened before.

(Then how come he told everyone how to find him on the back of each of his books?)

"I was just sort of wondering," I pressed on, "were you, that is, are you a fan of Arthur Conan Doyle's?"

Impossible to tell from the silence that followed what he made of me now. A literate psychopath? Someone who would bore him to death before bludgeoning him?

"I admire Doyle, of course," he said carefully, "though I'd guess I was rather more influenced by Poe."

Really. (I hadn't yet formed my theory about how pointless it is to ask people about their influences.)

"Really?"

He let the silence hang there. I thought I'd pushed this about as far as I could. I found I was gripping the receiver in a white-knuckled clench.

"Well, thanks very much for your time. I'll let you get on with your . . ." (what was it I interrupted?) "your life. So long."

"Good-bye."

I sank heavily onto the bed, covered in sweat.

LOS ANGELES

Los Angeles, when I arrived the next day, was just about as horrible as everyone predicted. I got off the San Diego freeway at Wilshire Boulevard (something that sounded vaguely familiar), and I headed east, assuming this broad thoroughfare would bring me downtown.

I had not yet heard Gertrude Stein's celebrated description of Oakland, her own hometown: "Once you get there there's no there there," which will apply equally to LA.

I now know I *would* have reached downtown if I'd only kept going far enough along Wilshire, but I gave up after about fifteen miles. Often I'd see a cluster of office buildings draw near and think I'd found the damn thing, only to grind my teeth with vexation when this same inexorable avenue spun past them, leaving the pathetic little group behind, to be replaced by more bungalows and a series of incongruous palm trees, their tall, thin trunks raveling pointlessly upward forever, crowned, finally, by an absurd thatch of fronds.

Where did they keep the damn city?

There was really no postponing the moment any longer. I fished out a dime, used a parking lot phone booth, and called the International Famous Agency. What was I going to do with my life if they said they weren't interested?

We'll never know the answer to that one because the call was forwarded to a young agent named John Ptak, who said he liked my stuff and wanted to meet me. I acquired directions and the rest is more or less history. After meeting with him, I opened the trunk of my car, checked my remaining supply of traveler's checks, and concluded that I could hold out till Christmas.

I rented an apartment in someplace called Culver City, more or less be-

28

neath the intersection of the Santa Monica and San Diego freeways. It was the same size or smaller than my flat in New York, but I thought it was great because it had a swimming pool the size of a postage stamp in the middle of a courtyard. I emptied the contents of my trunk into the little place and got into my car to look for dinner.

After dinner I got into my car again and began driving before I realized that I had no idea where I lived. I had forgot to learn my address. All my possessions (my music collection! my Ross Macdonald books!) were resting comfortably in some anonymous location, but for the life of me I couldn't recall where it was.

In my panic I began driving faster and faster up and down streets and boulevards, like a rat trapped in a maze. It dimly occurred to me that I would now be due for a fatal car accident in the wake of which all the authorities would find by way of identification would be my Colorado driver's license with its nonexistent address.

My parents would take it that I had simply disappeared from the face of the earth.

In a sweat-stained condition bordering on all-out hysteria, I stumbled on the place somehow, driving past it at about sixty miles an hour, U-turned, parked, went in, and lay on the bed, hyperventilating.

But things improved. The many and generous friends about whom Walter Mirisch spoke after Verna Fields's funeral began to make their appearance. A young man living in the apartment across from mine, originally from Illinois, was a film critic for *Variety*. He was so good that they booted him off the paper for having standards that were too high.

My little *Love Story* book came out, and that was a kick. They'd tried to make the cover look as much like Erich Segal's source novel as possible, which was embarrassing, but still I had written the thing and it had paid my way to California. I remember seeing the first copy in the drugstore across the street from my apartment about nine o'clock one evening.

A young mother was shopping with her child, stopping before the magazine rack. I pointed out the book and said I had written it.

"You wrote *Love Story?*" Her eyes widened slightly.

"Well, no, not *Love Story*," I explained. "See? *The Love Story Story.*"

"Oh." She looked at me dubiously. "No kidding . . ."

I pulled out my driver's license, which had my name, after all. She brightened.

"You're from Colorado . . . I went skiing there. . . ."

This was getting too complicated. I just bought her the damn book.

My first job was working for no money, developing a treatment for Elliot Silverstein, the director of the hit film *Cat Ballou* and later the amazing *A Man Called Horse*. I learned lots of stuff from Elliot, a former theater director from Boston who had staged the original production of Bernstein's opera *Trouble in Tahiti*. Silverstein was a sort of amalgam between Bill Schwartz and Howard Stein, my playwriting teacher at Iowa. Like them, he did not suffer fools gladly. Elliot had a short fuse and piercing blue eyes that glared at you from behind steel-rimmed spectacles. Working for him I began to realize that my background in theater was actually a sort of impediment to screenwriting.

"You want to solve all your problems with dialogue," Elliot observed bluntly. "But movies aren't dialogue, they're pictures. Contrast *Star Trek* with *Mission: Impossible*," he went on, ever the pedagogue. (*Star Trek* again. What was it with *Star Trek*?) "Turn off the video on both and listen. *Star Trek* works fine; it becomes a radio play—because it's all dialogue. On the other hand, *Misson: Impossible* without the visuals is just a series of sound effects. Now try it the other way round: if you turn on the picture and turn off the sound, *Star Trek* becomes essentially a series of talking heads. *Mission: Impossible*, by contrast, looks like a movie."

Compare and contrast, and remember, neatness counts. Elliot lived on a largish motor yacht in the marina, an area I got to know well, as well as his friends, a collection of Hollywood types, good, bad, big (big bosomed), small, and no account.

What surprised me was how generous Elliot's friends all were, how interested in a newcomer. They plied me with questions and encouragement. Later, more cynically, I could place another construction on their amiability: if the new boy had something to offer, they wanted to get in on it sooner rather than later, when the line got long.

But I don't think it was that cut and dried. Los Angeles just turned out to be a friendly place—more friendly than I had imagined. People were enthusiastic about things, excited about new people with new ideas. . . .

HIRED

When I began to focus on work I made myself a new rule: no speech in a screenplay by me was going to be more than ten lines long. This restriction was a killer. I was going to have to learn to write all over again, write in a way where literacy itself was a disadvantage. Later, watching the work of Steven Spielberg, I understand how much my verbal facility worked against me. It's better if you can *think* in pictures. What happens to your scene when you turn off the sound in your head?

Another rule: how many pages can you write of a screenplay before it is absolutely necessary for someone to speak?

I was certainly lucky. After three months my agent got me a job writing a movie for two producers at Warner Brothers. Warner Brothers! I was "on the lot." I had an office in the dream factory, I was one of the chosen few who was admitted by the guard at the gate. I even had a parking space, though the white-stenciled name on it read a sobering VISITOR. No matter. I trudged happily, deliriously, through the rows of soundstages and wardrobe departments, on my way to work in the movies. The first thing I did when the door was shut was slide a piece of Warner stationery into my typewriter and punch out the following:

> Dear Mom and Pop: I am writing this from my office on the
> Warner Brothers lot . . .

Don't let anyone tell you that being "on the lot" is not a thrill.
I was part of the circus at last.
Warner Brothers back then was still a real studio, complete with backlot.

Although it has more recently been converted to office buildings and parking spaces, in the early seventies you could still wander around back there and see "medieval" wrought-iron chandeliers from which you knew Errol Flynn had swung a million "Action!"s ago, all stacked in neat configurations next to submarines, airplane fuselages, spiral staircases, doors of all sorts, and even a huge castle, which had variously functioned in *Camelot* (in the eponymous, ill-starred musical) and as a monastery in the *Kung Fu* television series. There was a "New England" town square, an "Elizabethan" street, a generic "European" street, an Andy Hardy All-American type *Meet Me in St. Louis* street (the real one at MGM was already apartment houses in Culver City), and several "New York" or "big city" streets with brownstones, stores, and movie theaters. And of course your basic "Western" town street was still in use, though fading fast, even as I explored its dusty storefronts.

The film I was working on was nothing, in fact, to write home about. The producers wanted a horror film with a twist—a film in which men, and not women, were the victims. The idea pleased me. I recalled a letter to the editor I had read in the *Times* some years earlier, where a woman had complained about Hitchcock's *Frenzy*. "Just once," she wrote, "I'd like to see a movie where the *man's* eyes widen in fear . . ." Armed with the producers' mandate to that effect, I dreamt up a story about an etymological experiment gone wrong at a remote desert think tank, in which all the women are turned into "queen bees," whose biological urge to reproduce always resulted in the death of the chosen drone. As their colleagues start mysteriously dying off, the men become panic-stricken, have to resort to the buddy system at night, etc. while the girls grow redolent with health and well-being.

The film, as I finished it, was called *The Honey Factor*, a nice, oblique title for a film I felt could play the trendy Cinema I on Third Avenue or the Paramus drive-in with equal appeal.

The producers seemed pleased. By this time it was Christmas and I made my big mistake: never visit your parents during preproduction. When I returned from New York a week or so later, one of the producers made a big speech about how a screenplay is a blueprint for a building that hasn't been built yet, how there were always adjustments to be made, etc. "You know, maybe we need another window? A few more electrical outlets?" Made sense to me.

I sat down and read the revised script, puzzled to find that *The Honey Factor* by Nicholas Meyer was now *Invasion of the Bee Girls* by Nicholas Meyer and Amy Andrews.

Amy Andrews? Who the hell was Amy Andrews? Girlfriend of one of the producers, it turned out. All that had been witty and oblique (the Cinema I stuff) had been chucked in favor of dumbed-down stuff for the Paramus drive-in crowd.

I was furious. Mortified. Impotent. I rang my agent, bellowing like a wounded elephant.

"Get my name off these fucking credits."

"No," he responded, "get *her* name off the fucking credits."

"You don't understand," I whined, "this thing is a piece of shit."

"*You* don't understand," he corrected. "You need the credit."

In any case, the assignment of credits wasn't up to me or the studio; assigning the final credits for a film is the jealously guarded prerogative of the Writers Guild (of which I was now a member). On this occasion the Guild decided in my favor.

We will come back to this topic of credits by and by.

I never did manage to see *Invasion of the Bee Girls*. Maybe one day. People who see it on my résumé keep telling me it is a camp classic but I never know what this means or if it's a good thing.

Meantime it was back to the drawing board. *Invasion of the Bee Girls* was not going to be my passport to immortality. Looking back on an enterprise of this sort, one is inevitably tempted to gloss over the dry spells and concentrate on the positive events, to telescope time so that good and bad are conflated to the point almost of overlapping. Not the case. There was a year when I made four thousand dollars, in all. My parents were still of the opinion I was heading nowhere fast, but mercifully I heard about their anxieties only secondhand, through my sister and her husband, also now in Los Angeles. Still, a secondhand vote of no confidence was demoralizing enough. TV dinners were the order of the day. As was self-doubt. I spent a lot of time on my own—it had begun to seem like my natural state—wondering if I was ever going to have anything to show for my efforts besides a stash of model boats. I had a chip on my shoulder, exacerbated by an arrogance that erupted when I felt ignored. At the same time, like Groucho, I would never have belonged to any club that would have me for a member.

I lost my agent, who didn't trouble to tell me I had lost him, a familiar if unpleasant repetition. One morning the phone rang and someone named Kevin Sellers informed me that he would now be handling my affairs.

"What happened to John?" I asked, naively surprised that an agent who had been unable to sell anything by his client should wish to dump same.

"He's very busy," Kevin explained. He turned out to be a good kid, and I liked him a lot. He actually cared about writing and movies.

Of course he did not remain an agent very long.

Also I acquired a girlfriend. When I met Kelly she had been working for one of the two *Bee Girls* producers (not the one with the girlfriend-writer). I was instantly smitten. She had, after all, smiled at me, and we moved in together shortly thereafter, me shifting my Culver City digs for a small house in funky Laurel Canyon.

Kelly was beautiful, intelligent, musical, and neurotic, though I suppose I ran her a close second in that last department. It was a stormy romance, chockablock with scenes wherein she spoke long monologues about her life and times while I sat cowed and listened, wondering how had I gotten myself into this. Or could wangle my way out. The sort of thing Philip Roth describes so well. The affair last lasted two years, succumbing, finally, to a kind of attrition.

YOUR NAME HERE

Things weren't all or always terrible. During this time, I wrote a couple of television movies that were actually filmed. It's hard to convey what a thrill it was to finally hear actors speaking my lines. I wasn't always happy with their performances or the editing or the direction, or the lines themselves, for that matter (always too many words; I was always mentally reaching for a pencil to scratch things out—picky, picky, picky), but I was far from unhappy. This was exciting stuff. I wasn't making a great living but I was managing to support myself in a minimal sort of way. A young director with whom I was friendly, Jeremy Kagan, asked that I write the screenplay for what ABC assumed was going to be a Kung Fu TV movie, *Judge Dee*. Actually, the film was a horse of quite another color. Dee Jen Jay, a seventh-century Tang Dynasty circuit court judge, was China's first detective of record, and a large amount of detective literature in which he is featured was Westernized by a Dutch diplomat, Robert Van Gulik. The Judge Dee books are popular all around the world, except in the United States, for some reason. I adapted *Judge Dee and the Haunted Monastery* for Jeremy and, using an all-Asiatic cast, we filmed on the Warner backlot, converting the old Camelot castle into our monastery. The film looked great, the actors struggled with my rococo Mandarin English (too many words), but the studio/network were pleased with the result—pleased enough to order up a second Judge Dee movie, which I also wrote. I was getting the hang of all this seventh-century Tang Dynasty stuff and greatly anticipating the second movie when, unfortunately, Khigh Dhiegh, the lovely actor who played the Judge (you may also remem-

36

ber his droll turn in *The Manchurian Candidate*) succumbed abruptly to a heart attack.

As suddenly as all the activity started, it stopped. As I was to learn, this is a feast or famine business. You're hot, you're in demand, you're making a living. Then you're high and dry, out of fashion, out of cash . . .

And then the WGA goes on strike.

STRIKE!

The 1972 Writers Guild strike changed my life dramatically. There's lots to be said about the Guild, but for the moment I'll confine myself to the strike itself, which required me to picket outside the (then) Goldwyn studios at Santa Monica and Formosa for three hours a day, four days a week, carrying a placard. All writers are frustrated actors; now here we were, starring in our own production of *Waiting for Lefty Meets On the Waterfront While Waiting for Bardot*, shouldering our picket signs as though they were rifles and we, the workers on the front lines of the proletarian revolution. Writers of the world unite; we had nothing to lose but our subordinate clauses.

We all picketed with a partner. After three hours walking with him or her in a long oval, with the sun beating down on the pavement (and us), we learned more than we ever cared to know about him—and vice versa, natch. I picketed with an older man named Al Beich who had written a lot of *Mannix* episodes. One day when our shift was finished, he invited me back to his place for a drink.

"Just follow my car," he offered by way of directions. In LA you measure places by the time in takes to reach them, not how many miles there are between them. "It's about ten minutes," Al said.

The car of this proletarian revolutionary turned out to be a vintage green Rolls-Royce convertible. I followed it west on Sunset Boulevard until we turned into the driveway of the most opulent building north of Sunset, the one everyone stares at from his car and wonders about, a European-looking stone mansion of enormous proportions and (relative) age, situated on the primest real estate in town.

Mannix paid for this? Maybe I should think twice about episodic television.

It turned out that Al (who was in his sixties) was in fact part of the enormously wealthy Beich candy family, and that it was his (much older) sister, Mary—who was never there—who actually owned the place. It further turned out that Mary was herself the much younger widow of Wyatt Earp's lawyer, a man named McCarthy (you following this? you believe this?) for whom the place had been built by Italian artisans, imported from Italy for the purpose. (They probably stayed to work on Griffith's sets for *Intolerance* when they were finished.)

The estate was like Norma Desmond's mansion in *Sunset Blvd.*, a miniature palazzo, complete with marbled-floored ballroom, a kitchen larger than my entire one-room flat, a stage (for live theatrical productions) in the basement, along with hundreds of polo mallets suspended from the ceiling—McCarthy was an avid polo player; see the Polo Lounge in the Beverly Hills hotel—next to Renaissance canvases and even a blue, eighteenth-century sedan chair in the foyer, which sported a telephone within its recesses.

In the basement were all McCarthy's files and contracts of the day. You could pull open a drawer and see how much Vilma Bánky was getting. Or Rod La Rocque. Or Valentino. I felt a little like Joe Gillis. All I needed was the *Salome* script to work on. At least Al's pool had water in it, not rats.

The trip to Al's was an amusing break in an otherwise bleak and uninteresting time. The strike squelched everything. You were not allowed to write scripts. Just when I was getting started, too.

"Well, since you can't write screenplays," Kelly pointed out, washing the dishes as I dried, "now you've got ample time to write that novel you're always talking about." Ah, yes . . .

THE SEVEN-PER-CENT SOLUTION

That novel. As though I needed to bash my head against the brick wall of fiction one more time.

But the truth was that because of the Writers Guild strike, I had nothing better to do—at least when I wasn't literally walking around in circles on the picket line—so I started banging away at my long-gestating notion of a Doyle pastiche in which Sherlock Holmes met, matched wits with, and finally collaborated with Dr. Sigmund Freud. Freud cures Holmes's cocaine addiction; in return, Holmes's methodology sets Freud on the analytic path that will lead to psychoanalysis.

What became *The Seven-Per-Cent Solution* was the end result of many thoughts and influences converging. My long-standing fondness for the Holmes stories was, of course, the starting point. (In my early teens I had actually attempted to turn Holmes into a musical.) But it must also be said that my distaste for all the Holmes movies and other imitations played an almost equally important part. In a word, I have never seen a Holmes movie I didn't dislike; almost never read a Holmes pastiche (other than a couple of very early ones) that seemed to me to capture the essence of Holmes and his amanuensis. Holmes pastiches, in whatever medium, always emerge as campy and unreal, in stark contrast—to me, anyway—with the original stories. It's the difference between a live Bengal tiger and the taxidermic version. In most of these stuffed approximations, Watson is always depicted as an idiot, an admittedly tempting choice because it's so easy, but one that, on closer examination, makes no sense. Why would a genius choose to hang out with a buffoon? How can we reconcile bumbling Nigel Bruce as the bluff but reliable narrator of the original case histories? Holmes's vanity is a subtle thing: he wants the appreciation of a regular man, not a sub-regular man. At least part of my impetus, therefore, was this disgust with what I regarded as inferior imitation. I felt—innately *felt*—that I understood these characters, their nuances, and Doyle's narrative tone better than anyone else. Right or wrong, that notion helped goad me to the project.

Another catalyst was a question repeatedly asked when I was in high school, viz: Your old man's a shrink, right? Is he a Freudian? I had no idea (how would I?) and finally asked him outright, "Pop, are you a Freudian?"

"It's a silly question," he responded.

When I asked why it was a silly question, he pondered and then said, "Because it is no more possible to discuss the history of psychoanalysis without starting with Freud than it is possible to discuss the history of America without mention of Columbus—or the Vikings. But to suppose that nothing has happened since the Vikings is to be pretty rigid, pretty doctrinaire. When a patient comes to see me, I listen to what they say, I listen to how they say it; I am especially interested in what they do not say. In addition, I look at their body language, how they dress, whether they tend to show up on time . . . I am in short, searching for clues—from them—as to why they are not happy. And against this data, I apply some measure of clinical experience to interpret these clues." I interrupted to observe that this sounded rather like detective work. "Very like detective work," he conceded, and at that instant, I realized who my childhood hero, Sherlock Holmes, had always reminded me of: my father. From there, I fell to wondering how much Arthur Conan Doyle had known about the life and work of Sigmund Freud.

The answers were surprising. Doyle and Freud were essentially contemporaries, dying within nine years of each other in London, Doyle in 1930, Freud in 1939. Both were doctors; in fact Doyle had spent six months in Vienna (Freud's home) studying ophthalmology. Enticingly, Freud's first paper extolling the virtues of cocaine as an anesthetic during eye surgery had been written in collaboration with two eye doctors, Koenigstein and Koeller.

Cocaine. That was the real connection. Doyle probably never used the stuff—although it was not then illegal—but in making Holmes a cocaine fiend, he was treading in (pre-Freudian) Freudian waters.

Back in New York when I had first begun thinking about these coincidences, what I had contemplated was a nonfiction piece of research on the subject of Doyle and Freud, but I'm hopeless without a story. By the time of the Guild strike, years later, the book had pretty much taken shape in my mind as a Holmes pastiche.

A Holmes pastiche must play by its own set of rules, the main one being that you write as Watson and imagine the Holmes stories to be true. Doyle is relegated to the subordinate status of Watson's "literary agent." Under this umbrella there is room for all sorts of playful speculation. Resolving Watson's hilarious inconsistencies—was he wounded in the arm or leg during the Battle of Maiwand in the second Afghan war? was the landlady's name Mrs. Hudson or Mrs. Turner?—you can take on Holmes and women; Holmes and music; Moriarty and Higher Math; the Polyphonic Motets of Lassus, and on and on. There are at least two full-length biographies of Holmes, one of Watson, and even one of the landlady, for chrissake. There's a series of novels about Professor Moriarty; another series about Irene Adler, "The Woman." Walk down Baker Street in London and see plaques everywhere claiming to be the original of 221B, the most famous address in the world. At the time of this writing there are not one but two—count 'em, *two!*—annotated editions of the complete Sherlock Holmes.

Of course no one I knew personally was interested in this stuff, besides me. They weren't interested in Sherlock so how could they begin to be amused by what I was finding hilarious?

Once I got to work I quickly discovered that banging away—which is to say using my trusty Smith Corona—didn't work when trying to write like Arthur Conan Doyle. The typewriter encouraged a different sort of rhythm. I found I had to write the thing longhand, at least for the first draft. It was an interesting experience, getting tactile with the twirling tails of *R*'s, furiously dotting *I*'s, and slashing the crosses on *T*'s.

When I had finished, I felt that at the very least I had finally written something publishable. The question was how to go about it.

For starters I sent the manuscript back to the East Coast of IFA and asked their literary agents to read it. After what seemed an eternity, a well-known book agent got back to me.

"There's no point in my reading this," she advised me. "I've never read any Sherlock Holmes, so how could I tell if this was any good?"

As was typical of me at the time, I said what I thought: "Putting aside the astonishing fact that you're a literary agent and have never read any Holmes, I'd have to say that if this book depends on your knowing any other book, it's a flop already."

An excellent argument, you might say, except that she'd hung up before she could hear it. Always making friends and influencing people.

I thought about my dilemma. I knew one person in the publishing business, Jim Nederland, whom I had met when he was the editor of a novel by my old professor, Peter Arnott. Nederland was at Macmillan.

I tucked the manuscript into a suitcase and splurged on a ticket to New York. When I reached the city it was pissing rain and Nederland didn't work at Macmillan anymore.

A reasonable person would have called first. It never occurred to me that people moved from job to job in the real world. My father was a doctor; he stayed a doctor.

"Is he still in the publishing business?" I asked the puzzled receptionist at Macmillan as I dripped a large pool of rainwater before her fancy desk.

She rather thought he was and gave me the directions to another publisher, across town.

By the time I reached Hawthorne Books, I was sopping wet. Nederland was surprised to see me.

"What brings you here?" he wondered, helping me off with my wet things.

"I've written a novel," I explained brightly.

"Oh." I studied him as he gingerly hung up my coat. The "oh" was oh-so-studiously neutral.

"What do you mean, 'Oh'?"

He shrugged. "This is a nonfiction house," he explained. "I've tried to get five novels accepted here—they've all been turned down."

My turn.

"Oh." I had a cup of coffee in his office while I collected my thoughts, then rose and said, "Look, I'm leaving this book with you anyway. Frankly, I don't have any choice; I don't know anyone else in the business."

"I understand." He walked me to the elevator, and I got on the plane and flew back to Los Angeles. Win some, lose some.

I was pretty surprised when four or five days later I got an excited phone call from Nederland.

"This one they'll publish."

"Really?"

"Really. Wonderful fun."

Wonderful fun. Wow. Lemme think.

"Uh, Jim, let me, uh, let me think about this."

"We'll offer you six thousand dollars for it."

Wow. That made two wows in a row.

"I, uh, need to figure some stuff out here . . ."

"Don't keep me on tenterhooks."

"I'll try not to."

I hung up, rather stunned, and explained matters to Kelly.

"Now what do I do?"

"How do you mean?"

"I mean I'm damned if IFA is going to collect ten percent from a deal they didn't lift a finger to help, but I need someone who knows about this stuff."

"Good point." We thought about it some more.

"Why don't you give it to Tom and ask his advice?" Kelly suggested.

"Good idea."

In theory, Tom was my lawyer, a guy I'd met at a party somewhere who was in entertainment law. He said he'd be my lawyer if I ever needed one but I never had. You have to be halfway successful to need a lawyer. It was a year since we'd met. I hoped he remembered me.

I called him at his law firm and explained the situation to him. He was intrigued.

"Who's Hawthorne? And let me see your book," he added.

A few days later he was on the phone, sounding pretty excited.

"Listen, I've read your book and I've researched Hawthorne. They're a nonfiction house; the book'll get lost there. You can do better."

This was happening too fast for me.

"Hey, wait a minute. They're offering me six thousand dollars and I haven't made that much money since—"

"I know, I know. Trust me on this."

"But what about Jim Neder—?"

"He'll understand, believe me."

"What about IFA?" My agency.

"Fuck 'em. They weren't there for the kickoff."

Which is how Tom Pollock, for many years the head of Universal Pictures, became my literary agent and how I did very well indeed. He worked for a straight commission, a deal he must have regretted, since I got a great deal of lawyering for the rest of my life without fees.

The next thing I knew, Harcourt, Brace, Jovanovich had bought my book for ten thousand dollars.

That was when my troubles with the Doyle estate began. I could now digress with a long explanation of international copyright law and why and when the United States adopted the Berne Convention, but suffice to say the copyright issue and permission to publish my book from the heirs and assigns of Sir Arthur dragged on for months. There's a saying: Where ignorance is bliss, 'tis folly to be wise. If I had known all the difficulties that would have ensued regarding the rights to Holmes, I probably would never have attempted the book in the first place.

The negotiations took so long, in fact, that I sat down one day at my typewriter and wrote another book instead, one that wouldn't have legal problems attached to it. Called *Target Practice*, this novel, too, had a long gestation period, followed by a terribly short actual writing time: three weeks. The story was an attempt to discuss the Vietnam War (a subject that had been percolating in my brain since college) in the guise of a Lew Archer–type detective story.

Detective stories, at least to that time, had always struck me as far removed from any external reality with which the rest of us were familiar. They took place in their little villages or country houses or mean streets, or wherever, but they never seemed to intersect with real headlines (not until the late Ross Macdonald, and his headlines were always local).

My novel was another pastiche, to be sure, this one based on Macdonald and Raymond Chandler instead of Doyle. Me hiding behind other people's faces again. It was not a bad story, however, and did what I set out to do, namely address issues of moral culpability related to Vietnam in the guise of what Graham Greene called "an entertainment." It was nominated for an Edgar Award in the category of Best First Mystery Novel (didn't win). I dedicated it to my father.

Along the way to publication I learned a thing or two about the publishing business. Still spinning wheels while waiting for some kind of resolution with the Doyle estate, Harcourt Brace Etcetera agreed to published *Target Practice*. My editor was a swell gentleman named Ed Barber, and he worked on both *Target Practice* and *The Seven-Per-Cent Solution*. On *Target Practice* I had no difficulty with the editorial process, but my Holmes novel proved more tricky.

"Here's what I have done," Ed wrote in his cover letter, accompanying the "edited" version of my book. "Although your novel is supposedly written in the 1890s" (actually, it was supposed to have been written in 1939, but let that pass) "it is actually being penned for readers of 1974." (So far, so good.) "So what we need to do in editing, is present the *illusion* of a period novel, while keeping in mind the fact of its contemporary readership."

I had no problem with any of this until I read Ed's version of my story. Here I found myself on the horns of a classic dilemma: first-time novelist's instincts versus those of experienced editor. Whose judgment should I trust—his or my own?

I was luckier than some writers in similar situations; because my book was itself an imitation of something else, I had a preexisting yardstick by which to measure the success or failure of my effort. Since my editor's version of *The Seven-Per-Cent Solution* didn't read like Arthur Conan Doyle and my original did, it was easy for me to decide to insist on something much closer to my own draft.

Besides, always let your failures be your own. The world is full of advice; you must pick and choose what is useful or relevant versus what is merely safe and/or familiar. There's no getting around instinct; pray you have some.

Ed Barber left Harcourt Brace for another company (there seemed to be an awful lot of this lateral movement in the publishing business), which didn't publish fiction. Déjà vu. That left me with Julian Muller as my editor, the head of Harcourt. Muller (famous for having published *Auntie Mame* when everyone had turned it down) told me not to expect too much from *Target Practice*. It was, after all, another book among thousands competing for the public's attention.

I sat listening in his office, puzzled and, I suppose, hurt. I certainly hadn't expected *Target Practice* to set the world on fire, but I wasn't sure I relished hearing about its lack of prospects from its publisher. I may have mumbled something to that effect.

"Look," Muller went gamely on, "if you want to write a mighty book, you must choose a mighty theme." Only the word he used instead of "mighty" was "commercial."

Harcourt wasn't (seemingly) able or interested in helping me to resolve my dilemma with the Doyle crowd. And now I began getting calls from Juris Jurjevics, of all people, the man who had edited *The Love Story Story* when he was at Avon Books. He was now with E. P. Dutton, and someone had slipped him a copy of my novel.

I explained that I had a deal with Harcourt. He asked how much they were prepared to pay me. I told him. Jurjevics said he would top the offer by a thousand dollars. I told Tom.

"Wait," said Tom.

A week later Dutton had upped the offer by another thousand. And so on. Finally, since Harcourt seemed utterly passive in the face of my legal quagmire, I asked Muller to let me out of our deal. He didn't seem to mind a bit and my Holmes book was now at its third publisher, E. P. Dutton, which energetically pursued the matter of obtaining permission from the Doyle estate to publish. No seven-per-cent solution, I promise you.

The book came out in August 1974, hard on the heels of *Target Practice*, which had been released in March. After years of drought (and I mean years), I had suddenly published two novels within six months. What happened next still strikes me as highly improbable. *The Seven-Per-Cent Solution* quickly appeared on the *New York Times* bestseller list in the number-ten slot and began inching its way north. Abruptly I was lifted out of obscurity and (comparative) penury. I was sought after for interviews; my name began appearing in print here and there, and the reading public, for reasons of its own, decided my book was one to read. Sherlock Holmes was in vogue. And so was Freud. The late Anatole Broyard, reviewing the book in *The New York Times*, was kind. He noted that after all the Freud bashing lately, it was a pleasure to see him portrayed as the hero for a change, furiously throwing coal into the boiler of a locomotive as if it were the work to which he had been born. Freud, for the record, bore only a superficial resemblance to the actual father of psychoanalysis; in the book, he was modeled after an entirely different father: my own.

I was having my fifteen minutes of celebrity.

The paperback rights to the book sold for an enormous sum. I was in my parents' kitchen in New York when the phone call from Juris told me just how much. I went back to my coffee and related the figure to my astonished mother and father.

They looked at me, actually dazed. This was so far from what they had ever expected (or predicted) for me. It wasn't that they weren't pleased, but this was a totally different program. The fact that I had gone out on my own, kicked over the traces, and then succeeded beyond anyone and everyone's wildest expectations (and let's face it, those expectations were never particularly wild to begin with) was going to have psychological repercussions for every one of us. The sum I had just earned, for example, exceeded my father's income for the same year.

My father had enjoyed the book, to be sure, but he had subjected it to the same rigorous editorial acumen he gave to all my writing. It simply had never occurred to any of us—certainly myself included—that the thing was going to take off in this fashion.

I was even sued, the surest sign that you're a success. It seems droll now, but at the time I was devastated when a doctor at Yale insisted that I had plagiarized an essay he had written about Holmes and Freud. I had certainly read his essay, as I had gratefully acknowledged in my Acknowledgments at the back of the book, for Pete's sake. I also acknowledged a great many other articles and books, some of which had also suggested the link between Holmes and Freud—to say nothing of that conversation with my father.

I felt my success had been tarnished by the imputation of my honor. Old-fashioned word. Old-fashioned feeling, but there you are. I had done something on my own, brought it into being by the hair on my chinny-chin-chin, the first time I had even rung the chimes, grabbed the brass ring, amounted to anything in this world, and now I was accused of stealing it. What a funny feeling in my tummy. Like a knife being twisted there.

I defended myself and won, but even winning proved costly and time-consuming. There were lawyers. Depositions. Fees. The case was essentially quite simple since the facts, namely my exposure to the article in question, were not in dispute. The issue hinged on the definition of plagiarism, which turns out to be quite narrow. You cannot plagiarize an idea; you can only plagiarize the *expression* of an idea; in other words, the *words*. Did you copy the actual words? Of course I hadn't. I had written a novel (arguably what this gentleman was kicking himself for failing to have done) and, using no words of his, had made a deal of money. Case dismissed.

He appealed. Lost again. It now seems axiomatic to me that if you are successful enough you will be sued. Years later, someone in Philadelphia sued Paramount over *Star Trek VI*. Claimed he'd thought up the whole thing. I ask you.

In *The Seven-Per-Cent Solution* I did not believe that I had written a great novel. I was twenty-eight and too old for that sort of self-delusion, but I understood that I had written a hugely enjoyable book and maybe that was what I was good for. From the vantage point of today the book's virtues seem to me to be its cleverness and high spirits. They may not be "ultimate" virtues—the novel was by no means profound—but I think one may be justifiably proud of a clever, high-spirited book.

The Seven-Per-Cent Solution stayed on the *Times* list for forty weeks, making it the third-best-selling novel of the year, behind *Jaws* and Michener's *Centennial.*

All in all 1974 was a banner year for me. Although the rest of the country was in the grip of a depression, with people being thrown out of work, the oil embargo, and lines around the block for gasoline, my second TV movie, a fictionalized account of the notorious 1938 Orson Welles radio adaptation of *War of the Worlds* and the havoc it caused, was aired around Halloween. I had titled it *The Night the Martians Landed* but CBS in its infinite wisdom had re-named it *The Night That Panicked America.* Whatever the title, I was certainly having a run of luck. The film even won a prize at the Monte Carlo Television Festival. (The Monte Carlo Television Festival???)

Tom Pollock told me I must buy a house. There was a need to invest the money.

"What money?" I demanded. I hadn't yet seen a penny.

"Trust me, Nick, there's going to be a lot of it."

And there was, too. I bought a small house, again in Laurel Canyon, and there too I was fortunate. I found myself the proud owner of the best two-person home in LA—complete with obligatory swimming pool—tucked dis-cretely into the hills on a piece of uncharacteristically level ground, not subject to mudslides on or off. (Earthquakes and fires were another matter.)

In early 1975 I was sent to publicize the book in England, where it was serialized in the tabloids (shades of Dickens!) and where it received the Gold Dagger Award from the British Crime Writers' Association. I was on radio. I was on TV. I was on a roll. My kid agent, Kevin Sellers, sold the film rights to his mother, a producer named Arlene Sellers. Other agents at IFA criticized the deal he made, pointing out all the things wrong with it—chiefly that it should have been for a larger sum of money—but I thought they missed the point. No one else had liked or worked on selling the book at all.

The deal was made with the stipulation that I write the screenplay, which I did, under the aegis of Herb Ross, who was to direct it. Writing the screenplay of *The Seven-Per-Cent Solution* was an interesting experience. Ross largely left me to my own devices. I included too many speeches, as usual (it would be years before I could figure out the screenplay thing), but I made good use of the opportunity to improve on what I considered the novel's defects, chiefly, the mystery Holmes and Freud are called upon to solve once Freud has cured Holmes of his drug habit. I was quite prepared to be ruthless and even eliminated the tennis scene between Freud and the villain, Baron Von Leinsdorf. At this point Ross dug in his heels. "Eliminate the tennis scene? No way."

"But it's not germane," I countered. "You want the audience to sit still in a movie while two guys play tennis? Unless you got a guy planting an incriminating cigarette lighter on an island"—a reference to Hitchcock's *Strangers on a Train,* which did have a tennis game/cigarette lighter in it—"people will be bored."

"But it's a favorite scene from the book," Ross insisted. "We have to have it." That struck me as an odd rationale, but I yielded. Herb had great respect for the material, and I was frequently begging him to cut stuff—even in the editing room—while he kept defending my work. "You're de-balling your own script," he'd say. He also had the habit of ending sentences with the phrase, "Do you know what I mean?" which, while rhetorically irritating, I admit I found hard to resist, even when I *didn't* know what he meant. During one of our exchanges, I conceded something along these lines, saying, in effect, "You're the expert, I'm just the—" "No, no," he countered, "you can't get away with that. You're in the big leagues now; you can't go on pretending to be the kid. You have to fight for what your gut tells you."

Herb Ross's interest in my views was not limited to my contributions as writer of the novel and screenplay; he sought my opinion on other matters, including casting. I suggested Peter O'Toole as Holmes, a seemingly inevitable role for the tall, lanky Brit, but he and Herb had not had a good working relationship on the musical version of *Goodbye, Mr. Chips.* When I heard that Robert Duvall was interested in playing Watson, I sparked to the idea. In the novel, I tried hard to emphasize a revisionist doctor, not the bumbler offered by Nigel Bruce. Our aim was to get audiences to look at these people afresh, and what could be fresher than Robert Duvall as Dr. Watson? But can he do an English accent? wondered Herb.

Herb Ross, formerly a choreographer, was married to Nora Kaye, the greatest dramatic ballerina this country had ever produced, and he never made a move without her. Kaye had been a devastatingly powerful and dynamic dancer, and when she opened her mouth, Lower East Side New Yawk came out, and with it a shrewd intelligence. On the day Duvall came to meet with us (stars do not audition, they "meet"), Herb and Nora had been feuding on the phone, hanging up on each other all morning. Duvall was also up for the role of Woody Guthrie in the forthcoming *Bound for Glory* and to our consternation he arrived in character—as Woody Guthrie. Herb and I glanced at each other, bewildered, as Duvall conversed in his Oakie twang. After fifteen or twenty minutes, he rose to leave and then, as a seeming afterthought, produced an audiocassette. "I brung you this so's you kin hear me talk like Dr. Watson," he explained before departing.

Wouldn't you know, there was no cassette player around for love or money, except one in someone's BMW, parked outside Herb's office. The next thing, eight of us had crammed into that car like clowns in a circus and listened to Duvall's impeccable Oxbridge. "He can do it!" I exclaimed, vindicated.

Not so fast. Herb had to play the tape for Nora. In due course a cassette player was found and he held it to the office phone and prefaced playing it by saying, "Nora, listen to this. Can you tell this man isn't English?"

In light of their recent spat that was all the opening she needed. On the extension, I could hear her: "Hoibert—is dat Mel Brooks? You wanna trow de pichure in the terlit, just youse dat poison, whatever. Don't take my woid for it," she went on. "Ask an English poison. Ask Sam."

Herb hung up the phone, devastated. Me, too. I could see my actor getting away. . . . "Sam" turned out to be the Rosses' friend, actress Samantha Eggar (who would later play Mrs. Watson in the movie). Herb followed Nora's instructions and, with the same preface, played the tape for Eggar, who hesitated as I held my breath on the extension again. "Well, it's awfully good," she acknowledged carefully, "but he's trying too hard, isn't he?"

Damn. Now Herb was really spooked. "Can we call one other English person?" I begged. "And this time, can *I* ask the question?"

We found a British secretary in the office of a studio executive—having a British secretary is considered el swell out here—and I said to her, "We're having a debate over whether this person is Australian or South African. Can you tell us?" My knuckles were white on the receiver as Herb played the damn cassette again.

"Oh," she corrected, "neither. That's BBC English. That's an Englishman." Which is how Duvall became Dr. Watson.

Later, Herb asked me what I thought of getting Laurence Olivier to play Professor Moriarty. It took all my self-control to pretend this was a regular question. Laurence Olivier, my childhood idol, he who had introduced me to Shakespeare, whose movies *Hamlet*, *Richard III*, *Henry V*, *Wuthering Heights*, and *The Beggar's Opera* I had sat through a million times. Olivier, whom I had seen in Becket on Broadway—the English Brando.

"Sounds good to me," I managed.

In the months that followed, I couldn't imagine this ever coming to fruition. We wouldn't be able to make a deal. He wouldn't live to play the part. *I* wouldn't live to see him play the part. He'd live and I'd live but we'd never meet. . . . But we made the deal and Olivier lived. *I* lived . . . and we met.

I had experienced life's casual cruelties. My mother's excruciating and pointless early death, my isolated and unsuccessful high school years—but just as randomly, life can be kind. At the Pinewood Studios in 1975, I was introduced to the Great Man.

"Did he really take cocaine?" Olivier asked, regarding Holmes. When I assured him this was the case, he smiled. "I don't think my father let me read that one."

Taking a breath, I told him of a letter I'd written him after seeing his filmed production of *Three Sisters*, in which, after thanking him for having brought so much happiness into my life, I'd explained I was trying to be a writer and offered, by way of small recompense, to send him a copy of the book I'd written when it came out, the book he was now filming.

He had no recollection and yet he'd sent me a very kind (now framed) letter of acknowledgment. He was on the film for three days, during which I lunched with him and watched his acting very carefully. When it came time for his close-up as the evil professor during one of Holmes's cocaine-induced hallucinations, he said, "I shall do my Richard the Third face . . ." and he did, too. I might as well have been in heaven.

But I was also in school. While working film sets are normally boring to visitors after the first half hour—it seems that nothing is being accomplished—for me, an aspiring director, it was endlessly instructive to watch the filming of my script. What might appear to the casual observer as long periods of wasteful inactivity, more closely scrutinized, revealed a pattern of industrious efficiency. I got to watch the masterful sets of the great Ken Adam (designer of the James Bond films and the extraordinary *Barry Lyndon*), lit by the equally celebrated cinematographer Oswald Morris (a favorite of John Huston, Morris photographed the pioneering color advances of the original *Moulin Rouge*, mimicking the palette of its subject, Toulouse-Lautrec, as well such crowd pleasers as *Oliver!* and *The Man Who Would Be King*).

I got to watch Herb Ross work with his actors and tried to learn from their interaction. Ross was patient but most of all—crucial for a film director—he was observant. And he was good with actors, not always the case with film directors, who, increasingly, have devolved into technicians. Ross knew how to give actors their time and space. He knew when to speak and when to stay silent, letting them make their own discoveries.

And I got to watch dailies, or rushes, those snippets of the previous day's work. Dailies have been described as sentences in a book that hasn't been written yet. (Editing is the process of stringing together those sentences.) In the dailies of *The Seven-Per-Cent Solution*, one could evaluate the work of Morris and Adam, but also glimpse the performances of such celebrated actors as Nicol Williamson and Alan Arkin (Holmes and Freud, respectively). I

say "glimpse" because what you are witnessing in dailies is slivers of performances, not the totality such as you'd see on a live stage.

While Alan Arkin took more takes to figure out how to play the role, it
was evident that both actors were at the top of their game. More problematic
was Robert Duvall, whom I had hectored Herb Ross into hiring, despite his
misgivings on the fateful day of our meeting him. Watching Duvall's work,
piecemeal, I despaired. The actor was doing nothing, merely standing there,
saying his lines.

"Can't you *ootz ootz* him?" I implored Ross. "He's not doing a thing." Herb
acknowledged the problem and tried to approach Duvall, who scoffed testily,
"What do you want me to do?" and made a serious of exaggerated grimaces.
We were going to have to live with what we'd got.

In the end, Duvall almost steals the movie. What we took to be his static
performance, once stitched together, revealed itself to be the most sophisticated film acting. Duvall understood, better than most, how his performance
would come together in the cutting room, how gestures so tiny they could
not be perceived with the naked eye or indeed in the dailies, once combined,
would deliver the cumulative punch. The closer the camera came, the less he
knew he needed to do.

Looking at dailies turns out to be an art in itself.

At this time, I was being importuned by my publisher, E. P. Dutton, for
a second Holmes novel, a request that threw me into some confusion. I well
understood their reasoning while at the same time I worried that I would, by
repeating myself, do the one thing that as a writer—and filmmaker—I had
always vowed to avoid. Two conversations served to change my mind. The
first occurred in San Francisco at the home of Francis Ford Coppola, where I
found myself having dinner one night with the director and his large family. I
had the opportunity to ask Coppola why he had chosen to make the second
Godfather movie, which he had filmed the year before.

"Three reasons," Coppola told me, serving up pasta he had cooked for
about twenty people on a Saturday night. "In no special order, I was offered a
great deal of money; secondly, I was curious to see if I could mine the same

vein for more material, and lastly, there were elements of the first movie—chiefly a pervasive amorality—which troubled me and I saw in the chance to make another film over which I would arguably have more control, an opportunity to address what I considered this serious defect."

Two days later, in Los Angeles, *Godfather II* won a boatload of Oscars, including Best Picture of the Year and Best Director.

The second conversation took place with another director, Ulu Grosbard, in Los Angeles. We were on a soundstage, standing in a buffet line at a wrap party for some film I've forgotten, when I posed the question of a sequel to my book to Grosbard.

"Do it," he told me. "It gives you 'fuck you' money."

"Meaning?"

"It buys you the right to fail. Our business is very problematic," he elaborated. "You can have hits, you can have flops, you can be hot, you can be cold. It's good to make money when you can; it's something for a rainy day and it buys you the opportunity to take chances on material whose commercial prospects might otherwise scare you off."

Coppola's and Grosbard's arguments carried the day and I went back to the Holmes well.

In 1976, I published my second Sherlock Holmes pastiche, *The West End Horror*, in which Holmes solves a grisly case in London's theater district, crossing paths with the likes of Oscar Wilde, Gilbert and Sullivan, George Bernard Shaw, and Bram Stoker. Though it lacked the surprise engendered by its predecessor, and though it was not a story about Sherlock Holmes (rather, a Sherlock Holmes story), it gave me considerable pleasure, especially as I found the actual mystery superior to the one in *The Seven-Per-Cent Solution*, and creating good mysteries is not normally one of my strengths. I also thought my characterizations of Wilde et al. were pretty good and I was proud of the fact that all the real people Holmes encounters were doing what they were actually doing in the first week of March 1895. Like *Seven*, *The West End Horror* became a bestseller, remaining on the *Times* list for three months. I had definitely arrived.

To top off my heady year, I found myself nominated for an Academy Award for the screenplay of *The Seven-Per-Cent Solution*. I don't much hold with prizes for art, and Oscars seem especially spurious. If you want to know who the best actor is, let them all play Hamlet. Otherwise it doesn't make any sense.

Unless you get the nomination, of course. Then it's dead serious. I lost to William Goldman for *All The President's Men* and griped (to anyone who'd listen) that at least I'd generated my own source material and hadn't had to rely on Dick Nixon!

This was all fun. I was making a living making movies, my childhood dream. I was vaguely respectable. . . .

It was all too simple. All I needed to do was keep writing Holmes stories. Ulu Grosbard's advice had one, hidden pitfall. You could always rationalize repeating yourself with the idea that you were putting money away for yet another rainy day. Do it often enough and you'd get out of the habit of taking chances. I didn't know if I was an artist but I knew for sure what a hack was: someone who finds something they're good at and keeps doing it over and over. My ambitions may have exceeded my abilities, but I wasn't prepared to keep writing Holmes stories.

PART 2

TREK

TIME AFTER TIME

My directing debut came in 1979 with a film I wrote called *Time After Time*. The film was based on a then-incomplete novel by an acquaintance of mine, Karl Alexander, whom I had known from the playwrights' workshop at the University of Iowa. His time travel idea of H. G. Wells chasing Jack the Ripper to present-day San Francisco greatly appealed to me. I wished I'd had the idea myself but knew perfectly well that I wouldn't have dreamt it up—or anything like it—in a million years. I'm also a slow thinker so it was a couple of months after reading Karl's sixty-five pages that I woke up with my brainstorm: *If you like the thing so much, how come you don't option the rights and write the screenplay yourself?* Among other things, a film based on Karl's conceit would involve merely two men pursuing one another through an alien landscape—alien to them, not the audience, meaning our production would be cheap. I would need only two Victorian costumes, and most of the special effects would be in the minds of the viewers, now forced to view our own society from the perspective of Martians, albeit Victorian ones.

I felt this was the sort of project a studio might permit me to direct. I had been biding my time for this moment, slowly building up my credibility around town with produced television movies and my (entirely fortuitous) Oscar nomination. The iron was hot; it was time to strike. I optioned Karl's story with my own money and wrote the screenplay in a week. This figure, however, is deceptive. When folks ask how long it takes to write something, they never—I never—include how much mental work precedes the physical act of writing. Most of my writing takes place before I actually put pen to paper. In the case of *Time After Time*, I had lain awake for months contemplating Karl's clever conceit and how I'd make it into a movie if only I'd thought of it, before the penny dropped and I came up with the notion of optioning the thing. I thought a lot about Jean-Luc Godard's *Alphavillle*, a sci-fi movie I had reviewed in college, where all the props are ordinary items with extraordinary names. A book, for example, might be termed "an information container" and so forth. I didn't remember much of the Godard film except for this ingenious and provocative gimmick. When my script was finished I showed it to a producer friend of mine, Herb Jaffe, with whom I had always wanted to work. Jaffe was known throughout the business as a gent, which doesn't begin to do him justice. He was among the legion of people I'd met as a stranger in town who had befriended me—just as Walter Mirisch later reminded me in the aftermath of Verna Fields's funeral. Herb loved the script and was undaunted by the condition of my directing it, and slowly evolved into one of those father figures who seem to play such important roles in my life. In addition, his younger son, Steven-Charles, who coproduced the film, became my close friend and ultimately my producing partner. With Herb as my very reputable producer, another part of my "plausibility campaign" with the studios to direct was in place.

Although *Time After Time* bears a superficial resemblance to *The Seven-Per-Cent Solution* (Karl had said my book inspired him to write his), I think there are significant differences between the two. *The Seven-Per-Cent Solution* is about two specific people, Holmes and Freud, and how their intellectual gifts cross-fertilize. By contrast, *Time After Time* is a movie that juxtaposes types. Wells represents civilized, progressive, constructive humanity; the Ripper is his dark, destructive counterpart. If *The Seven-Per-Cent Solution* is about individuals, *Time After Time* is concerned with the flip sides of humanity.

That's my two cents, anyway. Artists are not the best—and certainly not the definitive—critics of their own work. Once that work is launched into the wide world, we lose all proprietary authority, and our opinions are of no more value than anyone else's. Possibly less. An author can't possibly follow his book into the hands of every reader, looking over his shoulder and telling him what to think about what he's read. Or what it means. Neither can a film director explain his intentions from the back of every theater where his film unspools. People will think what they're going to think, conclude what they will. The artist/author's opinion is simply and merely one additional view-point. The word "definitive" has no place in artistic or literary discussions. There is no such thing as a "definitive" biography, any more than there can be a "definitive" piano concerto or a "definitive" apple by Cézanne.

Warner Brothers and Orion competed for the screenplay and wound up cofinancing it. To become the director, I had essentially replicated the "leap-frog" system that had successfully led to my becoming a screenwriter: I had consented to sell the film rights to *The Seven-Per-Cent Solution* only if I wrote the script; this time I would sell my script only if I could direct the film.

They do say that fun is the past tense of shit, but, looking back, mak-ing *Time After Time* was perhaps the most fun I've ever had in the daytime. I barely knew what I was doing, had never directed a film of any kind before (unless you count my youthful contribution to *Around the World in Eighty Days*) and, though terrified, I enjoyed every heady minute of it. I worked with temperamental but excellent actors and I surrounded myself with an excellent and supportive crew, to all of whom I made the same speech: "I know noth-ing. You must teach me. You must not mind teaching me. And having taught me, you must not mind if I then want to do it my way, anyway. Don't go away angry. Don't go away at all." Those who could smilingly endure this catechism and say yes were the ones I wanted. I proposed Malcolm McDowell as H. G. Wells. Warner objected—"He always plays the villain!" "Yes, but this time he'll be the hero—that's acting," I explained, remembering Herb Ross's advice about sticking to my guns. A young, slow-talking brunette from Arkansas gave a terrific reading as the heroine. She was completely different from the blonde, fast-talking, city-chippie, Jean Arthur type I had contemplated when I wrote the script, but she'd made me see the part in a different light. I fought for and landed Mary Steenburgen. When Malcolm asked me who his leading lady was to be, I grinned and predicted, "You'll love her."

Warner Brothers suggested using Mick Jagger as the Ripper but I had trouble visualizing him—not as the Ripper (certainly!) but in his alter ego as a Harley Street surgeon. When I demurred they said, "You mean you won't even meet with him? I then realized—better late than never—that in order to appear reasonable I needed to go through the motions. Besides, there was always the possibility that they were right and I was missing a bet. A meeting with the living legend was duly convened at his hotel suite. Jagger's latest tour was coming to an end and he was understandably fatigued. We had beers and made self-conscious, desultory small talk for twenty minutes or so (about what? I can't recall), and then I departed, my mind unchanged. David Warner made a splendid Ripper—and a convincing Victorian doctor.

There's lots to say about making a movie; directing is fun. Orson Welles called it the biggest set of electric trains any kid was ever given to play with. There are also an astonishing number of moving parts and the director must keep track of all of them. It is therefore also extremely hard work, both intellectually and physically. You must be in top shape or you'll collapse. The job goes on seven days a week, twenty-four hours a day; there's no let-up. If you are not shooting, you are preparing to shoot, thinking about the film, watching dailies, dealing with actors, losing locations, answering to your backers, and always, *always* trying in the tumult to hear the small voice that whispered to you while you were writing the thing. *Is this what I imagined? Is it better? Is it worse? Should I settle or go for another take?* I remember reading someplace that Steven Spielberg said the hardest and most important thing to do while directing is to listen to that small voice in your head that reminds you of what kind of film you set out to make in the first place. It is almost impossible, sometimes, to hear that all-important voice amid the din of movie battle. The best directors have great inner hearing.

If you are both writer and director, you face a double-barreled pressure. When you're working on the script, you can't be directing; when you're directing you can't be working on the script. So: make sure that script is ready before you go. Directing a movie is like having a picnic on Mars—once you set out, there's no going back for the salt. The script *will* change as you work but try to have it in the kind of shape where it will be able to withstand change and still be true to itself. And you. Like the Constitution, which has had many amendments, but still manages to express the essential notions of the Founding Fathers.

Malcolm and Mary were great together—you really believed they were falling in love. I told myself I was a really good director. . . .

There are some strengths I bring to directing that are extremely useful and other qualities that are liabilities. In the main, I am healthy and haven't ever become incapacitated on a shoot; I know something about scripts and have become good at writing them; I understand the mechanics of storytelling and the integral part that character plays in narrative. We learn about a character from the choices he makes. (Character is destiny, says Aristotle.) My background in theater helps me to deal with actors and performances. You'd be surprised how many directors know nothing about stories or actors—or maybe you wouldn't. In addition, my writing ability is also of use in the editing room, where I know about cutting and pasting and being ruthless with what doesn't work. Also, I like people, which is useful if you're a director. I can usually charm or coax them to give me what I want.

So much for the good news.

The bad news is that I came to moviemaking late, especially working with the camera. While Steven Spielberg was playing with lenses, I was playing with typewriters, and the difference is all too obvious. The camera and its possibilities were alien to me—a fine situation for a film director. And remember, I'm a slow learner. The British have evolved a great system: you direct endless commercials and hone your technical skills along the way; in the U.S. commercial directors don't direct movies and vice versa. (The closest thing to that kind of training nowadays in America is music videos for MTV. But music videos arrived after I did.)

In addition, while I like people, I have difficulty confronting them. If I can't coax or manipulate them to get what I want, I sure as hell can't threaten them. Directing is government by consent of the governed. It's an agreement presumably made by actors and crew alike to trust the director and do what he says. But if an actor acts up and I can't figure out how to defuse him, I don't do head-to-head.

There are some directors who believe themselves—rightly or wrongly—to be omniscient. No one can tell them anything—about story, acting, filming, or editing. Crew members who make suggestions get fired.

That isn't the kind of director I ever believed I am or aspire to be. Film-making to me is a collaborative process, and that's much of what interested me about it. When I write, I write alone and I have complete control. I am limited by only my ability. When I direct, I work with gifted people and I try to take advantage of what they know and think, *always reserving the right to say no.* I am a pillager of other people's ideas, and on *Time After Time* I found that I (and the film) benefited from this policy.

Let one example suffice. We had just shot a scene with Malcolm and the unit had broken for lunch. A lighting man came down from high up in the gaiters (the scaffolding suspended on cables above sets on a soundstage, which supports crew and lights) and tapped me on the shoulder.

"You're the writer of this thing, as well as the director, aren't you?"

I owned that I was.

"Well, if you're asking me," the man went on, "he's saying the wrong thing there," meaning Malcolm as H. G. Wells in the scene we had just completed.

"Really?" I didn't know whether to pursue this or not. I was hungry. "What should he have said?"

"Well, if you're asking me . . ." and the man went on to supply a line far better than the one we had just shot. It was a reprise from an earlier moment in the script and so terrific, echoed in this scene, that I kicked myself before realizing that, as the director, I was entitled to come back after lunch and shoot the lighting man's line instead of my crappy piece of dialogue.

I cherished this moment (a) because it helped the film and (b) because the atmosphere on my set encouraged this sort of participation, of which there were to be many other instances. We sometimes limit people by using them to fulfill only their "official" job capacities. The cinematographer takes the pictures, the script girl sees to continuity and so forth, the gaffers arrange the lights.

This seems very shortsighted to me. These people have been around and seen a lot. Their ideas aren't always right, but I can always reject them. I carry in my head a vision of what the film is supposed to be (the little voice) but I can evaluate suggestions that may help me achieve that vision. Once my crew realized that I was interested in what they thought and had to say about the work, we became a much more cohesive and "European"-type unit. In America if the director turns to the prop man and asks what he thinks of a scene or a line, the man is terrified to respond; it's not his department. His department is props, a fiefdom he guards jealously, and when he looks at the dailies, he is interested in only whether his props did the job they are supposed to do. In Europe there's much less territoriality about job responsibilities and much more overlapping involvement with the total project. There's less fear, less concentration on covering your ass. To me this is a much more interesting and appealing way to work. Hollywood technicians and artisans are the equal if not the superior of any in the world; the problem lies with a system seemingly cribbed from the assembly line.

Warner Brothers wanted changes in the finished film. Some of their ideas were good; others I didn't like. They wanted more close-ups; I didn't see the need. They wanted Mary Steenburgen to appear more roughed up at the end and asked me to reshoot; again, I thought they were wrong. If audiences were studying whether she was "roughed up" instead of simply being flabbergasted to find her alive at this point in the tale, we were in big trouble.

A week or so later, my editor, Donn Cambern (who cut *Easy Rider*), found himself on an airplane with someone in the biz who asked him what he was working on. When he said, *Time After Time*, his seat partner sighed sympathetically, "Oh, that's the one they hate."

Cheerful tidings. Warner Brothers hated the film. Naturally. Among other things I had used the services of Hungarian film composer Miklós Rózsa (*Ben-Hur*, *The Asphalt Jungle*, *El Cid*, etc.), who was considered passé. Warner wanted a pop score, which would have been ludicrous. Our hero was a Victorian man, through whose sensibility we were seeing our world; I wanted the music to reflect his values and life experience, not ours; let rock music be another phenomenon he encounters in the late twentieth century, heard on radios or televisions.

Ted Ashley, then the head of the studio, saw the film in a screening room, talked on the phone most of the time as it ran, and then fled, saying, "Great job, talk to you later." Herb and I didn't hear from him for months. The word was out that we had made a stinker.

That *I* had made a stinker.

By the time we were due for our first preview, I was a total wreck. I had insisted and resisted, I had fought, I had refused so many of their suggestions, their well-meaning, but (to me) wrong-headed ideas, and now I was paying the price, my directorial career over before it had properly begun.

We previewed in Woodland Hills, just outside LA, because no executive could be bothered to travel anywhere to see this film. Some of them didn't even bother showing up in Woodland Hills. Those who did glared at me or pointedly ignored me. Even my two stars, demoralized by helpful remarks from their agents, wouldn't speak to me. I sat down behind them as the house-lights dimmed and felt as though I was going to my execution.

One of the fights I had had with Warner involved the use of their old logo (the Warner Bros. shield) and the fanfare written by Max Steiner to go with it. Warner was then using a logo that looked as though it should be stamped on office furniture; I had an old-fashioned film and I wanted an old-fashioned beginning. In the end (that is to say, the beginning), I had my way but they were enraged about it.

Now the Warner shield burst forth upon the screen, accompanied by the Steiner fanfare, and the audience erupted with applause and cheers.

And that was just the beginning. As the film unspooled, the audience responded enthusiastically in all the right places and applauded for some time when it was over. The picture was unquestionably a crowd pleaser. I can still remember Malcolm and Mary in the seats in front of me, staring at one another in disbelief as the film splashed across the screen behind their astonished silhouettes, to the accompaniment of laughter and cheers. I still remember a Warner exec looking at me in the lobby as I walked out and tearing up his notes like so much confetti, tossing them in the air.

People loved the film. At the end they didn't want to leave but milled about the theater, a sure sign of approval. The "cards," those terrifying mini-reviews by audiences that can result in a film's being recut, reshot, or even

shelved, were more wildly favorable than they had been about anything Warner had released in the previous three years.

I stood in the theater lobby, unable to grasp what had happened. And
stranger things were to follow. A second preview in Toronto the next day was
even bigger than the first in terms of audience size and enthusiasm. Woodland
Hills, after all, was a suburb of Hollywood, and the audience must have been
half industry. In Toronto, it was just folks, and they were much less inhibited
about manifesting their approval. The following Monday Frank Wells, chairman of the company, introduced himself to me by saying, "Failure is an or-
phan but success has many fathers. Congratulations."

We even got a handsome letter of apology from Ted Ashley, who quoted
Fiorello La Guardia—"When I make a mistake, it's a beaut. You've made a
great film," he went on. "Now the only question is whether the people will
come—whether you get the tom-tom factor," by which he meant word of
mouth.

Later still, Bob Shapiro, head of production at the studio, genially con-
fided over Diet Cokes in his office, "We admired you when you were flexible
and we admired you when you held firm."

Admired me? While I was trying not to heave with terror for having defied them? I had absorbed all these body blows personally, agonized over my
career prospects with every stand I took and all the while, from their point of
view, it was—what? Just business?

Ultimately, our film may have been victimized by its early success. Buoyed
by those preview results, the studio opened it very wide, perhaps too wide.
The movie needed time to build, time for those tom-toms to spread the word.
We were in so many theaters on day one that there was no time for word of
mouth to take hold. We also didn't have a big star, on the strength of whose
name alone people would hear about or be interested in the film. We had Malcolm and we had Mary, with whom Malcolm had fallen in love. After the film
they were married and had children. Perfect casting. In the end the picture did
do well, if not quite as well as those previews had led everyone to hope.

Time After Time is not a great film, but, like *The Seven-Per-Cent Solution,* it is enormous fun and, I think, does not insult the viewer's intelligence. Between the two movies there is something that seems to characterize the best of my work (in my subjective estimate, anyway): the fusing of a strong, often fantastical story with realistic characters, which makes the concept more plausible than might otherwise be the case. Looking at the movie today, I am struck by its homely appearance and its startlingly bitter social commentary. But both these aspects are easily—and mercifully—overwhelmed by the charm of Malcolm and Mary as Wells and Amy. Perhaps the fact of their falling in love as the cameras rolled didn't hurt. Movies are soufflés. Some rise, some don't. *Time After Time*, with all its first-time directing faults, is nevertheless a soufflé that rose and has remained aloft since its release. Steven Spielberg, producer of *Back to the Future*, told me that his team had studied *Time After Time*, running it again and again.

And to this day, all Warner Brothers movies start with the Warner shield.

We learn the lessons that life teaches us; sometimes they are the wrong lessons. The lesson I learned from *Time After Time* is that making good movies is easy, and that I knew how to do it.

I clearly couldn't distinguish between expertise and beginner's luck. Clever is not wise, as Odysseus learned to his cost.

Then it was back to the couch and more years of talking to myself. I was determined that my next film would be Robertson Davies's novel *Fifth Business*, for which I had written what I thought was a truly great script.

But the world wasn't ready for Robertson Davies's blend of mysticism and melodrama (it still isn't, apparently), and *Time After Time* was not so big a hit as to give me carte blanche. I waited for about two years, wrote a couple of other novels to pass the time, and got angrier and angrier.

Another thing about the movies and me; about art and me. I have always been more interested in content than in the form in which that content is expressed, which I believe is a defect on my part as an artist. Art is mainly about expression or execution and only secondarily about content. *Anything* can be made into art—even pornography or fascism, like it or not. (If you don't believe me, check out the wonderful *Carmina Burana*, which is comprised of both.) But I never was able fully to buy into the form-over-content argument. In my films, I care less for the photography and composition of the images than I do for what the people are saying and doing. I would a thousand times sooner direct actors and help shape their performance rather than work on special effects. I have this theory that the film can be anything but out of focus and audiences will tolerate it, so long as what they are watching is interesting. Ditto the sound. On the other hand, I, as an audience member, respond like everyone else to ravishing or original imagery in the movies, to nifty sound effects. I am as seducible as the next man. Even as I disapprove of the content-less image-makers, I envy them; envy their technical facility and their cheerful, absent-minded amorality. Hey, it's the movies—let's blow something up.

I had only half an idea what *Fifth Business* would look like; but I understood with perfect clarity that it was a terrific story, which was basically all I cared about, and I insisted on being allowed to tell it. Hollywood resisted. Time, meanwhile, was passing.

Star Trek II: The Wrath of Khan

Looking back on earlier portions of one's life, one is surprised by the turns it has taken. Things and events no imagination could have predicted unfold in a seemingly random manner, leading to equally unexpected and improbable results. Like pinballs in one of those arcade games, we bang into things and ricochet off in unanticipated directions. Detours become highways. I certainly could never have anticipated my involvement with the *Star Trek* series, let alone where that involvement would lead.

Had *Time After Time* been a bigger hit, I might've got my shot at *Fifth Business*, but it wasn't and I didn't. In the meanwhile the film had netted me Hollywood's (then) über agent, Stan Kamen, who called and said he wanted to represent me. I responded that he wouldn't when he heard that there was only one project in which I was interested. Agents must be used to all sorts of quaint notions and obsessions from clients, and mine didn't appear to faze him: agents know how to wait . . . Kamen would patiently send me scripts; I would send them back.

Time passed. I sat in my house and went to meetings only if they involved *Conjuring* (the screen name for *Fifth Business*). Months became years. I met with all sorts of people but *Conjuring* stubbornly resisted my efforts to give it life.

I got all sorts of advice, including of the "Make one for them—something commercial" (again that word!) "and then you can get your film financed" bromide.

It was on a Sunday afternoon in early 1982 and I was barbecuing hamburgers with a childhood friend, Karen Moore, now (i.e., then) an executive at Paramount, when she gave me a piece of blunt advice: "Nicky, if you want to learn how to direct, you should *direct*, and not sit up here holding your breath because you're not getting to make the film you want."

Had this counsel come unsolicited from, say, my parents, I doubt I would have paid it heed, but originating in a disinterested friend, it resonated, especially when she followed it up with, "Why don't you sit down with Harve Bennett over at Paramount? He's in charge of producing the next *Star Trek* movie and I think you'd like him."

I must have stared at her.

"*Star Trek?* Is that the one with the guy with pointy ears?" My experience of and exposure to the series had been limited to my Iowa City friend and since then had consisted only of seeing those ears flash by when channel surfing. One look and I kept going. The whole idea that, contrary to all scientific understanding and evidence to date, the cosmos was filled with other "life-forms," most of them walking around on two legs, speaking English, and always landing on planets with breathable air, seemed utterly absurd to me.

"You'll like him," Karen insisted, meaning Bennett, not Spock. With her earlier advice still ringing in my ears, I agreed to meet the man.

Each of Hollywood's studio lots has its own personality and feel. Warner is perhaps the most attractive, with a gardened, country-club sort of atmosphere; Universal most resembles a factory, while Fox and MGM are shadows of what they once were. Most of Fox's territory is now occupied by the high-rise office buildings known as Century City, while MGM, in some sort of irony, is now the home of another company entirely, Columbia (in turn owned by Sony), once known, due to its puny size, as Columbia the Germ of the Ocean.

The Paramount lot was the most "Hollywood" of the bunch, due to its location in the heart of that zip code, even though it shared space, eerily enough, with a cemetery. Aside from a "Western" street and some New York facades, there never had been a real backlot (exteriors had typically utilized the Paramount ranch in Agoura). In fact the smallish studio had actually been cobbled together from Paramount and what was formerly RKO, before it had been bought by Lucille Ball and turned into something called Desilu, combining Lucy's name with that of her Cuban husband, Desi Arnaz. Before the

Desilu incorporation, RKO had been largely owned and controlled by some-one named Howard Hughes. RKO (for Radio Keith Orpheum) was the place where they filmed *Citizen Kane*, and where Fred and Ginger had cavorted, personifying pure happiness. Over the wall that separated them, Paramount was home to Cecil B. DeMille, Ernst Lubitsch, and Billy Wilder.

Studios concentrated on different fare—MGM was wholesome and musi-cal, Warner made gangster melodramas, biopics, and "premature" anti-Nazi propaganda, Fox concerned itself with great domestic social issues, Universal with Frankenstein et al., while Columbia relied on Frank Capra populism and Rita Hayworth.

Paramount went for Marlene Dietrich, European sophistication, and De-Mille historical hokum, before going on to Hope and Crosby, then Martin and Lewis. By the time of my arrival that day in 1982, the wall that had sepa-rated the two studios had been long since been breached, and all was now Paramount.

Film studios not only don't look like one another, they tend not to look like anything else, either, with their huge soundstages and intermittent "bunga-lows." Although periodically gutted and refurbished with the latest decor and technology, the old wood and stucco exteriors at Paramount look pretty much the way they do as Billy Wilder showed them in *Sunset Blvd.*

In one of those bungalows, after I finally located it among its lookalike neighbors, I found myself chatting with an unpretentious gent some years older than myself. Harve Bennett had thinning light reddish hair, a friendly smile, and a keen, analytic intelligence he was at some pains to conceal under the cloak of "I'm just a regular guy" affability. Perhaps he saw himself in this light—or at any rate, wished to see himself in it—but if so, he was kidding himself along with others. At some point I learned Bennett had been a child radio star on a program called *Quiz Kids.* A native of Chicago, he'd migrated to Los Angeles, where he'd found a great deal of success in the world of televi-sion, having produced *The Mod Squad, The Bionic Woman*, and *The Six Mil-lion Dollar Man,* none of which I had seen.

My attitude toward television has always been ambivalent, to say the least. The constant interruption of the stories by commercials makes it hard for me to watch. The only shows I could stand were the comedies of my childhood: *Your Show of Shows* (Sid Caesar), *You'll Never Get Rich* (*Sgt. Bilko*), Ernie Kovacs, *The Honeymooners*, etc. The rest, as Hamlet might have said, was PBS.

On the other hand, *Star Wars* had recently come out and knocked my socks off (along with everyone else's), and the idea of doing a big-screen space opera had its appeal. I use the word "opera" advisedly. I am an unabashed opera fan and I recognized in Lucas's work, along with John Williams's ersatz Richard Straussian score and its enormous contribution to the goings-on, a cinematic opera, a sort of *Ring* Lite.

Bennett, who was tactful enough to laugh at my jokes, sipped beer from a bottle and showed me several episodes of the original *Star Trek*. I confess what I saw did not particularly excite me; neither did the first *Star Trek* movie, released in 1979. I couldn't quite place (not having Bennett's analytical mind) what it was I found so off-putting and could only grope toward insight. My groping took the form of noting all the things I didn't like: the uniforms, the acting, the sets, the solemnity.

Bennett then showed me "Space Seed," the television episode that introduced the supervillain Khan, and I did respond to that: Ricardo Montalban was a great actor and like most great actors was wasted in roles beneath his talents. When Bennett, who spoke in clipped, foreshortened English, not unreminiscent of *Star Trek* dialogue ("Message, Spock?"), suggested using Khan as a character in the new film, I began to become interested.

The reasons Paramount was intent on making a second *Star Trek* film are by now well-known: despite the fact that the original motion picture had been a "runaway" production, costing an astounding forty-five million dollars (in 1979!) and despite the fact that it had received indifferent notices, the movie wound up in profit, close to eighty-three million dollars. Barry Diller, then running the studio with Michael Eisner and Jeffrey Katzenberg, realized that if they could make another, better film, at a reasonable budget, they might develop a franchise to rival Lucas's. The first *Star Trek* had been a torturous learning process, originally to be helmed by Phil Kauffman and designed by the great Ken Adam; disagreements about scripts and budgets sent both men packing. Eventually the film was directed by Robert Wise, whose impressive credits included editing *Citizen Kane* and directing such successful films as *The Day the Earth Stood Still* and *West Side Story* (with Jerome Robbins), as well as the indestructible *The Sound of Music*.

The second *Trek* attempt had subsequently been farmed out to the television division of Paramount, headed by Gary Nardino, who would undertake to make the film for a quarter of the original movie's budget.

These considerations did not escape me. I didn't know if I could make a great movie (my jovial editor on *Star Trek II*, Bill Dornisch, wanted to call his production company "Miracle Pictures"—their soubriquet: *"If it's a good picture, it's a Miracle!"*) but I began to see that even if I made an okay one that cost a fraction of the original, it would be a shrewd career move.

Bennett explained that draft five of the screenplay would be arriving in two weeks and offered to send it to me. I said fine and went home, where my mind began to toy with the idea of my outer space *singspiel*, featuring the redoubtable Montalban.

Other events intervened—including some involving *Conjuring*, never far from the forefront of my consciousness—before I realized that a month had passed and a *Star Trek II* script had yet to appear at my door. I rang Bennett and asked him what had happened. He chuckled awkwardly and said, "Kid"—his usual term of address for me—"my tit's in a ringer."

"Come again?" I'd heard him; I just couldn't process the locution.

"I can't send it to you," he explained. "It isn't any good."

In my naïveté, this was the last thing I had expected to hear. Several "beats" (as screenwriters are fond of writing) of silence must have followed.

"Kid?"

"Well, what about draft four?" I inquired, remembering he had referred to the latest pass as five.

A second chuckle on the other end of the line. "Kid, you don't get it. Draft four, draft three, and all the rest—these are unrelated attempts to get a second *Star Trek* script, and none of them works."

"Let me read them," I said before realizing that I'd said it.

"There's no point."

The conversation continued in this vein, but I persisted—why, I am no longer certain. All I can offer is that the space opera idea wouldn't let me go, and Karen Moore's words about learning how to direct hadn't ceased reverberating in my cerebellum, either.

A day or so later a car drove up, and a ton of scripts were hefted in my direction. I began with draft number five. As Bennett had described, it was a failure. Reading it made me feel as if I was watching the episodes again, and I had no particular interest in, much less affection for them. I didn't understand the world, the people, or the language.

I picked up draft four with the same result, then doggedly plowed through the rest. The process must have taken a couple of days. Not only were the scripts uninvolving, but I happen to be a slow reader.

Idly I did some calculating. Figure at least two months, more likely three, to write a film script—there had been *five* of these attempts. That probably represented a cumulative year's fruitless gestation. Now add the standard contractual studio "reading period" of six weeks, and what I was reading had taken even longer. The attempt to get a second *Star Trek* feature in the works may have consumed upward of two years.

Write us another Star Trek *movie.* What marching orders had the studio given each of these writers? Any? Too many? Were there themes or ideas they had been offered, or did their labors represent merely their own imaginations and initiative? I didn't think to ask. What difference would the answer have made? In any case, as I have since learned, studio memos are never signed, thus avoiding the assignment of responsibility. Script notes typically arrive attributed to some collective euphemism, such as FROM: THE GROUP but that's as far as anyone goes since the heyday of David O. Selznick. Years later, when Paramount asked me to write other *Star Trek*s, they never specified storylines or themes, so it is reasonable to suppose they hadn't on *Star Trek II.* Just make us another one. Later, as I recall, I would give them the general idea to approve, but it related to the area and subject matter, rather than the specific plot. Whatever it was, they always said okay. Things are quite different today; today the studio wants a complete précis of the proposed film before authorizing the script. They want the story broken down by scenes in something referred to as a "beat sheet." (I am not very good at creating the "beat sheets" because I don't know how the film will break down until I have written it.)

One thing was certain: after all of their work and chopped-down trees, there were bits and pieces of interest in each of the five drafts I read, but no theme, character, or situation was sustained such that it added up to anything. (Maybe beat sheets would have helped.)

Two years for bits and pieces seemed to me an awful lot of dry wells, but what did I know? (Nothing, as it turned out; years later, on *Fatal Attraction*, I again marveled at studios' stubbornness about getting what they'd made up their minds to have. I could never figure out, half the time, why they chose to make the movies they did. David Picker, for years head of United Artists, once acknowledged that if he'd made all the movies he'd passed on and passed on all the films he'd made, he would probably have scored about the same. But on the other side, for every ridiculous financial disaster, we find ourselves grateful for stupendous follies that somehow got filmed thanks to the same incontrovertible zeal, movies that today number among cinema's triumphs. Think *Darling Lili* vs. *Reds*.)

Disappointed and disheartened after my perusal of the five *Star Trek* scripts, I prepared to write the whole thing off and went back to my routine, such as it was. In those days, after feeding my dogs, I rolled down from my home in Laurel Canyon to the public tennis courts in the Valley and slammed the ball around with Gary Lucchesi, who had, following Stan Kamen's untimely death, succeeded him as my agent. Lucchesi thrashed me with regularity before heading off for William Morris. I was an enthusiastic but inept player—rallying brilliantly in practice but always clutching when points were at stake.

While Lucchesi was cutting deals for his other clients, I was being psychoanalyzed. It must have been driving from tennis to my analyst's couch that two ideas began to take shape in my mind. The first involved a niggling association at the back of my brain that had been there since I first began watching the episodes and the original movie. *Star Trek* vaguely reminded me of something, something for which I had great affection. It took me quite a while before I realized what it was. I remember waking with a start one night and saying it aloud:

"Hornblower!"

When I was a teenager I had devoured a series of novels by the English author C. S. Forester (author of *The African Queen* and *Sink the Bismarck!*, among other favorites), concerning an English sea captain, Horatio Hornblower, and his adventures during the Napoleonic wars. "Horatio" as a first name was the giveaway; Hornblower was clearly based on Lord Nelson, though I've recently learned his surname derived from that of Hollywood producer Arthur Hornblow, Jr., a friend of Forester's. There was also a beloved movie version, Raoul Walsh's *Captain Horatio Hornblower R. N.*, starring Gregory Peck and Virginia Mayo. (In the picaresque film, Hornblower faces off with the malignant and memorable El Supremo. Watching the film later as an adult, I understood that El Supremo, the frothing megalomaniac, was a racist caricature, the more so as he was played by a Caucasian in "swarthy" face, the UK-born Alec Mango. Khan Noonian Singh, by contrast, was a genuine [if oddly named] superman, embodied by a superb actor who happened to be Hispanic. Khan was a cunning, remorseless, but witty adversary—his true triumph being that audiences adored his Lear-inflected villainy as much as they responded to Kirk's enraged heroism.)

Hornblower has had many descendants besides Kirk. Another Englishman, Alexander Kent, wrote a series of similar seafaring tales, and Patrick O'Brien's Aubrey-Maturin novels are an upmarket version of same—Jane Austen on the high seas—one of which became the splendid film *Master and Commander*. Still another Englishman, Bernard Cornwell, produced a landlocked version of Hornblower in the character of Sharpe, a swaggering, blue-collar hero of the Peninsular War.

I asked myself, What was *Star Trek* but Hornblower in outer space? The doughty captain with a girl in every port and adventure lurking in each latitude? Like Hornblower, whose gruff exterior conceals a heart of humanity, Kirk is the sort of captain any crew would like to serve under. Like his oceanic counterpart, he is intelligent but real, compassionate but fearless, attractive to women but not precisely a rake. For prepubescent (and for that matter postpubescent) boys such as myself, Hornblower-Kirk conceals the sort of Lone Ranger–d'Artagnan–Scarlet Pimpernel hero we liked to fantasize about being, the steady guy with a dashing secret identity. Hornblower-Kirk's secret identity was folded into his own persona, but the notion still holds. (A case might also be made, I suppose, that James Bond is yet another offspring of Forester's hero.)

Once I was possessed of this epiphany, a great many things fell readily into place. I suddenly knew what *Star Trek* wanted to be and how I could relate to it. The look of the film and the natures of the characters—even their language—suddenly became clear. And doable. I would write a Hornblower script, simply relocating in outer space.

That left the question of the script itself, and therein came my second brainstorm. I invited Bennett and his producing partner, Robert Sallin, to sit down with me at my place, where I laid it out for them.

Sallin, who owned his own commercial-producing company, was a dapper, diminutive ex-military man with a clipped, Ronald Colman mustache and agreeable manners. He and Bennett had been close friends at UCLA, and the *Star Trek* project was seen by Bennett as a chance for them to work together. (By the time the film was finished, they would no longer be speaking.)

They listened as I explained my Hornblower thesis and notion of reconfiguring the look and language of the original series. I didn't like the idea of everyone running around wearing what looked to me like Dr. Dentons and couldn't make out why people said "negative" when they meant "no," or why no one ever read a book or lit a cigarette.

In this, I was ignorant of *Star Trek*'s history and more especially of the contribution of its originator, a former bomber, later a Pan Am pilot, and later still a policeman named Gene Roddenberry. As producer, Roddenberry had been in charge of the original 1979 movie, made a decade after the original television series left the air. In the wake of its disastrous cost overruns Paramount had apparently reached an accommodation with him, whereby he was not to participate in the making of the second film but would receive a credit. The original film's difficulties appear to have been concentrated in two areas: (1) a script that kept mutating (I was told that cast members received pages changes stamped not by the day but by the *hour*, as in, "Did you get the 4:30 changes?") and (2) endless difficulties over the special effects. Nowadays, thanks to computer-generated imagery, much of what once consumed millions of dollars and thousands of man-hours seems like child's play. But listening to Douglas Trumbull detail what went into creating Stanley Kubrick's even earlier *2001: A Space Odyssey* (1968), one understands that all this eye candy had to be figured out literally frame by frame, utilizing endless trial and error by multiple FX houses as they experimented with spaceship models, how to photograph them convincingly, get rid of wires, create the illusion of activity inside them (would you believe tiny projectors, reflecting images off mirrors bounced *inside?*), etc. Special effects houses need huge sums of money for equipment to start up and later geeks to man them, change them, break them, and reconceive them.

But none of the foregoing altered the parameters of the universe Roddenberry had set up. He was emphatic that Starfleet was not a military organization but something akin to the Coast Guard. This struck me as manifestly absurd, for what were Kirk's adventures but a species of gunboat diplomacy wherein the Federation (read America, read the Anglo-Saxons) was always right and aliens were—in Kipling's queasy phrase—"lesser breeds"? Yes, there was lip service to minority participation, but it was clear who was driving the boat.

Ignorant, as I say, or arrogantly uninterested in precedent, I was intent on refashioning the second movie as a nautical homage.

"And the script?" Bennett prompted quietly.

"Well, here's my other idea," I told them, taking a deep breath and producing a yellow legal pad from under my chair. "Why don't we make a list of everything we like in these five drafts? Could be a plot, a subplot, a sequence, a scene, a character, a line even . . ."

"Yes?"

"And then I will write a new script and cobble together all the things we choose."

They stared at me blankly.

"What's wrong with that?" I had been rather proud of this idea.

Now they glanced at one another before answering.

"The problem is that unless we turn over a shooting script of some sort to ILM [Industrial Light & Magic, George Lucas's special effects house, contracted by Paramount to provide shots for the movie] in twelve days, they cannot guarantee delivery of the FX shots in time for the June release."

I wasn't sure I'd heard correctly.

"June release? *What* June release?"

That was when I was informed that the picture had already been booked into theaters—a factor that, in my ignorance, had never occurred to me.

I thought again. I must have been really stoked by this point, because the next thing that popped out was:

"Alright, I think I can do this in twelve days." Why I thought this, I cannot now recall.

Again they looked at me, then at each other, and then down at my rug, as if something inscrutable was written there.

"What's wrong with that?" I demanded.

Bennett sighed. "What's wrong is that we couldn't even make your *deal* in twelve days."

I blinked. I was still relatively new to the business—this would be only the second film I'd directed—and none of this made any sense to me.

"Look," I countered impatiently, "Forget about my deal. Forget about the credit. Forget about the money. I'm just talking about the writing part, not the directing," I inserted with emphasis. "All I know is that if we don't do what

I'm suggesting, make that list right here, right now—there isn't going to be any movie. Do you want the movie or not?"

What would have happened had I not made this offer? Clearly the film would have been canceled for the nonce, the booking dates forfeited. Whether the studio would have plowed forward with yet another script for an opening in another season is a question no one can answer.

Everything changes with hindsight. Do I remember what happened next? I recollect their astonishment, but perhaps this is mythopoesis. I mean, who knew I would ever be *trying* to remember this stuff? What I *do* know is that we then made the list. It included Bennett's original happy notion of using Khan (from the "Space Seed" episode, wherein Kirk rescues the genetically enhanced Khan and his followers, only to have Khan attempt to seize control of the *Enterprise* and, failing, marooned by Kirk along with a female member of the *Enterprise*'s crew who has fallen for him, on an asteroid or some such location); the Genesis Project (creating planetary life); Kirk meeting his son; Lieutenant Saavik (Spock's beautiful Vulcan protégée); the death of Spock; and the simulator sequence (in which the *Enterprise*, under Saavik's command, appears to be attacked in what later turns out to be what we would today call a war game; this sequence originally occurred—minus Spock's participation—in the middle of one of the drafts). All these materials were culled higgledy-piggledy from the five different drafts that I never—to the best of my recollection—consulted again.

"Why can't Kirk read a book?" I wondered, staring at the titles on my shelves. I pulled down *A Tale of Two Cities*, funnily enough the only novel of which it can be said that everyone knows the first and last lines.

Bennett and Sallin left and I went to work.

TWELVE DAYS

When my agent and cheerful tennis partner, Mr. Lucchesi, learned what I was doing, I thought he would have a seizure. Lucchesi had once considered studying for the priesthood, but this episode must have confirmed his wisdom in abandoning the clergy. He was in no mood to turn the other cheek. The idea that I had offered my services for nothing was not only illegal; from his standpoint it was unprofessional and made a mockery of his function.

"You must be out of your fucking mind," was his poetic rejoinder.

As it happened, being psychoanalyzed at the time, I had ample opportunity to explore my motives. While my original logic seemed clear enough (if there was to be a film we had to get on with it; we effectively had no choice), it soon became apparent that my unconscious reasoning in offering to be the anonymous author was not as simple as it appeared. In doing the whole script sub rosa, I was essentially letting myself off the hook in case it didn't work. The strategy was akin to that I used for my tennis game—the part where, when it didn't count for points, I could be brilliant. My enthusiasm and my passion are frequently misconstrued as confidence—arrogance, even. The fact is, I've never had a lot of confidence. By arranging to write the script in this fashion my confidence—or lack of it—was not at stake. If I bombed, who was to know? It wasn't a real tennis game.

And anyway, it would all be over, yea or nay, in twelve days.

It is hard, bordering on impossible, to reconstruct precisely what happened during those twelve days. There were no computers then, so I worked on yellow legal pads and my Smith Corona portable electric. Making changes involved scissors, paste, and a Wite-Out eraser that was applied with a small brush. Soon my hands were covered with the sticky stuff, along with paper cuts.

The process involved no sleep.

As I worked, juggling the plots, subplots, and characters we had agreed upon—materials first imagined in bits and pieces by five disparate authors—trying to weave them into a cohesive whole, it felt as if I were fiddling with a Rubik's Cube. With this difference: I cannot work the Rubik's Cube, but in the case of the script, the pieces arranged themselves fairly easily. Not being a *Star Trek* aficionado, I labored in blissful ignorance, including—for example—Mr. Chekov in the tale, even though fans subsequently delighted to point out that Chekov was not a member of the *Enterprise*'s crew in the television season when the Khan episode took place. (He was there, I would insist, but occupied on another deck—the *Enterprise* is a colossally large vessel. I had crossed the ocean on the original *Queen Mary* and knew how easy it would be to miss someone in her crew of five hundred, let alone passenger complement of three thousand.) I was not burdened by "reverence" for the series, as people have often wondered. Indeed, reverence was not an emotion that ever crossed my mind. Far from being sacrosanct, I was of the opinion that *Star Trek* could stand some fixing. I made up rules as I needed them and wrote my own dialogue.

Around this time, word leaked that the film would involve the death of Spock, a leak that I later learned some people had attributed to a disgruntled Roddenberry. Amid all the discussions that followed, I off-handedly suggested that we put Spock in the simulator sequence that would now open the film, and kill him off from the get-go. I thought I was being funny, but Bennett jumped on the idea, so I threw Spock into the sequence, killing him in scene one as a way of disarming the audience's expectations.

I was writing the movie I wanted to see, my own adventures of Captain Hornblower.

Later, reflecting on my *Star Trek* experiences at various panel discussions, I found myself likening the series to the Catholic mass. That is to say, like the mass, there are certain elements of *Star Trek* that are immutable, unchangeable. The mass has its Kyrie, its Sanctus, Agnus Dei, Dies Irae, and so on. . . . *Star Trek* has Kirk, Spock, McCoy, Klingons, Romulans, etc., and the rest of the universe Roddenbery bequeathed us. The words of the mass are carved in stone, as are fundamental elements—the *Enterprise*, Spock, the transporter beam, and so forth—in *Star Trek*.

It is the music to which they are set that differentiates one mass from another (yes, I know, there's a different text for requiem masses, but you get the idea). Mozart's *Coronation Mass* bears scant resemblance to Bach's *Mass in B Minor*, which, in turn, is nothing like the African *Missa Luba*. Similarly, each *Star Trek* episode (whether on television or film) is distinguished by the writing and directing personalities of those who create them. It is they who provide the new music to the *Star Trek* words, or, to switch metaphors, the wine may be new but the shape of the bottle is always the same. I was pouring my own brew into the bottle of *Star Trek II*, trying to fill it without breaking it. (Later, on *Star Trek VI*, I *did* wind up breaking it and found myself in a melancholy face-off with Roddenberry himself.)

And as I was putting the pieces together, I became aware of something else: certain themes in the story were beginning to emerge like the details of a brass rubbing, the consequence of plot juxtapositions I had made with no time to justify them. I was fiddling with that Rubik's Cube as fast as I could, trying juxtapositions and flinging them around with no more than instinct and intuition to guide me, because there wasn't time to write stuff down on three-by-five cards and stare at them on a bulletin board (something I've never done, in any case; it all stays in my head, somehow). These themes were friendship, old age—and death. As I became aware of these ideas—implicit in the new narrative—I began writing *into* them, so to speak, investigating, developing, and sharpening the story's implications as I discovered what they were. It's hard to explain the intuitive process and always very frustrating when the studio executive—or the fan—wants to know, Why did you do such-and-such? The artist goes a lot (most?) of the time on intuition. On his or her gut. Why is Kirk given a copy of *A Tale of Two Cities?* Because that was the book I grabbed off my shelf? Yes, but in the end, it also somehow became an organic part of the movie. According to Socrates, artists are like children, who make no sense except when they create, at which point they go into a kind of trance, during which time they take dictation from God—and this they term "inspiration." Afterward they are hard put to explain how they achieved what they did or the reasoning behind intuitive or "inspired" choices. So instead, they offer up colorful anecdotes, which may or may not be true. (W. S. Gilbert liked to tell people he got the idea for *The Mikado* when a Japanese sword hanging over his desk fell and almost decapitated him—colorful, to be sure, and possibly true, as well—but hardly revealing of anything germane to how he wrote *The Mikado*.)

Even as this book. I don't claim to have taken dictation from God (I'd never be able to keep up), but I was probably in some kind of a trancelike state, sleep-deprived and pumping adrenaline like an oil well gusher. I think neurologists refer to this as a State of Flow.

I remember wondering vaguely, as I worked, what my father, who, I was sure, had never even *heard* of *Star Trek*, would make of this movie. How to explain this world to that urbane New York shrink? I began the script with a title, *"In the 23rd century . . . ,"* as a clue for the uninitiated, but as the years have passed I have come to the realization that it was not merely my father whom I was attempting to orient, but also myself. Writing what became *The Wrath of Khan* was an ongoing attempt for me to translate the *Star Trek* universe into one that made sense to me. If fiction is the lie that tells the greater truth, it is as well to remember that fiction *is* a lie, what some folks would call a whopper or a stretcher or bullshit. How do we make the lie convincing? By loading it with circumstantial elements that *are* true ("Merely corroborative detail intended to lend artistic verisimilitude to an otherwise bald and unconvincing narrative," as Pooh-Bah has it in *The Mikado*). Without this kind of help—speaking for myself—much of science fiction will fail to convince. We try to blur the point at which the truth blends into the lie. If done correctly, the audience fails to notice the moment when they slip the bonds of reality and embark on the fantastic voyage. If done well, they are so involved that they miss the moment when they willingly agree to suspend disbelief.

The finished script of the second *Star Trek* movie revolves around a training cruise aboard the *Enterprise*, supervised by a reluctant Kirk, who, promoted to admiral, is now a depressed desk jockey, brooding about his age. Unbeknownst to the *Enterprise* and her youthful complement, another Federation starship, the *Reliant*, inadvertently lands on what is thought to be a desolate planet, searching for a place to help conduct a mysterious scientific experiment under the supervision of Kirk's old flame, Carol Marcus. The planet, however, proves to be inhabited by the treacherous Khan, whom Kirk had marooned there with his followers and wife years before. Thirsting for vengeance, Khan and his band hijack the *Reliant* and lay a trap for Kirk, who now finds himself marooned beneath the surface of another planet, where he rediscovers Carol and is introduced to the son he never knew he had. The climax of the film is a "submarine" battle (minus sonar) between Kirk and his nemesis in a lightning-splattered nebula, in which Spock sacrifices his life to save his captain, his friend, and the crew of the *Enterprise*, in the process miraculously rejuvenating Kirk.

When I finished the script, I turned it in and fell asleep with an aching back for fourteen hours, finally awakened by phone calls from Bennett and Sallin, saying how happy they were with my efforts. There remained the delicate problem of whose name to put on the title page. In the end, we gave a "story by" credit to the five authors of the five earlier drafts and decided on Harve Bennett's name as the author of the script. In this we were doubly naive. Bennett, who had cut his teeth on television, was a stranger to feature films and their protocols, and his ignorance was to cost him dear. In the present instance we were unaware that the WGA would rarely award a writing credit to anyone who was also a producer of the film in question.

I gave the screenplay its title: *The Undiscovered Country*. I thought this particularly elegant, coming as it does from Hamlet's "To be or not to be" soliloquy, in which he refers to death as "the undiscover'd country." After all, Spock would die in the movie.

And so would my title.

SHATNER

But all that was down the road. The script was finished. The studio professed itself delighted. Could it be adjusted? Of course, and it would need to be.

I arrive. *The Seven-Per-Cent Solution* gets the main window at the famous Hatchards bookstore in London in 1975, and I am famous for fifteen minutes.

Portrait of the artist as a young hairy person on the set of *The Seven-Per-Cent Solution* in Vienna, 1976. (You can't see my feet, but I am walking on air.)

Nicol Williamson as Holmes and Robert Duvall as Watson upstaged by Toby the bloodhound in old Vienna from *The Seven-Per-Cent Solution*. I wanted to take the dog back to the States with me until I saw him eat.

I sit in happy anticipation while cinematographer Paul Lohmann lights Malcolm McDowell and Mary Steenburgen in the revolving restaurant while shooting *Time After Time* in 1978. We had two hours to shoot six pages and then had to clear out so they could open the restaurant.

You can have your cake and eat it, too. Ricardo Montalban and I celebrating someone's birthday on the set of *Star Trek II: The Wrath of Khan* in 1981.

Anachronism? What anachronism? I inspect the troops in the *Enterprise* torpedo bay, soon to be the site of my favorite shot in the film and later still, Spock's funeral.

Building the sand planet for *Star Trek II: The Wrath of Khan*. "*Star Trek*—were you on location?" "Oh, yes, three weeks on Venus."

Khan confronts a stowaway, courtesy of the crew. Ricardo Montalban gets a kick out of a blow-up puppet of Hervé Villechaize from *Fantasy Island*.

Executive producer Harve Bennett on right and producer Bob Sallin on left—best friends. And later, not . . .

Directing Kirstie Alley as a Vulcan on the set of *Star Trek II: The Wrath of Khan*. She was so fixated on Spock was she that she told me she wore her Vulcan ears to bed. (Either that or she wanted a later makeup call.)

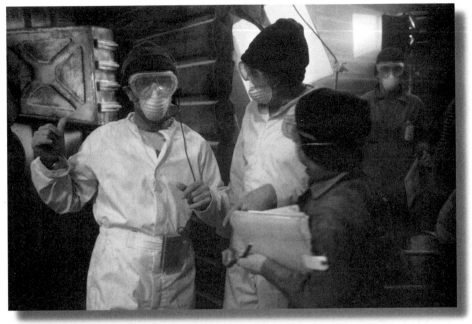

Work outfits for shooting on the sand planet, with me on left, cinematographer Gayne Rescher in middle, and script supervisor Mary Jane Ferguson on the right. Don't think all that gear kept out the sand, because it didn't.

Brainstorming with Leonard and Bill.

Khan and shipmates (Hell's Angels in space). Yes, yes, yes, those pecs are his.

Interior of the Genesis Cave minus all of the special effects. It remains a disappointment to me—what we could've done with CGI . . .

Part of the enormous crew of *Star Trek II*. I'm on the top with Mary Jane Ferguson, our script supervisor. Gayne Rescher our DP and Catherine Coulson are below left; below them, Jim Alexander, our sound mixer; Craig Denault, our camera operator, is below right; on the bottom, Doug Wise and Dick Espinza, our first and second ADs.

The Andropov Mystery

Newsweek
November 21, 1983 / $1.50

TV's Nuclear Nightmare
Public Service or Propaganda?
How Will It Affect Children?

ABC's 'The Day After'

Different from *Charlie's Angels, The Day After* brings the country to its knees with William F. Buckley Jr. and Phyllis Schlafly bouncing from coast to coast, like Chicken Littles, yelling that the sky is falling.

The jewel thieves' market in Parsola from *The Deceivers* in 1987. The set was fake, but the jewels were all real, with security men hovering everywhere just outside the frame.

Filming a cavalry charge for *The Deceivers*. Don't let anyone tell you making movies isn't fun.

At ease with the officers of the *Enterprise*. (See if you can pick out the perfidious Vulcan.)

Directing on the prison gulag set of *Star Trek VI: The Undiscovered Country* in early 1991—think cowboys and aliens.

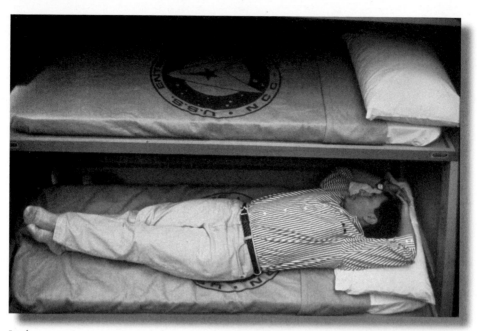

In the crews' quarters I catch forty winks and fall in love with the blankets, which I later attempt to merchandise. (I am the biggest buyer).

William Shatner offers advice.

Gorkon's Last Supper ("You've never heard Shakespeare until you've heard him in the original Klingon.") Wouldn't you know, there's no verb for "to be" in Klingon. Christopher Plummer, unhappy with the "authentic" Klingon-Shakespeare, substituted his own.

Producers of *Star Trek VI: The Undiscovered Country*. Ralph Winter on left and Steven-Charles Jaffe (also my longtime partner) on the right.

Herb Jaffe, (white hair, center), visits the set of *Star Trek VI*. From left to right: script supervisor Kathy Swor, sound mixer Gene Contemessa, me, Herb Jaffe, Herb's son Steven-Charles, and production designer Herman Zimmerman.

On the set of *Star Trek VI: The Undiscovered Country* with (from left) Kristin Glover, our camera operator, Kim Cattrall (pre-*Sex in the City*), me, and our script supervisor Faye Brenner.

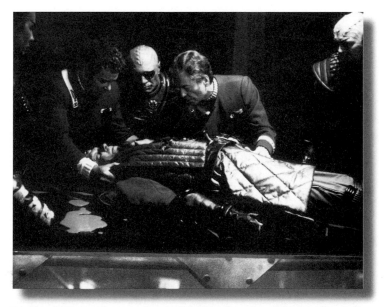

Death of Chancellor Gorkon, after Rembrandt, with (starting left) William Shatner, Christopher Plummer, DeForest Kelley, and David Warner (prone) as Gorkon.

Happily ever after with Stephanie.

(Bennett contributed some delectable moments, including the "would you like a tranquilizer?" exchange between Kirk and Bones as the *Enterprise* is piloted out of space dock by first-time helmsman Saavik.)

Nonetheless, the structure of the thing was sufficiently solid to send Bob Sallin and me up to Lucas's special effects house, ILM, in San Mateo, across the bay from San Francisco.

There we sat down with visual effects supervisor Ken Ralston and a roomful of agreeable technowizards to discuss the requirements of the script and how best to realize some of the tricky visuals.

Ralston et al. had read my draft with a microscope, breaking it down in purely visual terms. Deliberately or not I had created what I came to think of as an "indoor/outdoor" film—that is to say, the scenes aboard the spaceships were indoors and typically required no ILM shots (except those that appeared on the *Enterprise* bridge's forward viewing screen); and the bulk of the ILM material involved "outdoor," i.e., space shots, wherein the *Enterprise* and the *Reliant* played cat and mouse with each other or blasted away, tearing off bits of each other's armored hulls. This division greatly simplified my responsibilities as director. The ILM crowd had helpfully identified and numbered each of these "outdoor" shots and drawn preliminary cartoons, called storyboards, which resemble comic book panels, for Bob Sallin and me to evaluate. Did we see them differently from the ILM conceptions? Did we want more of them? Less of them? Did we have ideas of our own that they had failed to express? Had we imagined angles or perspectives they hadn't anticipated? In the following months, these cartoons would be refined, simplified, amplified, and then, when agreed upon, the relevant shots—often involving multiple "elements" (spaceships, wires, lighting, shadows, explosions, etc.)—would be "composited" at ILM and sent down to LA, piecemeal, to be again evaluated, criticized, and sent back, until Harve Bennett, Bob Sallin, and I had signed off on each one as completed. When *Star Trek II* was made, computers and e-mail were only beginning to make their appearance for most of us; back then all the shots were hand carried by messengers on planes between San Francisco and LA and back again. The explosion of the Genesis planet was later filmed by ILM inside nearby Candlestick Park, then the home of the San Francisco Giants. In addition, we scrounged other special effects shots leftover from the first movie. The *Enterprise* leaving space dock at the film's beginning was largely cobbled together from that source and included exquisite miniature work by John Dykstra and Robert Abel.

Nowadays, computers, e-mail, and video-conferencing simplify the entire process, though I don't believe they make it any better or less expensive. Computer-generated imagery has come a long way but has still, in my view, a long way to go before it can truly compete or compare with the three-dimensional reality provided by models.

I don't recall how long this initial ILM conversation had been in progress when I was called to the telephone. On the other end of the line in Los Angeles, Harve Bennett told me the bad news: William Shatner hated the script.

I can remember only the pounding in my ears, not whether I was sitting or standing or, having been standing, had subsided into a chair.

"He *hates* the script?"

"*Hates* it," Bennett repeated.

I couldn't think.

"So . . . what do we do now?"

He sighed. "Go back to your meeting. We'll see what happens."

There may be—and I know for a fact there are—people who can play their bad hand close to their vest, cooler heads than mine who can function equably while the house they inhabit tumbles around them. But I am not one of those people.

I sat through the afternoon's meeting numbly answering questions on autopilot all the while knowing that this was all total bullshit. There was no movie, the meeting was a charade, but only I was aware of it. And anyone who really knew me would have detected something amiss; my characteristic ebullience was nowhere in evidence. I kept replaying Bennett's blunt characterization of Shatner's response. *Hates the script?* How could he hate the script? Everyone loves the script. Everyone says what a great job I did. What's to hate?

A day or so later, William Shatner himself met with me in Bennett's office. I had known him slightly before this on a social basis, but today he was all agitated business.

"This script is simply terrible, a disaster," he began, and I don't remember much of what he said after that. I do recall that I had to keep getting up and going to the bathroom—so often that he finally remarked on it. "Are you okay?"

I mumbled something to justify my frequent egresses but the truth was that I was so distressed by what he was dishing out that my bladder kept filling up. A double humiliation.

The only time he sparked was when I brought up Hornblower.

"That's exactly what Gene [Roddenberry] said it was!" he exclaimed.

Later, I would learn just how infatuated with Hornblower Roddenberry had been.

After Shatner finally left, Bennett ruminated. Much more experienced than I, he was used to temperament and he had that analytic ability I so sorely lacked of being able to parse and dissect what was being said into manageable components. As he talked I began to calm down and form a plan of my own. What seemed so catastrophic to Shatner seemed eminently fixable to me now that I wasn't jumping up for the men's room every five minutes.

As part of my ongoing cinematic education, I was now learning how to write for a star. As a man, William Shatner is refreshingly free of ego. He is polite, attentive, unassuming, interested in other people and what they do. But as a leading actor, he is very protective, particularly of Kirk, his screen persona. Once I understood the paradoxical duality—no ego, but enormous vanity—of his character, it became easier to understand and address his concerns. Put simply (perhaps too simply), he wanted to be the first man through the door. If the messenger delivered the message, he didn't want that messenger to tower over him. He didn't mind that the film dealt with a man growing old; he just didn't want to specify that man's exact age. (Not unreasonable if you think about it. What actor wishes to find himself rejected for the role of a fifty-year-old because he's already played a character who owns to sixty-two?)

Later, rereading the above, it occurs to me that Shatner and I may not be all that different. I've been called egotistical but I think this is a misinterpretation. My narcissism has its own bespoke shape. I am passionate, enthusiastic, but not, I would argue, egotistical.

But vain . . . yes, I'll grant you vain.

I went back to my screenplay—malleable as the Constitution it would prove to be—and amended it per my new insights. The revisions proved remarkably simple, and in the end Shatner's needs were easily fulfilled. In a day or so—more paper cuts and more Wite-Out sticking to my fingers—I photocopied the revised result and sent it back to him.

When I turned on my answering machine a few hours later, I heard his voice: "Nick, you are a genius, I don't know what you've done but this is terrific . . ." etc.

Uh huh. I saved the tape with this precious recording for some future emergency and started preparing the movie in earnest.

PREP

As I have noted, directing a movie that you have also written is doubly taxing. You want to be prepping the film when you are still revising the script; you want to be tweaking the script when you are busy prepping the film.

Since *Star Trek II* was being made on the cheap, I would have no choice but to use hand-me-down sets and props, though I did hold fast on changing the costumes and gussying up those same drab interiors, which held all the interest for me of a Holiday Inn. I wanted blinking lights everywhere and I wanted uniforms that suggested a military, not to say nautical character. I wanted to understand rank, ratings, and function. I toured the *Enterprise* bridge, and it was hate at first sight, not least because I realized 40 percent of the film took place on a set in the shape of a circle, meaning that it would require coverage in 360 degrees. Typically, if you are shooting in a room, essentially a box, you can be very selective with your coverage and light everything for one direction before "turning around" and getting the rest. In a circular set, you are *always* turning around. Since the *Enterprise* bridge, with its removable, swappable pie-slice sections, also doubled as the bridge of the USS *Reliant*, I was actually forced into *double* 360-degree coverage. In order to fit or manipulate a camera in this confined space, we would be forever removing and reinserting these bulky, balky pie sections, each with its own elaborate wiring that brought light to the *Enterprise*'s endless controls and monitors, each hooked up to its own individual-playback VHS machine. Moviemaking frequently involves a lot of waiting around, but this was enough to grind all the enamel off my teeth, especially given our constricting schedule.

There was another difficulty I was obliged to face. Many of the changes I contemplated for the second *Star Trek* movie flew directly in the face of the "ground rules" established by the first, *Star Trek: The Motion Picture,* directed by the legendary Robert Wise. I knew Wise and admired him both professionally and personally, which put me in a tricky position. I was intent on making a very different movie. Many people find much to trash about the original *Star Trek* movie, but I am not among them. I am certain that without Robert Wise's pioneering effort, subsequent *Trek* films would not have been as successful. Say what you like, Wise and *Star Trek: The Motion Picture* went boldly where no one had gone before. And if those who preceded us made mistakes, those mistakes certainly pointed the way for people like me who came after. What some have described as the overarching solemnity of the original film drove me in the opposite direction. Tom Stoppard said somewhere that the first thing he looked for when writing was the jokes. This approach, coming from a writer I idolized, served to validate my own instincts to push back against the seriousness of *Star Trek: The Motion Picture*. Similarly, I rebelled against the look of Wise's film. For all I know, life aboard spaceships in the future will look bland and comfortable but in my opinion, it didn't look very *interesting*. In line with my nautical ideas, I would attempt something different.

The first *Star Trek* movie dealt in soft pastels and "updated" versions of the original Dr. Denton outfits. Doubtless the notion was that spaceships of the future would be user-friendly environments, where people could walk around in modified tracksuits, but in my opinion, however accurate such prognostications, the look was visually unexciting. What I wanted was the gritty interior of a destroyer or, better yet, the claustrophobic feeling of a submarine, with contrasting lighting to match the hard-edged, blinking lights of the sets. In my original inspection tour of the bridge, insisting on those flashing lights, I was told I had spent fifty thousand dollars. If I'd had the budget, I would've started from scratch and the result would have looked more like the spaceship freighter seen in *Alien*. (Gene Hackman once told me he thought the best film acting occurred in confined spaces. When I mentioned *Lawrence of Arabia*, he called it an exception.)

At Robert Sallin's suggestion, I hired Gayne Rescher as my director of photography and agreed to use the mercurial Bill Dornisch as the editor. It may be urged that these were not famous filmmakers. True. Like almost everyone connected with *Star Trek II*, they were drawn primarily from television (though Rescher had been Elia Kazan's DP for the extraordinary *A Face in the Crowd* and had shot *A New Leaf* for Elaine May). But as we were to learn, this was in no way a handicap. It turned out all many of these television folks needed was a chance to spread their wings.

Dornisch was a maddening talent with a high-pitched giggle that reminded me of Richard Widmark as Tommy Udo in *Kiss of Death*. All jolly intuition, he seldom read scripts but flew by the seat of his pants, juxtaposing images in the messiest cutting room I'd ever seen (not that I'd seen that many by that point), but ultimately throwing footage together in inspired fashion. Typically, I am able to get along with most people and once I succeeded in persuading Dornisch to read the script and could tell him what the film was trying to be about, he proved more than equal to the task. You meet a lot of walking wounded in my business, editors or actors or cinematographers who have been so abused by directors or studios that they have scars where there is no longer any skin. Handle with care and you may be able to bring them back to life, but it requires patience, tact, and, yes, affection.

A film editor in many ways resembles a psychoanalyst. In each case the director (or analysand) turns over the raw footage—dailies in one instance, free associations in the other—and these, in turn, are "assembled" by the editor or psychoanalyst, who then plays them back for the director/analysand. If the editor is good and understands the material and the director, what he shows you is recognizable as what you intended. You will tweak it here and there but you know you've been understood. If he's a *great* editor, he will take it further than you dreamed, finding, in the footage that you were so busy accumulating, the moments and "beats" you didn't even know you'd captured. The scene he plays back for you is richer, more textured than you'd imagined. Conversely, if he's a bad editor or the wrong one for this particular job, the result of his assembly is unrecognizable—you haven't been understood. (All this, incidentally, applies to the psychoanalyst, as well, who is stitching together the dailies from your head.)

Robert Fletcher was our costumer—again, a legacy, but one that made sense. He knew from *Star Trek* but he was a flexible, thorough professional and was excited, I believe, to be turned loose to rethink the uniforms of the Starfleet crew for the first time since the original series. For Khan and his genetically engineered shipmates, we settled on a sort of Hell's Angels from Outer Space look. Joe Jennings, our production designer, was another experienced *Star Trek* hand, but the chance to breathe new life into familiar material, to rethink the look of *Star Trek*'s world, even if not entirely from scratch, got his juices flowing as well.

I have a theory that art thrives on restrictions: It's when you haven't the money or the facilities to bring off your project that you are obliged to be imaginative and creative. When painters came to grips with the fact that paintings don't move, that they exist in only two dimensions, they had to find ways to give the sense of movement to their pictures and to provide the illusion of depth. One might even argue that without censorship there would be no art, for what are metaphors, similes, allegories, symbols, etc., but attempts to circumvent the limitations placed on what we can say or show? One of my all-time favorite movies, the Laurence Olivier–directed *Henry V*, made on a shoestring during World War II, exploits its lack of resources by emphasizing them. The film acknowledges (as Shakespeare's play also acknowledges) the fact that "this cockpit" cannot "hold the vasty fields of France." By starting in a re-creation of an Elizabethan theater and letting the Chorus urge us, "On your imaginary forces, work!" we, the audience, get to contribute to the film, fleshing out its two-dimensional sets (taken from the Duc de Berry's *Book of Hours*), until the battle of Agincourt, where cinematic realism is finally allowed to prevail (but never entirely—instead of realistic battle sounds, William Walton's music is there to remind us, yet again, that something has been left to our imagination).

Our production manager was the amazing Austen Jewell, who had performed the same function for me on *Time After Time*. Sometimes referred to as the unit production manager, or UPM, he prepares the budget (and sometimes the first shooting schedule as well). The UPM hires the key crew after consulting with the director and producer(s). The UPM is responsible for managing the production and making sure department heads keep to their respective budgets. He/she monitors the daily progress of the shooting schedule. Nowadays the title is occasionally gussied up to something called "line producer." Jewell was well-named, a taciturn but dryly humorous taskmaster who was a living, one-man history of the movies. He played the child in Von Stroheim's *Greed* (1924) and was one of two street toughs who gave the Little Tramp a hard time in *City Lights* (1931; the other "tough" was future director Robert Parrish); later still Jewell was Chaplin's first AD on *Monsieur Verdoux* (1947) and countless others over the next forty years, including his chores as UPM on the Christopher Reeve *Superman* (1978). Watching and listening to him on *Time After Time*, I had learned the etiquette of a film set. There are codes of conduct behind and before the cameras. (Does the star stick around to deliver his off-camera dialogue to the day player?) I was humbled and envious that Jewell had lived his entire life on one set or another.

Robert Wise's nephew, Doug Wise, was my first AD. Calm and professional, whatever opinions or reservations he may have held concerning my revisions of his uncle's *Star Trek* work, he never once uttered them. A good "first" is the director's right arm, his expeditor, strategist, enforcer, and coconspirator. I never could get below the surface of Doug's professionalism, which is perhaps for the best. For all I know, Doug Wise had no interest whatsoever in *Star Trek*; his interest was in a smooth-running shoot and he let nothing interfere with that goal.

THE USUAL SUSPECTS

I began to meet other members of the cast: Leonard Nimoy (Spock), DeForest Kelley (Dr. Leonard "Bones" McCoy), George Takei (helmsman Mr. Sulu), Nichelle Nichols (communications officer Uhura), James Doohan (Mr. Scott, aka "Scotty," chief engineer), and Walter Koenig (Commander Pavel Chekov). These folks were uniformly supportive. They didn't hold my inexperience as either a director or a *Star Trek* watcher against me but tactfully pointed out things in the script that they felt were uncharacteristic or untrue of their roles—*So-and-so would never say this line in these words*, etc. More adjustments were made.

The cast of *Star Trek*, almost to a man (or woman), I felt, harbored ambivalent feelings about their roles and participation in the series. The crew of the *Enterprise* had been struggling actors of greater or lesser talent when fate had selected them for a television series. For sixty-seven episodes, those roles had paid their bills (this was before residuals) before the show was canceled.

And then something unprecedented had happened. The fans, as we all know by now, would not let the series die. Years passed and finally—in the wake of *Star Wars*—Paramount decided to take the cast out of mothballs, dust them off, and pay them again.

The phenomenon of an actor chafing at being exclusively identified with one role is not new. Eugene O'Neill's father had been driven almost mad (and arguably to drink) because the public was interested in him only when he played Edmond Dantès, aka the Count of Monte Cristo. For years Sean Connery struggled to escape the embrace of James Bond. What *was* possibly unique in theatrical annals was an entire cast yoked together by the same imperative. For better. For worse. Forever. Whatever they thought about the series, about science fiction, about the characters themselves, or about one another, they were joined to their on-screen personae at the hip for eternity. Nowhere is their ambivalence more clear than in the titles of two of Leonard Nimoy's books: *I Am Not Spock* (1975) and—almost twenty years later—*I Am Spock* (1995). Perhaps the most amusing approximation of the cast's collective feelings is to be found in the hilarious film by Dean Parisot and David Howard, *Galaxy Quest*, which deftly sends the embittered cast of a *Star Trek*-like TV series off on an actual interstellar adventure, as the show's ambivalent "actors" come to grips with their divided feelings about the roles that have enslaved them, concluding, finally that, like turning eighty, it's not so bad when you consider the alternative.

Kelley, Nimoy, and Shatner had the longest résumés. Atlanta-born Kelley had appeared in such Western fare as John Sturges's *Gunfight at the O.K. Corral* and Fred Zinneman's *The Men* before his lengthy television career; Nimoy's résumé before *Star Trek* was almost exclusively in television, where the Boston native appeared in everything from episodes of *Perry Mason* to *Sea Hunt* to *Broken Arrow*, *Highway Patrol*, *The Untouchables*, *Mission: Impossible*, *Rawhide*, *Tales of Wells Fargo*, *Wagon Train*, *Bonanza*, ad infinitum.

Originally a stage actor, Shatner's initial appearances in live television, were followed by several features, among them Richard Brooks's unfortunate adaptation of *The Brothers Karamazov* and Stanley Kramer's *Judgment at Nuremeburg*, before also becoming a television stalwart in such shows as *Naked City*, *The Defenders*, *The Dick Powell Theatre*, *Boris Karloff's Thriller*, *Alfred Hitchcock Presents*, and, most memorably, an episode of *The Twilight Zone*.

Like Shatner, James Doohan (Scotty) hailed from Canada and specialized in television, appearing in *Gunsmoke*, *Gallant Men*, *Twilight Zone*, *Voyage to the Bottom of the Sea*, *Ben Casey*, and *The Fugitive*, among tons of others.

George Takei, born in California, spent part of his youth during World War II interned in a *Nisei* camp in Arkansas before going the TV route in *Twilight Zone*, *The Gallant Men*, *Hawaiian Eye*, *Assignment: Underwater*, *Perry Mason*, etc. In addition to his role as a nonvillainous Japanese officer aboard the *Enterprise* (he played the other kind in *Return from the River Kwai*), Takei was silently representing another minority on American television, one that had yet to emerge from the closet, though on satellite radio with Howard Stern, he has not been shy discussing his love life (or, for that matter, his opinion of William Shatner).

Walter Koenig was born in New York. His television career included episodes of *The Untouchables, Combat, Ben Casey*, and *General Hospital*. By an unlikely coincidence, Koenig and I had attended the same high school. Although we were some years apart, I was often tempted to compare notes about various teachers with him.

Nichelle Nichols (née Grace Nichols), from Illinois, started as a singer with the Duke Ellington and Lionel Hampton bands before being cast in her groundbreaking *Star Trek* role, the first African American to appear on "equal" footing with a white cast. Instead of "the maid," Nichols played an officer, and more racial barriers fell when she shared the first interracial television kiss with Shatner in one of the original episodes.

It is probable, if not inevitable, that the paths of these actors crossed on all those television shows before their *Star Trek* encounters.

But it is their work in *Star Trek* for which most are likely to be remembered. I suppose the wonder is that the *Star Trek* cast was not more embittered, that they managed to retain their freshness, their hospitality to a stranger, and their enthusiasm despite the knowledge that—for better or worse—this was what they would always been known for.

There were newcomers to the second *Star Trek* film, as well. I hired a girl from Wichita with striking blue-gray eyes, who said she was fixated on Spock, to play the Vulcan beauty, Lieutenant Saavik. (She *was* fixated, too—Kirstie Alley told me she used to sleep wearing her Vulcan ears.) Bibi Besch (who later acted for me to great effect in my television movie *The Day After*) played a former sweetheart of the libidinous Kirk, while a young actor named Merritt Butrick played their illegitimate son. Our ensemble was rounded out by the great Paul Winfield, who played Captain Terrill of the *Reliant*. As I've observed, one of the great treats in the movie business is that you sometimes actually get to meet your dreams. After seeing Winfield in *Sounder*, I longed to tell this wonderful actor how much he had affected me with his performance—and now I got to do just that.

The only major cast member with whom I did not get to spend time before the commencement of shooting was Ricardo Montalban. He was busy filming his television series, *Fantasy Island*. We managed only a brief lunch at the Paramount commissary, during which I found him replete with gentlemanly—one is tempted to say "formal"—but guarded courtesy. Actors are typically suspicious of new directors ("Is he crazy?") until set at ease. Or not. Actors are fragile, their feelings easily bruised, and they have a sixth sense for when the man or woman in charge doesn't know how to drive the bus—or where it's heading. Has no sense of direction, you might say.

Mexican-born Montalban could claim the longest résumé of anyone in the cast. His work began with Mexican features in 1942 before wartime short-ages of leading men in California brought him to Hollywood. Montalban had also twice appeared on Broadway to acclaim, in Shaw's *Don Juan in Hell* and in the musical *Jamaica,* opposite Lena Horne. He danced in the latter show, managing to conceal a limp, the result of a spinal injury incurred in 1951 when a horse rolled over him during the filming of *Across the Wide Missouri*. I was intimidated to meet him, and his reserved manner didn't assuage my awe. I discussed the role and gave him a copy of *Moby-Dick*, concluding, "It's all in this book." He thanked me with the same formal politesse and went back to his Island. We were not to see each other again before shooting started, and I hadn't an inkling of what a good friend he was to become.

MUSIC AND CREDITS

I had to find a composer for the film, but it couldn't be the great Jerry Goldsmith, who had done the rousing score for *Star Trek: The Motion Picture*, as there was no way our budget could afford him. When I wasn't meeting, greeting, rewriting, and making a thousand decisions connected with the film's preparation, I was listening to cassette tapes containing samples of undiscovered, aspiring composers who used this device as a means of auditioning.

It was a dispiriting exercise. So much of what I heard sounded the same, which is to say generic, devoid of personality, much the way modern automobiles seem to be boxy replications of themselves, no matter what brand name is stuck on them. When you listen to Beethoven you do not imagine you are listening to anyone else, and while it is a truism that good film composers must be adroit quick-change artists, the best of them always retain the stamp of their own personas, no matter what subject they are charged with embodying musically. Dmitri Tiomkin sounds like Tiomkin, whether he's accompanying the Old West, ancient Egypt, or the isles of Greece. To the degree that I wanted a score that would be the "voice" of our film, I wanted a composer who *had* a voice.

I can no longer recall the particular circumstances under which I found myself listening to the music of someone named James Horner, but I remember paraphrasing Wagner, who, when he heard Bizet, grudgingly conceded, "Well, at last, here is someone with ideas in his head."

I met and hired master Horner, a quiet young man who spoke with a vaguely English accent, acquired, as I learned, from years spent at school in England, during the time his father, Harry Horner, had worked as a production designer there. Young Horner had studied at the Royal College of Music before pursuing a PhD at UCLA. I asked James (somehow one did not think to address him as Jim or Jimmy) to listen to Debussy's *La Mer* and told him I wanted a score that suggested the sweep of the ocean—nautical but nice, I added.

He smiled, but I couldn't tell if he thought that was funny. Later I discovered he had his own droll sense of humor. When I asked during a subsequent recording session if a certain passage he composed for the movie didn't smack of Prokofiev's *Alexander Nevsky*, he squeaked, "Whatdya want from me? I'm a kid; I haven't outgrown my influences."

While all this was going on, a dilemma was unfolding between Harve Bennett and Bob Sallin, his college friend, whom Harve had hired to produce the film. This was another instance where Bennett's inexperience with the world and nomenclature of features did him harm. In television the key credit is executive producer. He is the main honcho; the producer title in television, by contrast, usually indicates what features refer to as the line producer (aka UPM), a lesser title bestowed on those who see to it that the trucks show up on time, are parked in the right places and that shooting permits have been obtained. Line producers are responsible for the physical logistics of the shoot.

Bennett had offered Sallin the title of producer, retaining the executive producer title for himself, unaware that the coveted credit in feature films was the former. Realizing his mistake, he contacted me and asked what I thought was the honorable thing to do. Sallin was sticking to the letter of his offer and wished to retain his producer title.

I was no more experienced in these matters than Bennett but I said what I felt, namely, that a deal was a deal and that if Sallin was taking Bennett up on his original offer, I felt he was obliged to stick to it. In any case, I assured him (rightly as it proved), everyone would know that *Star Trek II: The Undiscovered Country* was Harve Bennett's production.

Did Harve ever actually ask if Bob would change titles with him? Did Bob turn him down flat? I have no idea and am not likely ever to learn.

Young Horner came over to play themes for the movie on my piano. They sounded good to me. Henceforth while I was filming, those tunes would echo in my head. I was somewhat frustrated to learn of the studio's insistence that we use the fanfare from the original television series, composed by Alexander Courage, which I had never really liked. But the studio had so far stayed out of my hair to a surprising degree. and I had already learned that you must pick your battles. After all, it was only eight notes . . .

Years later, a new recording was made of the music that the English light classics composer Robert Farnon had written for the movie *Captain Horatio Hornblower R. N.* I was astonished to hear something that sounded, at least to me, very like the *Star Trek* theme leap out (much more effectively, I might add) in the opening bars.

Yes, indeed, Gene Roddenberry had certainly been a Hornblower fan.

REHEARSALS

Before shooting was to commence, I badly wished to rehearse, though in this desire I was swimming upstream. My background was in live theater, and I knew and understood the value of rehearsals. Rehearsals allow the actors to be freer on set when the meter is running. They have already become familiar with the script, with one another (admittedly hardly necessary for most of them in this case) and with the director. In rehearsals there is opportunity to experiment, to discover what lines need adjusting or can be deleted altogether. Actors like to rehearse, but agents wish them to be paid for it, which studios are (typically) reluctant to do. The result is that rehearsals are encouraged to be clandestine affairs, conducted off the lot, largely dependent on the professional good will (and pride) of the performers. Normally, a play rehearses for six weeks before opening. Most movie rehearsal periods are nothing like that long—nor should they be. Movies are a species of short-order cooking; rehearse too much and you lose the spontaneity whose absence the camera is prone to detect. The exceptions to this rule are chariot races and dance numbers. Movie rehearsing must therefore strike a middle ground, something between a read-through and individual scene work. While some directors—Mike Nichols, for example—request and receive extensive rehearsal time when they ask for it, the most I could hope for would be three or four days spent in Laurel Canyon around my dining room table. Montalban was unavailable for these sessions, but all the other actors showed up, and we noshed on deli eats while we read aloud, discussed, and then broke into smaller groups to work on specific scenes. I wanted to have my cheesecake and eat it, too, which is to say, while being "true" to the original *Star Trek* characters, I wanted to expand their range of feelings and emotional possibilities, not defined by their jobs or plot functions but by their natures and how this would influence their reactions to particular events. I knew I couldn't achieve this with all seven characters but I could certainly try making things more earthbound in terms of recognizable human reality.

We made many dialogue trims. Speeches or lines I had written I was now told by the actors could be "done with a look," and this was all to the good. One thing I had learned watching *The Seven-Per-Cent Solution* and directing *Time After Time*: too much dialogue and your film is in danger of becoming static. Movies must move, and faces as well as actions can often do the work of words. In fact, I have since computed that the attrition rate for dialogue in a screenplay of mine, between the first draft and the answer print, i.e., finished movie, is 50 percent. Half the words will go, and you will save yourself time and money if you lose as many as possible before the cameras start rolling. Cutting out the words in the editing room is possible, even inevitable, but cutting them beforehand is usually better.

There is another advantage to rehearsals. They allow the director to get to know his actors, how best to support them, exploit their strengths, conceal their weaknesses, absorb their work habits and personality quirks. Who will need help, and how best to give it? Who is likely to be best on take one? Who will need more takes? Who thrives on encouragement and coaching; who needs to work out problems and solutions for himself; etc.

I learned as well that though the crew of the *Enterprise* functions in space as a crack team, equal to any of the challenges it must confront, once off camera and subject to earth's gravitational pull, the cast was a microcosm of any other society, riven by factionalism, allegiances, and jealousies. These people were not only joined at the hip to the characters they played, they were anatomically connected to each other, as well. But because they were professionals, they made the best of it. They carried human baggage and toted it the best they knew how. (There was at least one solid friendship among them: Shatner and Nimoy, whose relationship had begun as rivalry early on, evolved from a competitive modus operandi into a mutual admiration society that endured long after the series' cancellation and the last of the features.)

Conversely, rehearsals allow the actors to know and grow comfortable with the director. As I intimated earlier, the one question cast and crew always need answered when there's an unfamiliar hand at the helm is: is he or she crazy? This person is in charge of the film and of my performance. Does he know what he's doing? Or are we being led over a cliff on some kind of suicide mission as a result of which I'll never work again—assuming I live? (Think Klaus Kinski dragging that steamboat over a jungle-covered mountain in South America in Werner Herzog's *Fitzcarraldo* if you want help visualizing how crazy crazy can get.)

The studio, as I have noted, pretty much left me alone. Studio conduct has changed a lot since then. In the beginning the studios were fiefdoms run by those for whom film was a passionate personal concern as well as a business. Those illiterate, mostly Russian immigrants for whom film was a fundamental means of communication never lost their enthusiasm for the medium. At private screenings they talked and argued about a film's merits or possibilities. But as corporations with their bean counters absorbed the studios into their spreadsheets and the prize became only the bottom line (admittedly costs skyrocketed as the years passed, as the studios' monopolies on theater chains were broken up, etc.), studio control over filmmaking became ever tighter. I'm not sure what purpose this has served (most films continue to stink or lose money), but when *Star Trek II* was made, the front office took no interest in who was cast as the maid. I was given a free hand to make the movie my way, with the studio content to let me show it to them when I'd finished my cut, at which point they would weigh in.

Later, I would learn that matters had not been quite that simple, but I will relate this revelation at the point I experienced it.

SHOOTING, PART 1

Shooting finally got underway on November 11, 1981, and went pretty smoothly for our allotted twelve (five-day) weeks. We almost had to replace our sound mixer, who was seemingly defeated by the baffling acoustics of our damned *Enterprise* bridge set with its domed overhead panels spreading echoes all over the place (and making it equally hard to light). But otherwise we quickly fell into a rhythm and began plowing ahead. Gayne Rescher proved more than equal to the task; the *Enterprise* looked like a real ship, and the lighting enhanced the claustrophobic feel of a submarine. Kirk and company had never looked better.

Unlike a television series, where casts and crews may continue together for years, each film crew is a one-time family, come together for a specific number of months, after which it will disintegrate, never to be reconstituted in exactly the same way again. Its personal dynamics and workings are therefore unique. Hollywood crews are renowned for their seamless perfectionism though as I've noted, unlike their European counterparts, they are hesitant to stray outside their purviews.

Of course there were hiccups. I had saved a close-up of Nichelle Nichols for the end of the day, and she was understandably distressed at being photographed when she was tired. In another instance, Leonard Nimoy was deeply disappointed by the set for Spock's stateroom. I had to agree with him, kicking myself when he pointed out the chintzy use of what looked like Sparklett's Water pointillism on the walls, so out of keeping with what ought to have been something mysterious and haunting, especially given Spock's place in this particular story. This is a perfect example of the director's need for perpetual vigilance. The attention to every detail, to all the moving parts, is unremitting and crucial and I had dropped the ball. Keeping track of incessant and myriad details, lighting, schedules, temperaments, weather, props, performances, vision—these relentless claims on the director's concentration are part of what is so exhausting about the director's job. Also what makes it so exhilarating.

(On *Star Trek VI*, I made sure Spock had a stateroom worthy of his character.)

MONTALBAN

And then there was Khan. Because of his television schedule, it was necessary to shoot Montalban's scenes first, even before the rest of the *Enterprise* and her crew appeared. We had begun filming with the "other" Starship, the *Reliant*, and her crew, and now segued into our bigger-than-life villain as he hijacked that ill-starred vessel.

Initially Montalban had thought his role rather too small, but as he reread the script he realized, "When I am not there, they are always talking about me," an observation that served to reassure him. He was also concerned that he would wind up playing Khan as Roarke (from *Fantasy Island*), but as he slipped into makeup and costume, such concerns fell by the wayside. He was Khan and then some . . .

The question I am most often asked about the movie is whether that chiseled sculpture was indeed Ricardo Montalban's actual torso. For the umpteenth time: those pecs are his.

Montalban was the wild card, the one actor with whom I had never rehearsed, and he showed up looking splendid in his muscular décolletage for his first day of work, which, as it happened, was one of the most difficult.

Khan, marooned with his followers on Ceti Alpha V by Kirk, confronts an astonished Chekov and Captain Terrill of the *Reliant* with a six-page monologue that serves the dual purpose of explaining to those unfamiliar with the original episode just who he is and why he is so enraged by Kirk's abandonment of him and his followers. In the original television episode "Space Seed," Kirk punished Khan and company for attempted mutiny, by marooning them on a habitable planet, never realizing that subsequent to the *Enterprise*'s departure the planet's orbit was altered by a nearby supernova. The once liveable place had now become a desert and Khan's people had begun dying, one by one, including his beloved wife. I had seen the television episode once and been struck by the fact that Khan had seduced one of the *Enterprise*'s crew, who devotedly shared his exile. The idea that she might now be dead, in addition to explaining her absence in the movie, struck me as a plausible springboard for Khan's rage. Working backward from this premise, I built up in my mind an offstage love story that had come to tragic grief and over time shaped Khan's monomania where Kirk was concerned. Working on the script, I had tried to imagine what cargo Kirk had allowed Khan to take with him into exile and concluded that books must have been among the resources permitted him. What books from the library aboard the *Enterprise* (it was at this point I recalled absently asking Bennett and Sallin why no one in *Star Trek* ever read a book) would Khan have chosen? Somewhat heavy-handedly, I had selected narratives of fallen angels—*Paradise Lost, King Lear,* and *Moby-Dick.* How many times must Khan, with his "superior intellect," have read and reread those tormented tales? How much time did he have to absorb and identify with their doomed protagonists? Plenty.

All of which I attempted to present in six pages, which I had the idea of shooting in one continuous take. Movies are inevitably comprised of snippets and fragments of film, close-ups, wide angles, etc., which place their own peculiar demands on the art of the actor. While many film actors are quite used to emoting in chopped-up sections, I, with my stage background, always wondered if even the most professional screen performer didn't experience this as coitus interruptus. In live theater, by contrast, the actor can work up a decent head of steam, and I had the notion that Montalban, with his stage history, might relish the chance to do just that. (Yes, in the editing room I would probably wind up using reaction footage and dialogue from the other people in the scene, yet I persuaded myself that it might serve Montalban well to turn him loose while doing the actual filming of his monologue.)

I told him my idea and showed him what I had in mind, how the camera would allow him to play the scene in toto, dancing (discreetly) around him. He listened politely and made no objection. I believe we worked out twenty-three marks he would need to hit. *Twenty-three.* (Some months later I was given a one-line role in a television movie where I was asked to hit *one mark* and found myself unable to do it.)

Of course, six pages of dialogue is a lot to memorize, but it did not occur to me that this would pose a problem and indeed it did not, though many of our greatest movie actors (think Marlon Brando) have extraordinary difficulties with even a single line. Billy Wilder recalled Marilyn Monroe needing *fifty-three* takes to say, "Now where did I put that bottle of whiskey?" in *Some Like It Hot.*

As cast and crew watched, Montalban stepped onto the set and, while hitting every one of those twenty-three marks, proved letter-perfect. It was astonishing.

There was just one difficulty: Montalban had ranted the entire speech at the top of his lungs, his bellowing voice piercing the rafters of the soundstage. As echoing silence fell Montalban looked at me, along with the company. "Like that?" he inquired, ever polite.

I reflected: *This man has been making movies since before I was born. This film is only my second. I do not know him and so far have been unable to penetrate the armor of his exquisite manners. What will he say if I try to direct him? Will he go ballistic over my presumption?*

I harrumphed something or other about this being the general idea and then added, as casually as I could, "Now that we've worked out the moves, let's let the crew do their lighting and have a chat in your trailer about . . . interpretation."

Montalban silently followed me back to his Winnebago while I wracked my brain for a way to broach the subject diplomatically. When we had settled ourselves and he favored me with a look of neutral attention, I began something like this: "You know, I read Laurence Olivier say somewhere that an actor should never show an audience his top. Once you show an audience your top, they know you have nowhere else to go. . . ."

Montalban did not jump up and toss me out but narrowed his eyes in attention. "Another thing," I went on before I could chicken out. "The really scary thing about crazy people is you never know what they're going to do next. They can be very quiet but that doesn't reduce the terror because at any second they might leap—"

At which point I abruptly feinted a thrust in his general direction, causing an instinctive flinch, because my action had come out of nowhere.

"Ah, yes, I see, I see!" Montalban got up, very excited, before I could continue, then turned and grinned at me, very different from all that had gone before. "You are going to direct me!" he chortled. "This is wonderful! I *need* direction! I have no idea what I'm doing out there but I usually don't get help." He then proceeded to relate a couple of choice, self-deprecating anecdotes about experiences that left him floundering. I remember one involved a Mervyn LeRoy production with Lana Turner, *Latin Lovers*, where LeRoy's sole comment before the cameras rolled (". . . and I had so been looking forward to working with the great director of *I Am a Fugitive from a Chain Gang*," Montalban recalled) had been, "Ricardo . . . Lana . . . make it a good scene."

As I sighed with relief—I think we both did, actually, as the ice had finally been broken—I still could not imagine where this partnership would lead. Montalban was highly intelligent, and I seldom needed to finish my sentences. He would finish them for me and then embellish my notions. I have never driven a Lamborghini but I imagine that directing Ricardo Montalban is as close as I will ever come. The slightest touch of the steering wheel or pedal, and he responded immediately. He never made a move without consulting me beforehand. "Nick, what if I pause here before I . . . ?" And still more interesting and exciting from my point of view was the fact that, once he got my thesis into his head he was able to take it and run with it. Khan jumped to life more three-dimensionally than many a screen villain, his rage fueled by his sorrow, blended with his intelligence. While I watched Montalban film Khan's initial monologue with his disordered, flying gray locks, it occurred to me that he really should be playing Lear. When I mentioned this to him later, he smiled sadly and alluded to his Hispanic accent. "It doesn't matter," I insisted, correctly. "You speak beautifully, you enunciate every syllable. No one will give a damn. You must do it."

Alas, he didn't, and it is our loss.

If the question I am most often asked regarding the movie concerns Montalban's chest, the scene that evokes the biggest reaction in the early part of the film is that same cargo bay encounter between Chekov and Terrill and Khan's "pets," the Ceti Alpha V eels. The eels are obviously not from Ceti Alpha V, a purely fictional designation. So what are they and where are they from? I think the story may now safely be told. The eels are not eels at all, but rather Andean shrimp, a mountainous cousin of the more familiar armadillo, though more fierce and in fact much rarer, as they are currently on the endangered species list. I can remember as if it were yesterday when I first met our shrimp wrangler, the infamous animal trafficker and trainer, Ole Machiado from Peruvia, who had hand carried the vicious critters through customs in a soundproof case and was now teaching Montalban how to hold the female in place with forceps on her neck while extracting her brood, nestled in the folds of her armor plating. Those are actually Montalban's unprotected arms in the shot, though the origin of his one glove can now be revealed. Unfortunately the actor did sustain at least one serious bite that entailed rabies and tetanus innoculations but, as always, Montalban was a good sport. The babies, by the way, were unharmed. They follow scent and Paul Winfield and Walter Koenig were obliged to daub their ears with Kaopectate in order to get the little things to dive toward their ear canals (models were used in the close-ups). To get them out again, we smeared a little Chanel No. 5 on their lobes.

No, I am not going to explain the Ceti Alpha V eels.

SHOOTING, PART II

Interestingly Kirk and Khan (how did their names both happen to start with the same letter?) never get to play a scene together in the film. Did I notice this would be the case? I can't say I did—nor did anyone else ever comment on or worry about it during the shooting, though Bill Shatner remembers a long discussion about the need to have a physical fight scene between the two men that he says was eventually scrapped for budgetary reasons. I can't say I miss it. Kirk and Khan do have a "phone" conversation of sorts of the type now common on iChat, and it was interesting to compare their styles and to learn how I could contribute to Shatner's performance.

On *Star Trek VI*, Christopher Plummer told me that he could tell that Shatner would be a star when he watched him subbing for him in *Henry V* one night at Stratford, Ontario. "He did everything different from me," Plummer recalled, "and that's when I knew . . ."

And if there was one thing Shatner knew, it was Captain Kirk. But the Kirk of *Star Trek II* was a bit different from the character of the TV series and the first film; he was aging, he was off his game, he was depressed (Captain Kirk depressed? This really was going to be different), and now he was in the fight of his life, up against a super-intelligent opponent whose only weakness was his obsessive hatred of Kirk. Khan has given him a minute to surrender the details of Project Genesis. Kirk, forced to put on reading glasses beneath the contemptuous glare of his implacable foe on the forward viewing screen, plays a desperate gambit and stalls until finally turning to Khan and telling him, "Here it comes," before he proceeds to hammer Khan's hijacked vessel with torpedoes.

The first time Shatner delivered "Here it comes," his sneer dripped off the lens. "Bill," says I, "this guy is some kind of über genius. You telegraph like that, he's gonna raise his shields in a second. Let's try it again."

The second take was similarly heavy-handed but, as it happened, no good for sound. (A stratagem I had contrived beforehand.) The third take, I think the focus was soft—and so on. Eventually Shatner became bored and when he got bored he got good. He dropped the attitudes he was prone to strike and instead *became* Kirk, with no trimmings. It was a good trick to stumble on and it happened early enough in the shoot that I was able to make good use of it throughout. (The only difficulty was ensuring that Shatner, who got better with every take, did not have to appear in a two-shot with someone who was at his best on take one and thereafter deteriorated.) When all's said and done, however, a director can only do so much; Shatner's triumph in the movie is his own, the product of his own intuition and his gift.

Montalban knew he was not a good judge of his own work ("I don't know what I'm doing out there . . ."), but many actors are convinced they are. And this despite the fact that so far from being objective, actors frequently pick the wrong roles in which to appear, let alone the wrong takes. Shatner was no exception. He would come up after the shot and say softly, "Take three was best for me." I would always nod and make a note of it, regardless of whether it was the take I wound up selecting. Similarly, if an actor wants another take and I have time, enough daylight, and I'm not blowing up a bridge behind him, I will always give it to him. Why should an actor have to go through the movie feeling his best work is getting away from him, even if he's mistaken? There's always the possibility that (a) it will get better or (b) he'll feel he's not been cheated or (c) it may not be better, but it may give you an idea for something you hadn't thought of that *will* be better.

William Wyler, Stanley Kubrick, and Warren Beatty are known for doing scores of takes, John Huston and Clint Eastwood for doing very few. Which is correct? Can you tell the difference watching their films?

Nimoy had long since figured out how to play Spock. "I never played Spock as a man with no emotions," he explained to me early on. "On the contrary, I always played him as a man of deep passions who was continually struggling to keep them in check."

I didn't need to say a word.

SHOOTING, PART III (LONG DAY´S JOURNEY INTO NIGHT)

Normally, a film is prepped, shot, and edited in that order. But in the case of *Star Trek II* (still known as *The Undiscovered Country*), the fact that the studio had already booked the film into theaters, coupled with our late start, forced me to shoot during the day and edit through most of the night. Fortunately I was in good health, and because we shot exclusively on soundstages, hours were pretty regular. Nonetheless, since I watched dailies in a screening room during lunch (fumbling with my sandwich in the dark, food and crumbs everywhere), I calculated that there was a monthlong period when I never saw daylight: I would sleep in the cutting room, head over to whatever soundstage we were on before sunrise, film indoors, then head for dailies, then back to the soundstage, from which I would emerge for only the brief walk to the cutting room again after dark. It grew to be an increasingly disorienting experience. My skin paled and, surreally, I became confused as to what day or time it was—was it day or night? (Later, when people would ask, "Oh, you directed *Star Trek*—were you on location?" I would always respond, "Yes, three weeks on Venus." Which was about how it felt.)

Because everyone liked the script and felt confident, shooting was nonetheless a pleasant, and even on occasion amusing experience. My friend from the University of Iowa, Dave Dierks, came from Iowa City to visit the set on the day we were shooting the entrance to the Genesis cave, a long corridor tunneled, ostensibly, through solid rock. For some reason joints in our fiberglass tunnel had split, occasioning what looked to be yet another dumb delay. The carpenters were on break, and no one would touch the thing for fear of inciting union issues. I turned to Dierks and wondered, "Could you get up there and hold the damn thing together for a couple of minutes?" He could and did, complaining afterward that he never got to witness any filming.

The Genesis cave was my biggest disappointment. It should have been filmed on location somewhere, but because of our omnipresent financial strait-jacket we were forced to use an implausible set, and everyone—including the brass, when they saw it—hated it. (Nowadays, with the advent of sophisticated CGI, we might have pulled it off.)

It was during this most frantic period of shooting and cutting that my as-sistant, Janna Wong, came up to me one evening (was it evening?) and said she thought the studio had changed the name of the movie.

"What're you talking about?" I demanded, frazzled as we walked from soundstage to our editing rooms. Janna wasn't certain but she'd heard rumors. I dismissed them.

A day or two later, she was certain: A Paramount executive in New York named Mancuso had renamed the movie *The Vengeance of Khan*. I was baf-fled and had more important things on my mind; still, I had to deal with this. I asked Janna to call the gentleman for me early the following morning.

"Mr. Mancuso, how do you do? I am Nicholas Meyer, the writer-director of *Star Trek II*."

"How do you do, Mr. Meyer?"

"Well, I am being told that you have changed the name of my film and that it is now to be called *Star Trek II: The Vengeance of Khan*."

"That is correct."

"Mr. Mancuso, have you seen any of the film?"

"No, I haven't." Nor had he read the script.

"Don't you think it would have been tactful to contact me as the maker of the film and discuss this decision?"

There followed what I took to be a puzzled pause three time zones away, and then:

"Mr. Meyer, I'm only trying to do what's best for the movie."

". . . I see," I responded, more to maintain the stichomythia than because I did. "Let me ask you something else," I proceeded, still stuck in this After You, Alphonse mode, "George Lucas's third *Star Wars* movie is being finished. It is called, as I'm sure you know, *The Revenge of the Jedi.* I know Paramount has extensive dealings with Lucas over the Indiana Jones franchise. . . . Do you think he will be pleased by your copycat title?"

"I assure you, that won't be a problem."

I wasn't sure what to say or do at this point. My job was to make the best possible movie I knew how and I couldn't do that and waste my time and energy on a tug-of-war about its title. Lots of arguments surround titles in general. Tennessee Williams's *A Streetcar Named Desire* was originally *The Poker Night*; *Death of a Salesman* was originally *The Inside of His Head.* In both cases the ultimate titles sound "classic" to us, reek of inevitability, but who is to say that *The Poker Night* wouldn't have had the same effect if it had been retained?

Movie titles generally don't mean much, though there are always exceptions. *Raiders of the Lost Ark*, I grant you, sounds thrilling, but what of *Forrest Gump*—is that a swamp in Louisiana? Both films were enormous hits.

In the event, George Lucas predictably lodged a strong objection to our title, which was thereupon altered, again by Mr. Mancuso, in consultation with no one, to *The Wrath of Khan* (after which Lucas himself changed his mind, realizing that the Jedi weren't revenge takers and substituting the now-familiar *Return of the Jedi* as that film's final moniker).

As the cutting room began to catch up, I started going home at night and allowing myself occasional treats. In those far-off times, Los Angeles had no opera company of its own but hosted the New York City Opera for a three-week visit each year. Their sojourn this year coincided with our shoot, enabling me to obtain my annual opera fix. On my opera nights I would stage a complicated shot for the last of the day. While the crew was lighting, I would shower and put on a suit so that I could head downtown immediately after we wrapped. I wound up directing looking like those directors of yore, who worked in jackets and ties.

Aside from the title wrangle, the studio seemed pleased with what we were shooting. I made my share of blunders. Bob Sallin was not happy with the way I staged Kirk's original entrance in the movie and he was perfectly right—it was pedestrian. As a maker of innumerable commercials, Sallin was far more experienced and visually sophisticated than I, with only one film under my belt. At his instigation we reshot Kirk's entrance, to far greater effect. On another occasion I lost my temper when I had no business doing so. Dee Kelley was having a hard time remembering a simple, single line: "Those people back there bought time for Genesis with their lives." For some reason he couldn't get it out, and the more we tried, the more spooked he became, like a horse who is now terrified of a big jump. Instead of calming him down or calming myself down, instead of taking a breather, I stubbornly couldn't understand what the difficulty was and allowed my gathering impatience to show. For a sensitive person like Dee, my irritation only compounded his nerves. Later, after we'd finally got it right, I went to him and apologized. I have a rigid streak that makes small allowances for the unexpected. I show up for work prepared and I always expect my cast and crew to do the same, which includes the actors knowing their lines. This is, to my way of thinking, part of what they're paid to do, and getting to do it (i.e., to make movies) is something that I regard as a great privilege. But mine wasn't always a great MO, as it made no allowances for the thousand variables that are an inevitable part of the filmmaking process, including other people's quirks and problems. It also made few allowances for spontaneity when spontaneity might help. In movies where the dialogue is stylized, for whatever reason, I believe that I am within my rights to insist that it be delivered letter perfect rather than improvised. Billy Wilder felt the same way, a precedent I relished since it helped to justify my own instincts and inclinations where the dialogue of *Star Trek* was concerned. But where Wilder was willing to put up with fifty-three takes for Monroe and her whiskey bottle ("I could get my aunt Hattie to do it right the first time, but who would pay to see my aunt Hattie?" Wilder pointed out), I did not possess the same professional cool. There are many reasons why an actor may not be able to say a line. It may be the actor's problem, it may be that there's something wrong with the line, but whatever it is, exacerbating the actor's terror is not what *I'm* being paid for.

Of the move to fire me I learned nothing until much later.

When I started directing *Time After Time* I was stylistically very conservative. I shot wide angles, close-ups, over-the-shoulders, POVs, etc., like any other director would . . . and then I remember thinking, *If you're going to shoot your film like the next man, why don't you move over and let the next man do it?* People say they want to direct, but what's the point of doing it if you're only going to do it the way other people do it? What's the point if you aren't bringing something unique to the process? At the end of the day, all you have to offer as an artist in any medium is *yourself.* And if the best you can do is simply to imitate what others have done, why bother? Could I still hear the small voice Spielberg describes, the inmost conscience of the film? That voice can easily get lost in the hubbub of the convoluted and noisy process. (Those who enjoy sausage would do well not to see how it is manufactured.)

As shooting had continued on *Time After Time*, I had become progressively bolder in many ways, more willing to try things that hadn't—so far as I knew—been done before. By the time I got to direct *Star Trek II*, I surrendered to my instincts much sooner. For example, in my zeal to pay homage to Hornblower (and, also, to favorite U-boat movies of my youth), I determined that there should be a scene in which we ran out the guns. To make this possible, I asked Joe Jennings to design a futuristic torpedo bay, complete with steel gratings that would be ripped up manually by the crew when the *Enterprise* prepared for action. I encountered many dubious reactions to what, after all, was bound to be (correctly) perceived as an anachronism, but I held fast, and the yanking up of those gratings as the torpedo is lowered into place remains my favorite shot of the movie.

Years later, listening to a fan rhapsodize over this shot, I asked if the anachronism hadn't troubled him. He was surprised—"What anachronism?" he demanded. "Half the ship's machinery had been put out of action by Khan; they *had* to rip up those torpedo gratings manually!" Here is a perfect instance of a movie lover making his own logic to paper over what to another viewer would be sheerest nonsense, a lovely instance of the collaboration that Coleridge described as the willing suspension of disbelief.

My instincts were not infallible, however.

I was wrong when I draped a sweater over David Marcus's shoulders toward the end of the movie. I was—as always—trying to keep things real but in this instance only succeeded in making them ludicrous. Similarly, I wanted a sign that read NO SMOKING ON THE BRIDGE but lost that one. Probably a good thing.

During the filming of Spock's funeral, Shatner was alarmed to see Saavik, Spock's Vulcan protégée, shedding tears. "Are you gonna let her do that?" he protested. "Vulcans can't cry!"

"That's why it will be so moving when this one does," I countered, and this time I was correct. Directors make a million such choices, and I expect it's their batting average that separates the good filmmakers from the mediocrities. (Vulcans don't lose their tempers, either—except when Spock becomes enraged in *Star Trek VI*.)

SPOCK'S DEATH

The shooting schedule of a movie is usually drawn up for maximum efficiency. All the scenes occurring on a given set are likely to be scheduled together, no matter how far apart they are in the story, and actors are expected to shoot out of sequence, calibrating their performances accordingly.

But there is one exception to this scheduling imperative: when the actors' emotional complexities must be taken into consideration—if possible. (I was astonished to learn that Marion Cottilard's Oscar-winning tour de force as Edith Piaf in the French film *La Vie en Rose*, during which she ages decades, was shot out of sequence. How she managed this, I have no idea.) In *Star Trek II*, respecting the highly emotional nature of the material involved, we saved the death of Spock for almost the end of the shoot.

How the original decision to kill Spock was made, I do not know. I have heard rumors that it was Nimoy who, disillusioned with the first film and tired of the carapace of Spock's identity, agreed as part of his contract to appear in the second movie only with the promise of a heroic death scene. I cannot say. In any case, no matter what its origin, it was my job to make Spock's death plausible, meaningful, and moving and this, to the best of my ability, I set out to do, starting with the script and shepherding it through the filming and the editing.

Throughout the making of the film, rumors of Spock's demise fueled the rage of fans. I received a helpful letter that ran: *If Spock dies, you die.*

Great. But in the final analysis, art is not a democracy. Nor, notwithstanding the collaborative nature of the medium, are films made by committee.

The French director Robert Bresson made the observation: "My job is not to find out what the public want and give it to them; my job is to make the public want what *I* want."

The question, as I offered it to nervous Paramount executives, was not whether we killed Spock, but whether we killed him *well*. If we botched the job and the death appeared to be nothing more than the working-out of a clause in Nimoy's contract, people would throw things at the screen and they'd be right to throw them. But if we did it correctly and that death proceeded organically from the material, no one would ever question it.

That was my theory and my rationale.

Nimoy was uncharacteristically restive on the day of Spock's death. There may have been several reasons for this but I suspect his nerves were brought on (a) by the knowledge that he was (we thought at the time) taking an irrevocable step as regards an alter ego he had lived with for almost fifteen years and (b) by the fact that there was now a feeling on the lot that this film might be something special, and there were already whispers about continuing with a sequel. Was Nimoy now having second thoughts?

Whatever the cause, our actor was understandably on edge. I was interested years later, on reading his memoir (everyone connected with *Star Trek* writes a memoir), to discover that part of his annoyance was caused by my showing up to shoot his death scene dressed as Sherlock Holmes.

At the outset of this book, I cited the observation of trial lawyers as to the unreliability of eyewitnesses, and here is a perfect instance of that principle. I have never on any occasion in my life dressed as Sherlock Holmes. But it *is* true that I was wearing a suit, because it happened to be one of the nights when I was going directly downtown to the opera after we wrapped. It was likely my suit and not a Holmes costume that distressed Nimoy, though I suspect he would have been upset no matter what. The scene we were about to film was especially tricky for him.

I have also owned at the outset of this memoir that I was unfamiliar with *Star Trek* and its television history and the devotion of its fan base. And this may have contributed to my surprise while we were rolling when, out of the corner of my eye, I saw my cinematographer, Gayne Rescher, with tears streaming down his cheeks. I looked around and beheld more of the crew weeping as the dying Spock held up his splayed hand and enjoined Kirk to live long and prosper. (I had wanted his blood to be green—Dr. McCoy was always referring to Spock as "You green-blooded, inhuman" etc.—but Nimoy vetoed it.)

I felt my own eyes begin to sting but I squelched my tears and concentrated on my job, which was not to weep but to make others weep. I had written this scene as best I knew how; I photographed and choreographed it the same way and hoped it would be okay.

I asked Nimoy about the spread-fingered salute (which, incidentally, Shatner could not duplicate in return, though most audiences never notice), and he told me that it originated from a childhood experience in Boston. His father took him to temple, he recalled, "And there was a moment during the service when the congregation was supposed to turn away from the altar but I turned back and peeked—and they were all holding their hands like this," at which point he demonstrated Spock's trademark gesture with the palm held away like a cop stopping traffic, only with the third and fourth fingers held together, split from the first and second in like configuration.

Spock turns out to be Jewish.

Despite whatever efforts we may make, we live in the present. What happened yesterday is done and each day the train we ride in called Life will take us further from it. Only madmen can take up residence in their memories while the future remains an undiscovered country.

But movies are different.

Jimmy Stewart memorably described movies as little pieces of captured time. This felicitous and poetic image comes as close as anything I've read to encapsulating the phenomenon of film, the idea, in effect, of putting a frame around a moment for eternity. The creation of that moment may have been meticulously prepared or it may have been simply improvised; a thousand variables may have contributed to it and God knows, more dreadful moments than magical ones have doubtless been preserved in this fashion, but the major point I'm endeavoring to make is this: what more or less took place in an instant, or a day, thanks to the phenomenon of movies, morphs into a piece of the permanent record.

In physical terms, it took about a day to film the death of Spock. In another sense that day was more than a decade aborning. The confluence of Gene Roddenberry, of Leonard Nimoy, Bill Shatner and the rest of the *Star Trek* ensemble, the work of many writers and directors, the devotion of countless legions of fans and, yes, my own happenstance contribution, all combined on that day. Some of us understood the significance (small *s*) of that eternal moment while it was unfolding; some were just doing their jobs. I am not prepared to argue that the Death of Spock ranks with *Aristotle Contemplating a Bust of Homer*, but I think it facile to altogether dismiss its significance. I am certainly pleased to have played my small part, even as the train called Life carried me inexorably forward.

One further consequence of wearing my suit during that day's filming led to my acting debut. While directing a week or so later, I was summoned to the soundstage phone, a novelty for me. In the absence of the now ubiquitous cell phone, its primitive soundstage predecessor was typically monopolized by all sorts of people, many of them, by this point in the shoot, intent on lining up their next gigs. My call turned out to be a double novelty, for it was from a casting director named Toni Howard.

"Nick," she greeted me. "Are you still acting?" This, I fancied, was a little bit akin to asking a man when he had stopped beating his wife. Acting? How did she know I had *ever* acted? Nonetheless, my vanity instantly aroused, I assured her that I still acted and why did she want to know? It seemed she was casting a TV movie, *Mae West*, and wondered if I might be interested in playing the young George Raft.

"It's not a large role," she warned me. How large? I asked. One line—perfect. In January—even better. While my cast and crew dithered behind me, fiddling with lights and wardrobe, I continued to indulge myself. How did you come to ask me about playing George Raft? I asked. It turns out she'd seen a still photographer's shot of me, in my suit, riding a camera crane, my hair slicked back from my pre-opera shower.

"You look like Valentino," Toni stated. "And, as you may know, George Raft was brought to Hollywood as a lookalike replacement for Valentino, after his sudden death."

Vain, I grant you. Hah. I was in.

Come January, we were still mopping up what is known as "principal photography" but in actual fact all we were doing the day I departed for my one-line debut was close-ups of hands flipping switches and turning instrument dials. My crew wished me jolly good luck as I abandoned them in search of a new career.

It was a surreal experience. I had begun (typically) with grandiose notions of myself, like John Huston, doing a "guest starring" role in Otto Preminger's film *The Cardinal* and ended with cold sweats. I was mailed not the entire script but only the page with my single line, which, when I read it, I knew at once was wrong. (*"Oh, Jeez,"* I could imagine the director groaning, *"he wants to change his one line?"*) But I did have a point. My character, George Raft, was supposed to be exiting a sneak preview of his own film, when he gets accosted in the theater lobby by studio execs asking his opinion of the movie. He was supposed to snarl in reply, "Mae West stole everything but the cameras," before stalking off. Surely, I reasoned, we know by this point that the movie's about Mae West. Shouldn't my line be, "That broad stole everything but the cameras?" "That bitch"? "That tomato"? Anything but the fearfully on-the-nose "Mae West."

But I had other problems, such as hitting my mark—and unlike Montalban, who had effortlessly nailed twenty-three, I was too spooked to manage my one and only. During rehearsals, when it was indicated by a huge, black electrical tape cross, I experienced no difficulty. Imagine my surprise when, just prior to rolling, the big X was replaced by something the size of a beauty mark.

I have never seen my performance, which is probably just as well.

With shooting finally completed, I could concentrate on work in the cutting room.

CLIPPERS ON THE SIDES

Editing is a part of filmmaking I greatly enjoy. Like writing, where the name of the game is rewriting, I love the process of experimentation that editing affords. Though computers have simplified the mechanics of this process, even with time-consuming Moviolas or KEMs, the experiments were where the fun was. The work—no matter how electronically simplified—generally conforms to the following stages: (1) the editor strings together an assembly of what you've shot, trying to include as much as possible so you can be reminded of the possibilities; (2) the director views the assembly, after which he contemplates suicide (it is a maxim that no movie is ever as good as its dailies or as bad as its first cut); (3) the director starts slashing away and may jettison as much as an hour out of the assembly; (4) he looks at it again and still wants to kill himself but perhaps more humanely; (5) he then cuts another fifteen minutes; and so on. Eventually, he is no longer cutting minutes but seconds, endlessly refining the moments in the film, ultimately down to frames. Sometimes, hit by a brainstorm, the order of scenes is rearranged, or it occurs to someone that maybe a voice-over here or a flashback there might help and the continuity itself undergoes a transformation. You are no longer bound by the screenplay, for now the film has assumed a life of its own and you are molding celluloid instead of paper. Finally, at the end of the time contractually granted the director for his cut, the movie is turned over to the studio, and the fun ends as a tug-of-war commences. But let us leave that until its proper place.

Bill Dornisch the giggler took some getting used to. And he had a tendency to tear film, which led to a battered workprint. But he also had a sure-footed instinct about the footage itself and an impeccable sense of rhythm, essential for an editor. Unlike Bennett, with his shrewdly analytic temperament, Dornisch operated on pure instinct. He could seldom explain his choices, but they startled you with their rightness. I learned much from him when he'd offer certain truisms over his shoulder: "I can make 'em talk sooner but I can't make 'em talk faster."

You can lose track of time in an editing room. Typically, there are no windows or, if they exist, they've been blacked out. Day, night, these distinctions become meaningless as you sit, hypnotized, before your footage, amazed at what editing can do. Show a man entering a room and smiling. Cut to a baby gurgling in its crib, and the man is a nice man, smiling at the baby. Now substitute a shot of a bloody, headless corpse, and that same man with the same smile has been transformed into a sadistic killer. If movies are a director's medium rather than an actor's (let's omit writers for purposes of this discussion), it is because the actor's performance ultimately lies in the hands of the director and his editor and, as such, is at their mercy. Whereas an actor in a play is in complete control (the director can rage from the back of the theater but he can't stop the performance once the curtain is up), here the choices—the particular takes, which close-up (if any), the length of the pauses—will determine how that performance goes over. Performances have indeed been made and lost in the cutting room. If the filmmakers start to panic over the movie, decisions may become draconian. Maybe the solution is to look at another take! This is an especially seductive notion, since we've all become so bored with the one we've been playing with all these months. The "new" take suddenly seems better, more vivid, etc., even though it typically is no such thing—merely different.

Star Trek II was in fact the first feature film to utilize computer-generated imagery. The informational Project Genesis video presented on Kirk's monitor by Dr. Carol Marcus, was, I believe, the first time CGI found its way into a movie.

Throughout the postproduction process, each individual FX shot, like missing pieces of a jigsaw puzzle, would trickle down from San Francisco to be viewed, criticized, redone, and eventually slipped into its proper place in the film. Until such time as the finished shot was approved, a blank piece of film was inserted with the words SCENE MISSING. Some slugs had descriptions on them ("*Enterprise* fires back"), while on others there was a crude storyboard sketch of the missing scene. I learned the hard way not to preview a movie without all the finished effects shots. No matter how many times or how emphatically you attempt to explain to the preview audience that some shots are missing or incomplete, that they must understand these are yet to be included, please ignore this, we're sorry, blah blah, when the cartoon version or the SCENE MISSING title appears instead of the real thing, audiences always erupt in laughter, bounced out of the tale.

"In Space No One Can Hear You Scream" ran the tagline of the original *Alien* movie. From a scientific standpoint, this is certainly the case. But when we viewed the ILM spaceships flying around without sound to accompany their motion, they did indeed resemble nothing so much as the plastic models they were. It was sound that gave them their heft, their gravity, if you will, even though they were in an ostensibly weightless environment. Too bad, as I had been intrigued by breaking with spaceship movie tradition and having the ships glide silently, accompanied only by music when appropriate.

About spaceship sound *inside* the *Enterprise*, I was much more certain: There had to be some. I didn't care what speculation had informed the previous movie or how silent the engines of the *Enterprise* had been heretofore. As far as I was concerned, *this Enterprise* was going to have a throbbing heartbeat. Our discussion on this subject happened to take place in one of the Paramount screening rooms, where during a pause in the conversation I became aware of a rhythmic, reverberating pounding. It was the air conditioning unit for the entire building, located next door. "Listen!" I said. "That's just how I want the *Enterprise* to sound." Cecelia Hall, our sound effects editor, duly recorded it and used it at various volumes whenever we were anywhere inside the ship.

At some point during this period, those whispers about our film began to get louder. People who hadn't seen a frame were spreading the buzz that it was terrific. I was pleased but uneasy hearing this, mainly because I couldn't imagine how this rumor had gotten started or on what it had been based.

It was also during this period that I encountered my taciturn production manager, Austen Jewell, one day in the parking lot. Jewell, whom I had met and whose work I had so admired on *Time After Time*, asked me how the editing was coming. In the course of telling him, Bob Sallin's name came up, and Austin (at different times in his career he spelled his first name both ways) held up his hand like a traffic cop. "Don't mistake him for your friend," he warned me. "He tried to have you fired during the first week of shooting."

I must've stood in that parking lot with my mouth opening and closing like a goldfish's. "He—?"

"He wasn't happy with the footage so he tried to have you fired. I was in the screening room when he showed your stuff to Michael Eisner." (Eisner was Paramount's president and chief operating officer at the time.) "Eisner said, 'I don't know what your problem is; I only wish *Grease* looked this good,' and that was the end of it."

We chatted for a few moments more and then Jewell got into his car, leaving me to my confused thoughts. I now recalled Sallin's disappointment with my staging of Kirk's original entrance. He had been correct about that. I liked Bob Sallin and admired his understated style. Evidently, the reverse was not the case. Or perhaps, despite liking me, he had been disappointed in my performance as director. If our positions had been reversed, what would I have done? Or, more to the point, how would I have done it? And what to do with this information now? In the end I elected to do nothing. I hadn't been fired. It was water over the dam or under the bridge or whatever it was. The film was finished, the buzz was positive, and I had bigger fish to keep frying.

It was also sometime during this period that I got a call from Harve Bennett, summoning me to his office. Wondering what excrement had now tumbled into the wind machine, I trudged wearily across the nighttime lot and sat opposite his cluttered desk.

"Kid, we have a problem," Bennett began, pausing to sip his beer. "I've lost the credit arbitration. What do you think I should do?"

Determining screen credits on a movie is the prerogative of the Writers Guild, not the studios. The studio submits its proposed screen credits to the Guild, but the WGA has the final say. Writers may appeal to the Guild for arbitration if they feel they have been unjustly credited (or uncredited) but only on narrow, procedural grounds. There is, as I have noted, a prejudice against according a producer a writing credit on the same film. In our blithe innocence, we had placed Bennett's name on the screenplay, and now he was telling me it had been rejected and asking me what I thought he should do.

Something in his expression told me this was not the moment to hesitate.

"You've been robbed," I said quickly, "and if you appeal, I'll go in there as a witness."

Which, surreally enough, was exactly what happened. I felt as if I was one-upping Tom Sawyer, who got to observe his own funeral. In my case I got to deliver the eulogy as well. "Gentlemen, this script, one of the swellest it has ever been my privilege to read, let alone direct," and so on.

One of the reasons credits are so hotly and frequently contested is the pernicious system of awarding bonuses tied to the amount of screen credit received. If a writer gets sole credit, so much more money; half credit, less; and so on. In the end, Bennett and Jack B. Sowards (author of one of the five original screenplay drafts), received story credit and Sowards received the sole screenplay credit.

At a meeting in Michael Eisner's office, Barry Diller fumed at the title of the movie. "No one knows what the fuck 'wrath' means!" he shouted, glaring at me. "How did we wind up with this stupid title?"

"Don't look at me," I responded. "The title is the handiwork of Mr. Mancuso in New York."

We showed our cut of the film to Eisner and company. Shots were still missing, and there was a musical "temp" track in place of Horner's anticipated score, but it was evident the studio was much pleased. The buzz continued to grow. I was spared the ordeal of sitting through the movie in the executives' presence (I always have trouble watching my own work, anyway; all I can see are mistakes), but I did screen the cut for myself and sat there, trying to figure out what I had done—or failed to do. It was no use; I couldn't be objective. I couldn't make head or tail of the movie, except to know every cut, every line, every scratch on our very scratched-up work print. I had no idea what the studio's enthusiasm was based on. I might as well have been looking at the thing through the wrong end of a telescope.

The studio's notes, when they arrived, were few and mostly reasonable. One interesting plot issue they felt needed to be addressed: In the present cut (and script) of the film, Kirk is aware that he has an illegitimate son. But given the fact that in the previous twenty years (which is to say, throughout the period covered by the series and first movie) no mention has been made of this fact, Kirk emerges as a schmuck for having ignored the boy all this time. The studio felt this was not only unsympathetic but perhaps also implausible, and requested that the scene in which Kirk and David meet be reshot so as to resolve this. Kirk's line, "Why didn't you tell him?" delivered to the boy's mother would now be changed to, "Why didn't you tell me?" which would require Carol to present a rationale for having completely cut Kirk out of David's life. This made sense to me, and we reshot the exchange. Reshooting is a surreal feeling. The cast and crew have long departed, the sets have been dismantled, etc., and now a skeletal version of all must be reconstituted. Sometimes key components are no longer available, which coerces you into close-ups. If your cameraman is now off on another film, someone must attempt to replicate his style and use the same lenses, but you can usually spot the difference in the lighting or framing when you watch the finished film. A battle I lost involved eliminating the identity of midshipman Peter Preston (as Scotty's nephew); also Kirk's line, "Midshipman, you're a tiger," which they felt came out sort of gay. In subsequent versions of the film, I managed to restore Preston's identity without Kirk's questionable line reading.

Our first "public" showing, or preview, took place on the lot at the Paramount Theater. Because of the secretive nature of our film's plot, all *Star Trek II*'s previews were likewise held on the lot. (For all I know, the viewers had to sign loyalty oaths.) First screenings, before no matter how friendly an audience, are among the most terrifying parts of the filmmaking process. When we had first screened *Time After Time*, my intestines entwined themselves like a horse's, and I would have colicked if I could. The same symptoms obtained now: I stood in the back of the theater and fought the urge to flee to the men's room and be sick. That Hydra-headed monster, the audience, can, on a whim, destroy you and all you've worked for.

True, some things can be fixed; that's what previews are for. With plays in "tryouts" you can rewrite; in film you can reedit or reshoot if necessary (if you can afford it). Here, though, we faced a greater challenge: How would an audience react to the death of a beloved character?

We had no idea how the audience would in fact respond to Spock's death but we all knew the moment when they would be bluntly reminded that it was imminent: a shot of Spock's empty chair on the bridge after he'd quietly gone below in an effort to save the ship. Suddenly the opening scene came back to them and they remembered: this is the movie where Spock dies. If they were going to throw things, this was when they'd do it.

There was dead silence at the sight of that chair.

And there always would be. What one audience does, every audience does. Similarly, if a joke doesn't work with one audience, it will never work with any audience.

The audience giggled at the SCENE MISSING slugs but otherwise was enraptured by the film beyond anything I could've imagined. The movie played like gangbusters, with the audience laughing, cheering, and weeping in all the right places. You could hear people sobbing throughout Spock's death.

At the end, they were simply stunned.

Was this what we wanted?

I had certainly thought so.

But by this point another thought began percolating through everyone's head. As enthusiasm for the film mounted, some people were beginning to think beyond *Star Trek II*. It was not a foregone conclusion that we had saved the franchise—the film could always flop—but the question was now being asked: What If? And, as a corollary, how could there be another *Star Trek* movie without Spock? Kirk might well be the anchor of the series, but it was hard to escape the conclusion that Spock was its most popular character. Was there any way of keeping him alive, or, failing that, bringing him back to life or, at the very least, hinting at that possibility? Instead of stunned silence, should we heed Harvey Milk's credo: you gotta give them hope?

Something to cheer about?

It is hard to describe how infuriated I was by what I took to be these crass commercial considerations. I had by now come to realize how devoted the show's fan base was, how seriously people took the idea of Spock's death, something for which I had fought long and hard, confident in the belief that, if it proceeded organically, it would be more than justified; it would be inevitable. From my point of view, bringing him back to life would constitute a complete dry hustle of people's emotions, an unforgivable breach of trust. Yes, we'll get you all worked up, we'll wring tears at the passing of Spock, and then we'll reveal it was all a crock. Someone once observed that Americans like their tragedies with happy endings, an idea that I found morbidly repellent as it negated the tragedy in the first place.

Bennett's concern—possibly influenced by his overall deal on the Paramount lot (he would be here when the rest of us had cleaned out our offices), but also perhaps the product of his shrewd analytical abilities—was whether the film was making a mistake when it simply deprived people of anything that could be construed as "hope."

Pick your battles, I learned—and this is the battle I picked. I did not want the death of Spock to end in a betrayal of the audience's emotional investment in that moment. In this I had no hesitation in believing that I was in the right. I fought the proposed idea of hinting at Spock's resurrection every way I knew how. I argued against it. I stalled. I lied. I refused to cooperate, trying to let the clock run out against the moment when it was time to cut negative or miss our release date.

I even came up with what I thought was an elegant compromise. At the beginning of each *Star Trek* television episode, we hear Kirk's voice-over in the log of the *Enterprise*: "*These are the continuing voyages of the starship*

Enterprise; her ongoing [originally *"five-year"*] *mission: to explore strange new worlds, to seek out new life and new civilizations . . . to boldly go where no man has gone before."*

I proposed letting Spock's sepulchral voice read these lines at the end of our film. The audience wouldn't know how he came to be saying them— was it his ghost speaking?—but they would get the idea of Spock's own "ongoingness."

But bigger gears had been set in motion than I could clog. My Spock log-entry idea was merely incorporated into a more literal hint that he was— somehow—not dead.

When Bennett indicated he would go along and try to come up with a satisfying compromise, I viewed it as a cave-in. Bennett, by contrast, was a realist. He had an overall studio contract and explained it to me like this: "Kid, you're the squadron leader, no question. But I'm the base commander. And after you're long gone, I'll still be here." Trying to make other movies, he didn't need to add.

"Don't you know who you are?" I countered, passionately. "You're Harve fucking Bennett! They *need* you. If you take a stand, we'll win!"

In the end Bennett, admittedly conflicted but obliged to take the long view, came up with the scenario that pleased everyone (except me, of course): first a shot was added in the engine room: Spock's fingers splayed on Dr. Mc-Coy's unconscious face right before Spock enters the lethal radiation chamber as he utters the somber admonition "Remember," and later Spock's coffin, shot from within a photon torpedo, would land on the Genesis planet, and Kirk would vow to return to see what had become of it. "If Genesis is indeed life from death," he would proclaim, "I must return here . . ." blah, blah. . . .

Since I refused to shoot it, Sallin was dispatched to San Francisco with a team to film the surface of the Genesis planet with Spock's coffin lying among the bull(shit) rushes in a botanical museum. At one point, he and I had an explosive encounter—again in the Paramount parking lot—in which he yelled, accusing me of being "morally bankrupt" and added for good measure, "You'd walk over your own mother to get the film your way."

"I would!" I admitted at equally high volume. "But as long as anybody around here is filing for Chapter 11, maybe you should go over your own accounts and look into the business of trying to get me fired."

And so on.

In the end none of my stonewalling did any good. Sallin's San Francisco footage looked beautiful, and when James Horner added music to help sell it, Bennett saw the result and wept. "I don't know if it's right or wrong," he confessed, "but I believe it."

Horner's music did indeed crown the movie, with or without what I viewed as its vulgar compromise. Music is always added at the end of the process, and if it works it is one of the most exciting parts of making a film. Sound *always* dominates image. If you doubt this, simply drive around town (or country) and listen to your radio. The music will determine the character of the landscape, never the reverse. Show a laughing girl bounding across a field of yellow daisies and underscore that child with Chopin's "Funeral March" and you will know the kid is doomed to die of an incurable disease. Horner's music captured the essence of the film; he even made sense of *Star Trek*'s fanfare.

But oh, the satisfaction when you subdue the beast. Comedians talk about "killing" an audience, "knocking them dead," and I understand the sense in which the relationship is an adversarial one. And when the monster is defeated, when you have a hundred or a thousand or ten thousand people eating out of the palm of your hand, laughing or crying at your command, you can pound your chest like King Kong. The delirious sense of accomplishment is nonetheless the high that we in the theater—any theater—are constantly chasing, the reason we're going through all this hell in the first place: to make strangers laugh or cry. Nothing is more important to us. To outsiders, such a goal may seem absurd, puerile, incomprehensible—but only because they haven't inhaled the opium of a smash. The bliss is ultimately indescribable, but Sondheim's song, "It's a Hit!" comes closest to capturing the feeling.

And once you know your film plays, once you have ironed out every last frame so that it works from beginning to end (rarely!), you can relax and revel in that power, that high.

How calm, how serene you are watching that celluloid unspool . . .

Later I attended another showing of the film in the executive screening room with Harve Bennett, Gary Nardino (head of the television division), and Paramount chairman Barry Diller. When the lights came up, the others waited in silence for Diller's reaction.

"I didn't know this movie was about the death of Spock," he began. "You can't kill Spock."

This was less than a month before the film was to open. Bennett stared at the floor, Nardino gazed at the ceiling, or perhaps it was the other way around. Regardless, neither man spoke.

I wanted to ask how it was that the boss of a studio with this much money involved (admittedly less than 25 percent of the previous film's gargantuan budget) could not have been bothered to read the script, but I confined myself to replying, "Yes, you *can* kill him—if you do it well." I had all the courage of the preview audience's convictions.

"And another thing," Diller went on as though I hadn't spoken. "The reconciliation scene between Kirk and his son doesn't work."

"In your opinion," I responded, my intestines contracting and my heart pounding so that it could be heard across the room.

He turned to look at me, as if seeing me for the first time, a vein throbbing in his forehead.

"Look, I can say it to you politely or I can just say it: the scene doesn't work. If I were that kid I'd want to know where the hell my father had been my whole life."

I took a deep breath. "Here's where I come out," I said, speaking very slowly so as to keep my voice steady. "I filmed the script we all agreed upon. I was asked to make editorial changes and I made them. I was asked to reshoot material and I reshot it. More material was reshot without my agreement, but this is where I draw the line. If any further cuts or reshoots take place they will take place without me, and if this film is further touched, I will get a sandwich board and picket Paramount Pictures in Westwood when the film opens, and if this is the sort of reputation you want to attract other directors to this lot, that is, of course, entirely your affair."

Neither Bennett nor Nardino moved. Diller stared at me. The closest I could come to looking him back in the eye was to stare at the adjacent pulsing vein on his forehead. Finally he said, "Well, if you feel that strongly, it's your movie."

With which he walked out.

At some point during all of this, Bennett had to check into the hospital for several days with an infected cat scratch.

Our next preview also took place again on the Paramount lot with another recruited audience; once again I was a complete wreck. What if this crowd—in unique contradiction to the show biz rule cited above—felt differently? What if they ridiculed what had made others weep? I had stuck to my guns, defied the head of the studio, and now I was—predictably—panicked about my stand. Unlike Bennett (and a lot of other folks), I came late to the concept of considering "the big picture," which in my case was whether I'd ever work for Paramount again—or indeed anywhere else, as word of my intransigent behavior would certainly get around town.

The "reconciliation" scene between Kirk and his son received applause, and no one seemed to object to Spock's coffin on the Genesis planet with its—to me—unforgivable implications. "'There are always possibilities,' Spock would say," Kirk reflects.

Exiting the theater, I caught sight of Diller's sour expression. When he saw me, he said: "Yes, yes, I know what I'm supposed to say but I still don't think it works."

Was there any point in replying that it no longer mattered what either of us thought? That audiences may be stupid but they are never wrong? No, but I said it anyway.

As other wildly successful previews followed, the struggle for credit became even more intense. One night I received a call from a distraught Bennett.

"Were you aware that Bob Sallin has hired his own publicist?" he asked.

I told him I was not.

"I called him when I heard this," Harve went on, a catch in his voice. "I asked him if this was true. He said, 'What business is it of yours?'"

I was silent on my end of the phone. What was there to say? On the other end of the line I could hear Harve's breathing.

Contrary to all the clichés, Hollywood is in fact comprised of human beings, who, in addition to their ambition, are possessed of sentiment and sentience. Bennett and Sallin had been friends for years, always dreaming of the time they would work together.

And it ended like this.

On June 4, 1982, the film opened to the biggest weekend gross to date and I had my fifteen seconds of fame. At the (now demolished) National Theatre in Westwood, I was stunned to see lines around the block with folks seated before TV trays, eating their dinner. But that wasn't the biggest surprise. The biggest surprise was how many of them were already wearing the brand-new uniforms of the *Enterprise* crew. This was long before all the Internet sites that now render any secrecy impossible. How had these people learned about and copied our uniforms?

I flew to New York, saw the film in Times Square with my parents, had the thrill of waiting up with heart-pounding anticipation for the morning papers to come out with their notices (another treat now denied us by the internet), and can still remember the first line of Janet Maslin's *New York Times* review: "Well, this is more like it."

Later I did the television and VHS cuts, where, with the studio no longer interested, I got to reinsert midshipman Preston to his rightful place in the plot but otherwise made no particular alterations. In my experience of watching them, so called "director's cuts" are rarely superior to the release version of the picture. (Orson Welles's *Touch of Evil*, as reconstructed by Walter Murch, being the conspicuous exception that proves the rule.) They are usually longer but not better.

The Wrath of Khan was now part of cinema history, and history would judge it.

Postmortem

As the years passed I was pleased, proud, and always surprised and touched to see the film continue to garner affection and respect from critics and audiences. It was a long time before I saw *The Wrath of Khan* again. The occasion was a twentieth-anniversary screening in 2002 at the new, wonderfully appointed Paramount Theater on the lot, which—no coincidence—was also the occasion to launch the special DVD edition. In the intervening years, Kirstie Alley had become a television star. Gayne Rescher, Bill Dornisch, Joe Jennings, Bibi Besch and Merritt Butrick (mother and son in the film), and art director Mike Minor had all passed away (the latter two of a new and deadly scourge). The film had already appeared on DVD, but the studio was by now aware of the whole ancillary arena known as "special features," to which I had somewhat reluctantly contributed. I had not wished to do the "director's commentary" (I can think of nothing worse than trying to watch a movie with someone yammering in my ear throughout), but I sold out when I was offered DVDs from the Paramount catalog to jump-start my own collection.

When I was interviewed for a separate feature concerning the origins of the film and my contribution to them, I narrated the events surrounding the screenplay as I have recounted them here. Paramount's lawyers became alarmed, and the DVD producers were told they could not use parts of the story that might appear to put Paramount in jeopardy with the Writers Guild. I, in turn, responded that if they didn't include the truth, I would back out of the project entirely. In the end a compromise was reached and I was responsible for a clause that is now standard in all studio DVDs, the disclaimer that states that the studio is in no way responsible for any of the content or comments made by people appearing in the interviews on the disc. It is hard to overstate the importance of this clause: It enables those supplementary DVD segments to be more than mere puff pieces but a valuable form of oral history. People can tell their differing, multiple versions and perceptions of the truth (as Rashomon tries to explain), in all their fascinating variety, without the studio worrying about the consequences.

That night the Paramount Theater was full to overflowing with friends and fans. Ricardo Montalban was the guest of honor. There were speeches, including a brief one by me. (Brief because, who wants speeches in a movie theater?) Then *Star Trek II* in its DVD format was projected on the huge screen with incredible fidelity, and I had a chance to sit back and try to be objective about the movie, just another member of the audience.

Mindful that I had long ago surrendered all proprietary authority over the film (all artists, as I've claimed, lose that authority when their creations go out into the wide world), and mindful that my opinion was no more or less "definitive" than anyone else's, I decided that *The Wrath of Khan* was a pretty good film. It also struck me as *sui generis*. It wasn't really *Star Trek* in the sense that its predecessor or the TV series was; it existed as a kind of one-off tale, set in a unique landscape of its own devising. As for Spock's coffin on the Genesis planet . . . it seemed so innocuous now that I marveled at having made such a fuss about it. I found the movie involving, affecting, well-acted, and well-photographed, with a lovely "nautical" score, all in all a rousing adventure that put me in mind of Captain Horatio Hornblower. In short, I was able to enjoy something I had done, an infrequent occurrence.

But in another sense, *The Wrath of Khan was* a *Star Trek* movie, and it was in that sense that I finally began to understand what it was that made the series special. I had been mistaken when first exposed to the *Star Trek* universe. All I could see then was its ludicrous science—but I had missed the fiction.

As I wrote elsewhere:

> At its best, *Star Trek* appears to function as pop-allegory/
> pop metaphor, taking current events and issues (ecology,
> war, racism) and objectifying them for us to contemplate
> in a sci-fi setting. The world it presents may make no sci-
> entific sense but it is well and truly sufficient to lay out
> human questions for us to think about. Removed from
> our immediate neighborhoods, it is refreshing and even

intriguing to consider earth matters from the distance of a few light years.

Like the best science fiction, *Star Trek* does not show us other worlds so meaningfully as it shows us our own—for better or worse, in sickness and in health. In truth, *Star Trek* doesn't really even pretend to show us other worlds—only humanity refracted in a vaguely hi-tech mirror.

More years have passed since that twentieth-anniversary showing of the film, and since then more cast members have passed away. Dee Kelley and Jimmy Doohan have left the sick bay and the engine room of the *Enterprise*, and lately Kirk's archnemesis, the redoubtable Khan, has joined them in another space and possibly another dimension, going boldly to the undiscovered country where the rest of us have yet to journey. It goes without saying that I shall miss them; even if I didn't see them often, I confess it comforted me somehow to know they were on the planet. Perhaps now Ricardo will finally get to play Lear for the ultimate audience.

I, who never watched the show when it first aired, now always pause when, flicking around the dial at home or in hotel rooms on the road, I behold again, those familiar, cherished faces. I stay with them—as they have remained with me.

THE DAY AFTER

Someone said that Hollywood is like an extension of high school. I am not sure exactly what this means but I do acknowledge the place's stratified aspects, among which is the difference between having a hit and having a flop. With the success of *The Wrath of Khan* I was suddenly popular. If *Time After Time* had registered in the town's eyes, as a *succès d'estime*, *The Wrath of Khan* was just a big, fat hit and it catapulted me into the ranks of "bankable" directors. It was time, I thought, to go back to *Conjuring*.

But that still wasn't happening, and for the life of me I couldn't understand why. Hadn't I "made one for them"? And, from my perspective, more to the point, what was wrong with *Conjuring*? People always began their response by telling me how well written it was. It took me years to figure out that this was not a compliment. They were taking shelter behind, "It's well written." "Well written" is, "These are beautiful blueprints but I don't intend to build this house." When someone tells you your screenplay is "so well written," that's the kiss of death. "Well written" is code for "I don't love you." Normally, when someone says, "I don't love you," you don't find yourself asking "Why?" but when it's your script instead of you, the temptation to masochistically pursue this absence of love is well nigh irresistible. Now you're really pressing people to the wall. Most of the time, who knows why someone doesn't love someone? In the case of *Conjuring*, people said they couldn't tell if it was "commercial," to which I always responded: How can you *tell* if anything's commercial until it's made a ton of money? Be reasonable, people. If you *knew* what "commercial" was, all films would make millions, but it's a crapshoot every time. Why are you always trying to figure out what "the people" want, instead of figuring out what you think is terrific? I always seem to get into this pissing match of unprovables. I was once talking to someone about the movie business, and when I pointed out that *Romeo and Juliet* had always been a hit despite the fact that the lovers die at the end, he responded, "It would've been an even bigger hit if they lived." You can't win. "I don't love you" trumps any and all logic.

In the midst of a period of what *Variety* would call "mulling offers," ABC gave me the opportunity to direct *The Day After*, a TV movie about a nuclear holocaust, written by Ed Hume. I was the fourth director to be offered the script and I could see why others had turned it down. Who wanted to learn about this god-awful stuff? The great and terrible paradox about the nuclear issue is that while it remains the single most important dilemma (latterly twined with global warming) to confront the human race, it is at the same time so dreadful that no one in his right mind can bear to contemplate it. Like most people, I preferred to avoid the entire terrifying topic. What sort of person willingly immerses himself in the prospect of nuclear annihilation? Everyone knows the bombs are out there, Damoclean swords dangling over our necks, and that knowledge—semiconsciously carried around inside our heads—is more than sufficient for most of us.

As it happened, during this heady time of professional success, I was being psychoanalyzed. (*Still!*). I spent a lot of time on the couch (and else-where) trying to rationalize my way out of doing this movie. I could think of endless reasons.

My analyst was Dr. Lewis J. Fielding, famous at the time for having had his office burgled by Nixon's "plumbers" in search of dirt to use on another of his patients, Daniel Ellsberg, in the hopes of discrediting the Pentagon Papers he had secretly photocopied from the Rand Corporation and given to *The New York Times*. When I first began my analysis, I wasted a lot of Fielding's time (and my own) making nervous jokes revolving around my anxiety of following in Ellsberg's footsteps. "Look, doc, I've brought you the Pentagon Papers!"

"Interesting," Fielding responded, to my chagrin. "You know you're the second guy today who's trooped into my office with these things?" Et cetera.

Under normal circumstances Fielding seldom spoke, other than to reca-pitulate or string together my associations at the end of the hour (see my notes on editing above), but on the occasion of my *Day After* soul-searching, he surprised me by interrupting my monologue:

"I think this is where we find out who you really are," he suggested quietly.

Which is one of the most dreadful (and useful) things anyone has ever said to me. I knew the moment the words were out of his mouth that I would have to direct *The Day After*. I had entered psychoanalysis to find out who I was—and now I was going to.

It wasn't all that easy rounding up people to be in the movie or work on it, either. Everyone was as spooked as I was. When I approached Gayne Rescher, my cinematographer from *Star Trek II*, and asked him to photograph the movie, he said he wasn't up for it.

"You mean," I badgered, "that you prefer to sit around at dinner parties and bitch about the state of the world, but when someone offers you the chance to put your work in the service of your beliefs, you're gonna turn it down?" He frowned unhappily. "I think," I pressed shamelessly on, "that this is where we find out who you really are."

Damned useful, that phrase. I crowbarred a lot of people with it.

Jason Robards didn't need that kind of pressure. I'd met him once at a friend's house and now bumped into him on a flight to New York. I can't say it wasn't a thrill to chat with the man. By way of making small talk, Robards asked me what I was up to. I told him I would be shooting a film that summer in Lawrence, Kansas, about nuclear war.

"Really."

Suddenly I was seized by a weird impulse. We were at 36,000 feet with no TV executives or agents in sight.

"So, Jason, what are you doing this August?" Maybe I had had some cognac; can't remember now.

"Not a thing."

"Would you like to be in this movie?"

"Beats signing petitions," he answered without hesitation. I promised to show him Ed Hume's compelling script when we landed, as I had a copy in my suitcase.

"Great." We shook on it, and I hoped nobody in LA was going to have a fit. It was slightly anticlimactic to land in New York and find that TWA had managed to lose my bag. Robards didn't know me that well; perhaps this would convince him I was out of my mind.

"It's a really good script," I told him, vamping like mad next to the luggage carousel, desperate for a sight of my errant suitcase.

"Don't worry about it," he soothed. "Just have someone get it to me one of these days."

As it happened, ABC wasn't bent too out of shape by my hiring one of the best American actors of his generation, but my relations with them and with television in general were congenitally stormy.

Brandon Stoddard was the head of ABC Circle Films, the branch of the corporation that was going to make the movie, which in fact was his idea (apparently inspired by his having viewed the nuclear themed feature *The China Syndrome*). Stoddard had an assistant whom I shall refer to as "X." When X first showed me the script and asked me to direct, the film was planned as a four-hour "event" to be spread over two nights. The screenplay I read, while undeniably powerful, seemed also to be padded. I figured you could shake an hour out of it easily, and the material would benefit from being tightened.

"Why don't you whack out an hour of this thing, do it all in one night, and zap the audience right between the eyes?" I suggested to X. "I don't believe folks are going to tune in for night two of Armageddon."

"You're right about the script being padded," X conceded, "but what you don't understand is the economics of TV. ABC doesn't expect to make any money on *The Day After*, but there is a limit on how much we can afford to lose. The hour that you propose to eliminate represents essential advertising for us. Those four hours literally translate into three hours of film: ninety minutes a night and thirty minutes a night of advertising."

"Ah."

"So you see," went on X, who always spoke as though he saw himself explaining things to a child (and who knows?), "we need the film time to justify the revenue."

"Ah ha. Let me ask you something else," I pursued. "You don't really think you're going to get this thing on the air, do you? I mean, the American people watch *Charlie's Angels*—they're not prepared to be exposed to anything like this."

"Oh, it'll go on the air alright," prophesied X blithely.

The producer of *The Day After* was a genial, unpretentious fellow named Bob Papazian, who knew as much about television movies as anyone in the business. He had produced some excellent "prestige" movies about such things as the federal desegregation of Little Rock Central High and would later go on to manage the impossible logistics of *North and South, Book II*, fighting the entire Civil War in about a week. I liked him; he liked me; we've been friends ever since.

What had intrigued me about the script of *The Day After* was its seductive banality. It was just a TV movie about average Americans going about business as usual until they get fried. Since Americans (and, for all I knew, everyone else as well) were constitutionally incapable of reading the "antinuclear" books and articles or watching the alarmist TV documentaries, and were equally unwilling to watch such nuclear-themed movies as *On the Beach*, I had the idea that maybe the comforting familiarity of our script might work for us, would enable the film to sneak in the back door of everyone's consciousness, so to speak, in the guise of the good old reliable movie of the week. I knew, however, that whatever its soap opera camouflage, *The Day After* was no movie of the week.

Like Stoddard and X, Bob Papazian also seemed to be unable to appreciate what was so clear to me from the beginning—namely, the political, financial, and psychological impossibility represented by the film as a project for American network television. When I tried to explain my fears, Papazian just laughed—his laugh, like Bill Dornisch's (whom I had cajoled into editing the film), being another sort of giggle. Nonetheless, we got along splendidly and went to work preparing the project. I figured I'd cross the bridge of the padded script (somehow) when I got to it but meanwhile immersed myself in Jonathan Schell's *The Fate of the Earth* and other light reading, the sort of thing that—like everyone else—I had hitherto avoided.

Nicholas Meyer

Everyone is aware that a nuclear war would be fatal, but no one knows—or, understandably, wants to know—the precise details. Since our only model for the consequences of nuclear bombs being dropped on humans was Hiroshima and Nagasaki, two horse-and-buggy A-bombs from forty years earlier, any attempt at modeling the effects of a nuclear catastrophe was all guesswork and computerized extrapolation. At the time that we made our film, for example, scientists had not yet discovered the phenomenon known as nuclear winter. But they had discovered a lot of other alarming consequences, including electromagnetic pulsation, known familiarly as EMP, to say nothing of what radiation does to living things not obliterated outright. It was hard to read this stuff, to concentrate on it, to figure out where and when (and how) it belonged in our script—and keep your head out of the oven.

I had yet to cope with the Byzantine politics that characterizes network television. To take but one example, Bob announced to me one day that we had a meeting to attend.

"What meeting?" I asked as we got into his car.

"Standards and Practices," he answered as we pulled out of the garage.

"Standards and Practices?" I echoed. "What's that?"

Bob defined Standards and Practices. My eyes widened.

"Censors. You're describing censors!" I squeaked as we headed west on Pico Boulevard toward ABC corporate offices in Century City.

"They call it Standards and Practices," Bob explained with one of his giggles.

I mulled on this. "What happens when we get there?" I asked.

"Well, you go through the script, and they tell you what you can't film. You can argue about some stuff," he added, casting me a sideways look.

I said nothing but cogitated some more as we drove on for three more traffic lights. I am not the fastest thinker in the world but I was slowly coming to the conclusion that I had been blindsided. Bushwhacked. Ambushed.

"Bob."

"Uh huh . . ."

"Lemme ask you something."

"Shoot."

"If they were gonna censor this script, wouldn't it have been more appropriate to censor it *before* I was offered it to direct?"

"Whaddaya mean?"

"I mean, you guys showed me a script, and I agreed to direct this script. Now I find out that some people can take it apart before I ever roll a camera. Seems to me if they had wanted to tone it down they should have done that *before* I agreed to direct it."

"This is how it's always done," Bob explained, puzzled.

I thought about this as we headed into the ABC garage.

"Bob."

"Still here, Nick."

"I just want to say that I can't be bound to honor anything that happens in this meeting."

Nervous guffaw from Bob.

"Hey, take it easy."

"I'm just telling you. This"—I hefted my copy of the script—"this is the script I signed on to shoot, nothing less."

More uneasy laughter from Bob.

The meeting was even stranger than I had imagined. A man and a woman who never smiled went through our script page by page.

"On page two," the woman indicated, "where the patient calls the Japanese doctor *tojo*, that's out."

"How come?" I found myself asking despite myself.

"Because the term is racially offensive to Japanese viewers, and we will not knowingly insult a portion of our viewing public."

"Did you ever make a film and use the term 'nigger'?" I asked.

"Never."

"Didn't you make a miniseries called *Roots*?" I pursued. "Seems to me the term 'nigger' was all over the place."

"Yes," admitted the man, "but that was in context."

"What does that mean—'in context'? Means it was *about* 'niggers'?"

They shifted their positions in their seats. To my left, Bob squirmed.

"It's out," the woman said flatly.

"Completely," added the other.

I said nothing.

Later on they objected to a scene where one of the characters purchases a diaphragm.

"How come?" I replied, dutifully maintaining my proscribed part of the exchange, as ritualistic as the responses of the congregation. They seemed to expect it.

"Because the network will not take a position that could be construed as endorsing birth control."

It took another kind of control to just sit there. Where do the people come from who do this job? Did they have childhoods like the rest of us? Go to school? Get drunk, laid, laugh, cry? Or are they born, Athena-like, full-blown from the head of some executive?

"You mean you guys have never made a film where birth control devices were used or discussed?"

"Never."

"Didn't you make a film about teenage pregnancy a year or so back? Seems like there was all sorts of talk about diaphragms, pills and such."

"Yes, but that was—"

"In context," I finished for him. "Anyway," I reasoned, unable to stop myself from engaging in this discourse any more than I could prevent myself from debating with the Jehovah's Witnesses who knocked on my dorm room in college, "this character later bitterly regrets having used a diaphragm. That certainly would seem to be the opposite of an endorsement of birth control."

"It's out."

"Completely."

I said nothing.

And so it went. Where nuclear war was concerned, they also objected to scenes that depicted the electromagnetic pulse and its consequences. They were scientific experts now. We found ourselves arguing over scientific data none of us was qualified to evaluate.

They told me the EMP was "out." I said nothing but sat with the script in my lap, making not a single note. Bob was writing stuff down, but for the life of me I couldn't see why.

Later, filming in Lawrence, Kansas, I ignored every one of their directives. Matters came to a head about ten days into shooting. We were filming one of the family subplots (which took place while the United States and the Russians were getting ready to launch their missiles), when I got tapped on the shoulder by Bob.

"There's a call for you from LA."

"Can you take a message?"

He shook his head.

"It's the ABC brass."

I took the phone. The voice on the other end was apoplectic. He was on a speakerphone, and I sensed a bunch of other execs in the room with him.

"Nick, what do you think you're doing!?"

"Shooting the script you offered me to direct."

"But we agreed, *you* agreed—" the voice expostulated.

"I agreed to nothing," I pointed out, having been waiting for this moment, "except to shoot the script you offered me. But rather than have this discussion," I went on, by way of preempting his next expostulation, "let me make this easy for you. Fire me."

"What?"

"Fire me. I didn't want to make this depressing movie anyway. Fire me, and I'll have a perfect out."

"You're kidding."

"Not me. Look, you're only ten days in, it shouldn't be too hard to reshoot. You just get a new director and some new actors—"

"New actors?"

"Well, if I walk, Jason's gonna walk, maybe JoBeth Williams, too, but that shouldn't be a problem," I hastened to assure him, warming to my topic. "You just replace Jason, replace JoBeth, replace Gayne Rescher, and before you know it, you'll be—"

"Hang on."

I could hear voices mumbling and thought I caught the phrase "that son-ovabitch" before my correspondent got back on the line.

"Nick, we'll get back to you."

"Do that."

The next day the phone rang again, this time in the Kansas farmhouse where we were shooting. This time the voice—the same voice—crooned with patronizing serenity.

"N-i-c-k, it's your movie, you shoot it the way you want, but, as an officer of ABC Circle films, I must tell you that legally none of that stuff can be in the picture."

"Fine, you've told me."

And there that particular brouhaha ended. In the event, not one of the items I shot was deleted, including the celebrated diaphragm and the scenes involving the effect of the electromagnetic pulse, which depicted all electricity cutting out in the wake of an airborne nuclear explosion.

Following the shootout with the network, actual shooting, first in Law-rence, Kansas, and later at an abandoned LA hospital, went very well. For all the bad rap Kansas has garnered in recent years, what with trying to turn back the clock on Darwin, the people of Lawrence were as sophisticated as any I've ever met and they came out by the thousands to make the film work and achieve a scale it could otherwise never have afforded. Now, granted, some of these folks were just there because the idea of being in a movie struck them as fun, but I talked to a large number who had come out of political convic-tions and genuine concern at the prospect of a nuclear war. *The Day After* is dedicated to them. (The night the film aired, they held a candlelight vigil for peace in Lawrence that hundreds attended; twenty-five years later, at an anni-versary reunion and screening in Lawrence, the people who showed up were not movie freaks, but peace junkies.)

There were other problems, however. When it came time to edit the film

I was confronted with the hour's worth of padding in the script. I had never edited scenes "to length" before and the process as well as the concept I found confounding. Why should a scene play longer than it could justify itself on the screen? I placed a call to X.

"Listen, X," I said, "I know that you want this film for two nights, but candidly, I think it will be significantly weakened if we keep in all this extra stuff. I believe in putting my best foot forward and making the best possible impression on you guys that I can. Can't I edit the film the way I think it should go and then, if you still want the rest back in, we can restore it?"

"I'll get back to you," said X. A day later, he called.

"We, too, believe in the doctrine of first impressions," said X. "Edit the film your way, and we'll look at it."

I was astonished by this response, which only made sense when I later learned how difficult it had become for ABC to get any sponsors for the film. As I had anticipated, the political landscape was beginning to register seismic tremors, and the withdrawal of sponsors was one of the earliest manifestations of the difficulties we were to have broadcasting *The Day After*. General Motors, General Mills, General Foods—all the generals had headed for the hills. Certainly if ABC couldn't get advertisers, it made no sense to stretch out the movie beyond a single night. In the end my hatred for the commercials that insistently interrupt the action on network television, and my dream that they might be magically dispensed with, was gratified. The only advertisers to hang in were Commodore computers and one of the smaller car rental companies. Tactfully, the network decided to have no commercials after the bomb dropped. (I wonder if their tact would have obtained if they'd been getting prime ad rates.)

I was in the cutting room one day with our little radio turned on, listening to President Reagan speak. He began by describing the dreadful potential of nuclear weapons, and as I listened, I stopped work, convinced by his tone that something momentous and just possibly wonderful was about to be announced. A freeze on nuclear weapons? Was it possible?

No, the president had something else in mind, a nuclear space shield, an umbrella of missiles to shoot down other missiles, by which to protect Americans in the event of a nuclear missile attack. The press soon dubbed it Star Wars (to George Lucas's consternation), and I went back to work, convinced—if I needed any convincing by this point—that this film needed to be made.

Bob and I finished our one-night version of *The Day After* and showed it to the group of ABC execs. It ran about two hours and twenty minutes. When it was over these guys were all sobbing. These were television executives, but they were also human beings—they had families, they had children, they had lives of their own, a stake in the planet like everyone else—and they had been deeply and obviously affected by what they had seen.

Based on their response, I imagined I was home free.

In fact our troubles had just begun, as a six-month-long tug-of-war soon began over the final shape of the film. Some battles I won; others I lost. When my editor, Bill Dornisch, loyally refused to recut the movie per ABC's samurai approach (now that there was no advertising revenue at stake, why not trim it to the bone?) he was summarily sacked. At one point I actually walked off the picture for three months while X went into the editing room himself, accompanied by his own editor (Y?), and went to town on the film.

Talk about being the hatchet man . . .

A lot of times in this business, confronted by your own impotence in the face of corporate and contractual reality, you think you will die. That all these corporate honchos had wept buckets when they saw the first cut of the film only compounded my misery. That I had labored so hard and given so much of myself (not to mention the people who worked on the film both in Hollywood and by the thousands in Lawrence, Kansas, who had all trusted me) to something I thought so terribly important and then to see it ripped to meaningless shreds was enough to make me contemplate suicide.

Really.

It was the first of many such contemplations. I crawled into bed and stayed there for days while my long-suffering agent, Gary Lucchesi, labored behind the scenes on my behalf to effect some kind of rapprochement. Agents must take the long view; they don't want their clients blackballed from future projects because they made waves, a reputation with which I was already flirting. The only good news about being so desperately hurt and angry was that I couldn't eat, which, in my case, did have some benefits. I simply couldn't get my head around the fact of my powerlessness against a large corporation; even though I had brought the film into being, given it life, made them weep when they saw it, then fended off all their absurd compromises, I finally couldn't fend off *them*. The film was theirs; it was their idea, they commissioned it, they paid for it; I was merely the hired hand. Any *droit morale* was theirs. Why was I unable to accept this reality? Grow up.

In the end, X's cut of the film was so ridiculous that even his superiors blanched, for he had inadvertently managed to make plain what we had struggled to conceal: Who started the war? In X's version, it was unambiguously the Soviets. ABC was contractually obliged to let me see it, and I was shattered afresh, all the stitches on my wounds popping open and the bleeding recommencing. Of course with my reputation for being "difficult" now firmly in place, it didn't seem to matter much what I did to cement or redeem it. I lay on my bed of pain, stared at the ceiling, and tried to think. It now occurred to me that the last thing ABC wanted for this hot potato was public dissension from the filmmakers' ranks. Accordingly, when Marilyn Reed, a columnist from the *Chicago Sun-Times*, called and asked me about the film, I hinted darkly of pressure to recut the movie from corporate sources. I took care to be oblique and nonspecific, but my message was clear. Next thing I knew, I was brought back in from the cold to repair X's carnage in the cutting room.

In the end, the film *was* censored, and many things weren't the way I intended them. In addition, it was preceded and succeeded by all manner of disclaimers but it still packed enough of a wallop to drive Bill Buckley and Phyllis Schlafly crazy. They ran around the country like Chicken Littles, warning anyone who'd listen that the sky was falling, while on its editorial page the *New York Post* demanded to know why Nicholas Meyer was doing Yuri Andropov's work for him. (Andropov, lest you have forgotten, was the Soviet premier at the time.) I ask you. The press surprised me by taking no interest in the film itself; all they were obsessed by was the issue of who started the nuclear war depicted in it—we or the Russians? I couldn't for the life of me figure out why this was the only issue that commanded their attention but later came to understand what I had earlier intuited, namely that nuclear war and its consequences per se were simply too dreadful to contemplate head-on and probably wouldn't sell newspapers. It was easier and doubtless more reassuring for the press to concentrate on the more familiar terrain of who began it. Never mind the horrendous consequences of nuclear war; safer to concentrate on whom to blame for starting it. X's version probably would have sent Rupert Murdoch into ecstasies, even as it scotched any possible improvement in U.S.-Soviet relations. I went on CNN's *Crossfire* and tried to get in a word edgewise while Pat Buchanan and Michael Kinsley yelled at each other.

The Reagan White House saw the film before it aired and called us with editing "notes"! In retrospect I don't find this surprising. The President, an old Hollywood pro, doubtless had always longed for final cut. (So did the Army, when we asked for their cooperation before shooting. We didn't get their helicopters; they didn't get to rewrite our script.)

In the years to come I would hear all sorts of amazing stories connected with *The Day After* and the effect it had on people. How a general in Havana saw the picture and said the Cuban Missile Crisis had never been real to him before viewing it; how the Joint Chiefs had screened it at the Pentagon, searching for a way to discredit it—and me. How the White House felt the crucial need to put someone on television directly following the picture to say how off-base the thing was. They considered Jeane Kirkpatrick, which would have been fun, but unfortunately wiser heads prevailed and we were all treated to the benign presence of Secretary of State George Shultz, reassuring Ted Koppel that everything was going to be just fine. Then followed an all-star session of *Nightline* (the most highly watched edition of the program ever), featuring Elie Wiesel squaring off with Henry Kissinger and William Buckley, with Kissinger opining that scaring ourselves to death was no way to make nuclear policy.

Seeing as that is just what we had been doing for the previous forty years, I felt his argument had some holes in it.

I tried to watch the film the night it aired but couldn't imagine anyone sitting through it. After all, it wasn't a very good movie; that had been, in a way, the point. If the movie had been "good" in the conventional sense, we could have let ourselves off the hook, talking about how wonderful Jason Robards was, how effective the music was, etc.—anything other than contemplating its stark nuclear message. (As far as music went, there wasn't any, other than some Virgil Thomson over the credits and a few bars to link a couple of scenes, as I hadn't wanted to "goose" anyone's reactions.) As a director, I had made the film as a counterintuitive exercise. I knew if people discussed the movie instead of what the movie was about, we'd have failed. I wanted all the script's banality to work for me, to entice the audience past our subject matter until they were drowning in it. Seeing the film that night on television, however, all I got was the banality.

And thank God there was no CGI technology available to make nuclear destruction spectacular and "fun," which was how *The New York Times* some thirty years later reviewed an end-of-New York movie called *The Day After Tomorrow*—global warming as a special effects extravaganza.

The morning following our telecast I was stupefied to learn that over a hundred million viewers had stuck with the thing to the end, often watching in hand-holding groups. Ed Hume had known exactly what he was doing. It is my understanding that the hundred-million mark for a TV movie has yet to be surpassed. And with all the channels currently available to fragment the viewing audience, it seems unlikely a single event will ever again capture so large a portion of the population.

The Day After is probably the most worthwhile thing I ever got to do with my life to date. In the immediate aftermath of the broadcast, though, I wasn't convinced it had done any good. Who wants to admit that his mind was changed by anything as dumb as a TV movie, anyway?

Following the telecast, an instant survey was taken in which people were asked if the movie had changed their minds about nuclear war. The press then gleefully informed me that according to their stats, no one's mind had been changed and what did I have to say to that?

I answered truthfully that it was too soon to say what effect the film had had on viewers and whether any were prepared to admit—even to themselves—if it had. What do people really believe about anything? People aver all sorts of positions and ideologies—but do they mean what they say? Or are they saying what they want to believe? Hope to believe? Want *you* to think they believe? Maybe we only learn what we really believe on our deathbeds or with a gun to our heads.

But at least one person's mind *was* changed by the film. When President Reagan signed the intermediate range missile treaty in Iceland, I got a lovely card from someone that said, "Don't think your film didn't have something to do with this," which turned out to be intuitively prescient. Some years after I had a weird confirmation of this fact. I was speaking at Oxford, and a student asked if I'd ever read Reagan's autobiography. I said I hadn't, whereupon he handily produced a photocopied page for me in which the president described his reaction to the film, essentially allowing as to how it had altered his perception of the nuclear subject. Remember, this was a president who saw life in terms of movies, and it had taken a movie to help him see that nuclear wars are unwinnable. Later, when I met Edmund Morris, author of Reagan's biography *Dutch*, he confirmed the paragraph in his book that stipulates the only time he ever saw Reagan depressed was after viewing *The Day After*. Reagan, who had come to power contemplating a winnable nuclear war ("if we have enough shovels . . ." etc.), had changed his mind.

Take it where you find it. *The Day After* received a staggering twelve Emmy nominations. In the end, it won only two; a smaller film, *Special Bulletin*, rushed into production on tape by NBC, took the "nuclear" TV movie Emmy a year earlier while we were fighting over our film's final cut. In *Special Bulletin*, the anti-nuke activists are the baddies who set off an A-bomb. Go figure.

When it was time to make the VHS and later DVD versions of the movie, I was allowed to reinsert some of the cut footage that the network had deemed too controversial to air.

Since its initial broadcast, a number of books and PhD theses have been written and (continue to be written) about *The Day After,* not counting Reagan's memoir. Many of these contain a great deal of information regarding the politics—national as well as network—behind the production and subsequent reaction to the film of which I was unaware. I have chosen to relate the making and airing of the movie as I experienced it, rather than including information to which I had no access at the time.

Before ending this chapter, there is an incident I feel bound to relate that occurred somewhere around this time and that had a profound effect upon me.

I was in New York and had, for some reason I cannot now recollect, been invited to attend a party in a Fifth Avenue apartment, given for members of the French film industry. I was there by myself, wandering around, knowing no one, but happily eyeing French filmmakers and actors whom I had long admired, as they ate and chatted in French among themselves, convivial, charming, and effortlessly Gallic. I spied a director who had long been an idol of mine. We had not been introduced, but I hovered nearby, watching his every move, hoping to glean I knew not what. He was standing by the buffet table, now laden with desserts, and the hostess passed and said, "Oh, Louis, darling, would you be an angel and cut these cakes?" before moving on to other obligations.

Having nothing better to do than indulge my fascination for this director, a slim, dark-haired gentleman, not especially tall, I watched him cut dessert cakes and as I did, I died a thousand deaths. I don't know about you, but as far as I am concerned there is only one way to cut a round cake; you start in the middle and carve out pie-sliced wedges to the edge. I daresay not one man or woman in ten million has gone about it otherwise for ten thousand years of human cake-cutting.

And yet here was this French director carving out triangles, parallelograms, squares, ovals, and what-have-yous, cutting the cake as no one before had ever cut the cake, thinking through (or not even thinking, doing it on instinct or intuition) the whole cake-cutting business as if it was for the first time.

I sidled up to him and tried to keep my voice casual.

"How come you're cutting the cake like that?"

He shrugged, didn't look up, and went on sculpting. "Well, this way everyone can have the size and shape that they want."

A perfect answer to go with his unprecedented act. I was in the presence of a genius. No wonder Louis Malle had been able to make a comedy about incest. I stumbled away in a daze, left the party, and walked alone up Fifth Avenue in the dead of night, stunned, indeed humiliated by the thoughtless feat of originality that I had witnessed.

My first response was that I couldn't wait to cut the cake like that. I am not brilliant. As I continued my lonely hike uptown, I realized that I would never cut the cake like that, nor do anything so profoundly original, as long as I lived. The first man who said a woman's lips were like a rose was a genius; the second guy who said it was a plodder. It was a sobering moment. I had come face to face with my limitations and in a fashion that I could not ignore. It was as if I was a pianist and had finally listened to Horowitz. What was the point of going on if you know you were never going to play like Horowitz?

In years to come I had another insight that was somewhat comforting: While it was true that I would never be capable of that sort of act, I *had*, on the other hand, recognized it when it had occurred. I *did* understand its significance at the time and preserved it in my memory; I am relating it to you now. That is the sort of artist I am; not of the first rank, perhaps not even of the second, but I do recognize something original when I see it; I can preserve it for others to savor, even if the originator of the act is unaware or unappreciative of just what it is he or she has done. I could never write *The Odyssey*, but I can probably make it into a very good screenplay. That is the other thing I am besides being a teacher. A storyteller. Not the creator of stories, but rather the re-creator. I would never have imagined anything as original as Sherlock Holmes—but I might, with some success, imagine him meeting Sigmund Freud. If someone had said their two names together first.

STAR TREK IV: THE VOYAGE HOME

Based on *Khan*'s spectacular success, it was by now a foregone conclusion that there would be a third *Star Trek* feature and that it would involve the resurrection of Spock. The year was 1983, and I was deeply involved in cutting *The Day After*. I was also falling in love.

Paramount Pictures asked if I would write and direct the third *Star Trek* movie, an offer I declined. I still felt passionately that Spock ought not to be brought back to life and in any case, bringing dead people back to life was something I didn't know how to do, because, I suppose, I have trouble believing such a thing is possible. The tale of Jesus's resurrection is one of the most prominent in our culture, but I have difficulty with that one, as well.

When Leonard Nimoy learned I was not going to direct the film, he perceived a challenge that suddenly made the whole project interesting to him and he perceived some leverage as well: He wanted to direct the film in exchange for his participation as the resurrected Spock.

Michael Eisner tried to talk him out of this, pointing out that directing a film is hard enough, but a directing debut in which you are also the star places you under a triple burden.

At which point Nimoy called and sought my advice. My reply was very simple: "Are you prepared to let this ship sail without you?" I asked.

"Absolutely," he answered.

"Then sit tight; you're gonna direct the movie."

Which is exactly what happened. Did I feel a pang when I learned the film was going forward with Nimoy at the helm? Possibly. I had become friends with many of these people, and there was certainly something alluring in the promise of directing a film that had all a studio's resources—production and distribution—behind it. If you're doing a studio film, nothing is too good for you; the red carpet of money and expertise is yours. Ever since the French gave us the auteur theory, the director has become king, and if you don't keep a cool head, you may confuse yourself with the job description. All the importance, all the deference attached to your every whim and opinion is there only so long as you are doing what the studio wants you to do. You ride first class—but only for the duration of the film.

Of course, if you are Kubrick or Huston or Coppola or Scorsese, you really *are* king.

Nonetheless, I don't believe I lost much sleep over *Star Trek III*. Nimoy and Harve Bennett wrote the screenplay together, Bennett produced (minus the participation of Bob Sallin, whose place and function were assumed by the very capable Ralph Winter), Nimoy directed, and *Star Trek III: The Search for Spock* was released in June of 1984. This was the second pairing of Bennett and Nimoy, and they worked well together. Kirstie Alley declined to reprise the role of Lieutenant Saavik, and her place was taken by Robin Curtis. It was a thankless task for the newcomer; it's far easier to create a character than reprise someone else's performance (James Bond being the exception that proves the rule).

The movie and its fate were largely unknown to me as I got married on June 6 and headed off on my honeymoon. I heard in distant fashion that the film was a success and learned occasionally of doings on the Paramount lot. Incomprehensibly to me, Diller, Eisner, and Katzenberg had been summarily dismissed. As I understood it, their firings had to do with a photograph of all three on the cover of *New York* magazine for an article extolling the value and virtues of the most successful studio chiefs at the time. Martin Davis, CEO of Gulf & Western, Paramount's corporate owner in New York (he had succeeded Charles Bluhdorn following the latter's death in 1983), was, according to this version of events, incensed that he had not been included in the photo or accompanying article.

With the Eisner-Katzenberg-Diller triumvirate gone (the first two would save Walt Disney and turn it into an entertainment behemoth; the third would found the wildly successful Fox television network), Davis picked Frank Mancuso to head the studio. Originally a film salesman from Buffalo, Mancuso headed west. With no hands-on production experience, he asked the recently retired head of Universal Pictures, Ned Tanen, to run Paramount's feature division. Tanen agreed to undertake the job on condition that he be given a free hand, answerable to no one and limited to what I think was a two-year contract. Dawn Steel (née Spielberg, a cousin) was made production chief, the second woman ever to reach the position (Sherry Lansing was first, at 20th Century Fox). Steel had begun in Paramount's marketing division and would go on to an extremely successful career, working on such projects as *Flashdance* and *Top Gun* with Don Simpson before succumbing tragically to a brain tumor in 1997.

Tanen was not unknown to me; as head of Universal (he of the Verna Fields eulogy) he had bought the rights to my Sherlock Holmes novel, *The Seven-Per-Cent Solution*, and had green-lit the film in 1975. A mercurial, brilliant, and witty man, he had led Universal for so long, he knew how to run a film studio in his sleep, which was probably why he didn't want to do it again for very long.

Tanen looked at the Paramount slate and computed what was needed. He green-lit a new Eddie Murphy feature, *The Golden Child*, and he ordered up the fourth *Star Trek*. Tanen's production slate would always include films he believed were more or less surefire so that he could—judiciously—experiment with other fare.

When Mancuso demurred at the price for both films, Tanen reminded him—brusquely, as I heard it—of the terms of his contract. As events proved, Tanen knew his stuff, and both films were successful. *Star Trek IV*, in fact, made the most money of any film in the series, for reasons that we'll examine shortly.

Paramount hired two screenwriters to deliver the script for *Star Trek IV*, both unknown to me. Following my honeymoon, I was preparing a comedy, *Volunteers* (written by David Isaacs and Ken Levine), that would star Tom Hanks and John Candy, when I was surprised to receive a phone call from Dawn Steel, an old friend whom I had first met through Karen Moore.

"Nicky, we have an emergency," she began without preamble. "Can you come over here right away?" "Here" meaning Paramount.

I could and did, to be told that the studio (read Tanen and Steel) were not happy with the screenplay for *Star Trek IV*, later aptly subtitled by studio exec David Kirkpatrick *The Voyage Home*.

"We're four weeks away from starting prep," Dawn explained, "And we need a whole new script. We want to keep the central story but start over with the screenplay. Can you help us?"

I wasn't sure how to answer that, since I had no idea what was being contemplated. I asked to speak with Bennett and Nimoy, who were to produce and direct the film. I left Dawn's office and trudged across the lot to Bennett's.

There was a comforting familiarity to our reunion. These were my friends, and I hadn't realized—or allowed myself to realize—how much I had missed them.

"What's the idea?" I asked, when we had shaken hands and settled into our old chairs.

"The idea," responded Nimoy with a smile, "is to do something nice."

He then told me the story he and Bennett had concocted, which I thought was terrific. I rarely get ideas myself and when I do, most of them stink. I am a pretty shrewd judge of other people's ideas, however, and I was convinced this one was a doozy. It would not only be *Star Trek* with all its special effects bells and whistles, but at the same time a cautionary ecological fable, the sort of effortless fusing of fantasy and reality that embodies *Star Trek* at its best.

Mind you, when all's said and done, you can make a movie out of even the most unpromising idea. Like most art, it's all in the doing.

In the present instance, the idea was: A "probe" from deep space approaches Earth, causing havoc on the planet, until it is realized that the probe is merely asking a question and becoming impatient with the lack of response. It wants to hear from humpback whales—the only hitch being that at this time (i.e., the twenty-third century) the creatures have become extinct, collateral damage in man's ongoing war against nature. With no reply from the whales, the probe becomes increasingly aggressive. Bridges topple, forests burn, etc.

The only solution for Kirk and his crew: to go back in time, procure two humpbacks, export them to the twenty-third century, and hope they will sing in such a fashion as to placate the probe.

The *Enterprise* crew, having lost their own ship in the previous movie, goes through time travel aboard a captured Klingon vessel known as a Bird of Prey (which features an invisibility "cloaking device"). The ship deposits members of her prize crew in twentieth-century San Francisco, there to take part in what amounts to a scavenger hunt: crew members (the *Star Trek* cast) must locate and capture two humpback whales and transport them into a future ocean aboard the ship. In addition to capturing the cetaceans, a male and female of the species, this involves tracking down and assembling the components of a huge aquarium in which said whales can be housed aboard the Klingon vessel until safely delivered to a twenty-third-century ocean, there, presumably to sing for our supper.

At this point, I interrupted. "Does it have to be San Francisco?" I had already made a movie in which time travelers wind up in San Francisco. "Can't they go someplace else for a change? What about Paris?"

Bennett and Nimoy glanced briefly at each other before telling me, No, it had to be San Francisco. Ostensibly this had something to do with the fact of Starfleet Headquarters being based there but may more likely have been related to the fact that filming in San Francisco would be cheaper than attempting it in Paris.

Bennett and I agreed to split up the work. Bennett would write Acts I and IV, the outer space bookends of the movie, while I would do Acts II and III, those that took place on Earth.

"Should I read the previous draft?" I asked.

They preferred I didn't. "We just want to use the same story," Nimoy explained, "and I'd prefer you weren't influenced by anything but what we've just told you."

This was fine with me, as I knew that once I read another version of the same narrative I would (a) be unable to forget it and (b) that would only confuse and hamper my effort to rethink the material.

(Later I would learn that the discarded draft had been written to include a major role for Eddie Murphy, an avowed *Trek* fan. Paramount executives had ultimately nixed the idea, reluctant to put their two biggest franchises in one basket.)

In blissful ignorance—my preferred condition—I went home and set to work. The job was pleasant and fun. As usual I got to indulge my love of comedy. My first lines in the script follow the time travel sequence, after which someone asks, "When are we?" and Spock replies, "Judging by the pollution content of the atmosphere, I believe we have arrived at the late twentieth century."

The Klingon Bird of Prey then does something Gene Roddenberry had always avoided on the television series: showing a spaceship actually landing on a planet. In the original series Roddenberry created the ingenious "beam me up" transporter gadget to avoid having to show enormous hardware on the surface of any planet. But now, using the famous Klingon "cloaking device," we again circumvented the problem by having an invisible spaceship land near the Golden Gate Tea Gardens.

"Everyone remember where we parked," Kirk cautions as they debark, much to my amusement. There was in the story, notwithstanding its cataclysmic, earth-ending potential, an element of gaiety that was hard to suppress. I didn't see the need to try and, in the process, discovered some personal payoffs as well.

When I wrote and directed *Time After Time*, I had been obliged to cut scenes from the film that, for one reason or another, didn't play. They had either been badly written or ineptly staged. Or both. In one instance I had the notion of trashing rock and roll from H. G. Wells's point of view. He's wandering around the city, a stranger in 1979 (to which he had been transported by his time machine), and finds himself stranded next to a Chinese youth, waiting for a traffic light to change. Having already caused one accident, Wells knows he must wait until the light turns green—but the young man next to him is carrying a ghetto blaster, which is emitting the most appalling sounds. Finally the light turns, and Wells makes his escape. Later, cooking dinner for Wells at her apartment, a young woman asks what kind of music he likes, and Wells responds, "Anything but Oriental."

That line should have worked like gangbusters but it fell flat. So much film time had elapsed between Wells's encounter with the young Chinese man and his boom box and the girl and her dinnertime question that audiences had completely forgotten the earlier encounter. "Anything but Oriental" made no sense to them. I still tried to save the scene with the Chinese boy, which I thought might play on its own, without the later punch line, but I had staged it so clumsily that it was unusable.

But on *Star Trek IV* I got to recycle my joke. In my new version—very ably staged by director Nimoy—Kirk and Spock find themselves sharing a bus with a ghetto blaster carried by an invincibly punk creature sporting a purple Mohawk (memorably played by the film's associate producer, Kirk Thatcher). After their polite attempts to get this apparition to modulate the volume on his boom box are rudely rebuffed, Spock, poker-faced, applies the Vulcan nerve pinch, bringing blessed peace and grateful applause from the relieved bus passengers.

Some movies take years to get made; others fall into place rapidly. I'm not sure that those made on the fly don't come out with more energy and élan than the ones that plod into their starting gates over decades. *Star Trek IV* was on a round-the-clock assembly line, much as *Star Trek II* had been, with delivery dates and release dates already in place. There was no time for a lot of second-guessing, and I recall only one studio note over which we wrangled.

While Ned Tanen loved the script and told me over lunch he thought it so good he would have made the film even if it hadn't been part of the *Trek* franchise, Dawn had one concern: she wanted to know about the probe and, in particular, what the actual question was that it kept posing to the whales.

Later I was to learn this kettle of whales was just the tip of the iceberg. Bennett and Nimoy, who had become as successful a collaboration as Gilbert & Sullivan, were now—like those storied partners—having serious interpersonal difficulties. Though not reflected in their work (to anyone's knowledge), at issue seemed to be a question of who was running the show. Bennett, the producer in residence, would be around long after Nimoy had departed, presumably working for the studio on other projects. (He had advanced this logic with me when I had found myself at loggerheads with the studio on *Star Trek II*.) On the other hand Nimoy was indispensable to *Star Trek*, now having added director to his other role as the incarnation of a certain Vulcan.

Their differences seemingly came to a head over Dawn's request that the probe's query to the whales be translated. Nimoy felt strongly that the message should be left to the audience's imagination while Bennett bowed to the studio in agreeing with their point of view, a defection that enraged his partner. Later, when I was the one under contract with an overall deal at the studio, and acting as I thought my responsibilities were defined, Nimoy would be infuriated all over again.

In the present instance, ignorant of their heated dispute, I unknowingly took Nimoy's side in vehemently opposing our supplying any answers or explanation for the probe's behavior. I argued that it didn't *matter* why the probe had shown up, what or who it was, or precisely what it wanted to know. "It will only diminish and trivialize the event if we answer these questions," I urged. In art, questions are always more interesting than answers. Once you give the answer, the gas goes out of the balloon. Who wants to see the Lone Ranger without his mask? Resolving artistic questions is akin to revealing the secrets behind the magician's trick. The audience won't thank you for it.

Dawn was a forceful personality and her Bronx passion was known to intimidate people. But as it happens I had attended high school in the Bronx and was of the opinion that what others took to be abrasive or scary was for Dawn nothing more than a typical argument in a kitchen situated in that locality. She yelled; I yelled back. "Fuck you!"s were liberally exchanged. As a studio executive, her inclination—indeed her training—was to assume an audience comprised of idiots: every *t* had to be crossed and every *i* dotted; everything to be explained on their behalf. There was nothing personal at stake for her; it was merely studio thinking. For the filmmaker (or writer, in this case), such things *are* personal, or they ought to be. All you have to go on in this business is your gut. As William Goldman famously explained, "No one knows any-

---

thing." I held my ground, and finally Dawn yielded with good humor ("You're wrong, Nicky Meyer!") and the matter was never raised again, either by her or the audiences that flocked to the film. Yet it is interesting how these choices and the passions behind them can linger and rankle. *Thirty-six years* after she made *The Letter*, Bette Davis spoke at an American Film Institute tribute to director William Wyler. During her laudatory speech Davis found herself still arguing with Wyler over the way he had insisted she deliver a line in the film. ("I was *right!*")

Such arguments are always unanswerable. To the charge that failing to explain the probe's motives did not affect the film's success, the studio executive can always maintain: "Yes, but had you explained it, the movie would've been even more successful." ("If Romeo and Juliet hadn't died at the end . . ." etc.) Aside from the financial yardstick by which to judge a film, questions of pure aesthetics can never be resolved.

Once matters of text were concluded, my involvement with *Star Trek IV* ceased and I resumed work on *Volunteers*, my Tom Hanks–John Candy comedy, shortly afterward leaving for location in Mexico in the fall of 1984.

VOLUNTEERS

Each time I agree to direct a film, I tell myself I am going to keep a record of all the decisions I make from start to finish—and then I forget to do so, or I begin my list and then lose track. Commencing with the decision to direct a given script, the list of choices the director makes is never-ending: the cast, the crew, what locations are available, what budget compromises will be necessary, how the movie will be cut, etc., ad infinitum. Be wrong on any one of these, and you seriously injure if not doom the film. During the course of my honeymoon in 1984, I had read and laughed myself silly over a script about the Peace Corps. Written by Ken Levine and David Isaacs and called *Volunteers*, the movie was already (perfectly) packaged with Tom Hanks and John Candy committed to play a pair of mismatched Peace Corps workers in Thailand. The film was a hodgepodge of wit and slapstick and it was consistently *smart*, which may have been a black mark against it. In keeping with my eclectic temperament, the idea of a comedy held terrific appeal. Perhaps the comedic opportunities presented by *Star Trek IV* had whetted my appetite. I said I would be happy to do it. Other directors may have shrewd, long-range goals and strategies for achieving them; I only wanted to keep doing different things. Join the movies and see the world. Be a storyteller. More objective observers may discern thematic consistencies in my work; I only know I love stories and have never much concerned myself with whether those stories were happy or sad, past or present, comical or pastoral or tragical, whether they were movies, plays, books, operas, or jokes—I just want them to be good stories. When someone once asked me what my definition of a good story was, I said, A good story is one that after I've told it to you, you understand *why* I wanted to tell it. I never knew *why* I was offered *Volunteers* or who it

166

was who thought I could direct a comedy. Perhaps, all those years ago, directors hadn't yet been slotted into genres. For whatever reason the chance came my way, I can only be grateful.

I hired cinematographer Ric Waite and production designer Jim Schoppe, and we determined to shoot Mexico for Thailand and flew down for a recce (short for "reconnaissance"), which is arguably the most fun part of filmmaking. Essentially, you are being paid to look around at anything that interests you and eat well along the way. We flew to Mexico City and thence to Veracruz (landing place of Cortés, whose roofless, ruined house with tentacular tree roots we saw on the coast; it reminded me of Geiger's beast in *Alien*). The town itself reminded me of the one in my favorite film noir, *Out of the Past*, also of Tampico in *The Treasure of the Sierra Madre*, only in vivid, eye-aching color. From Veracruz we motored south for three hours along treacherous roads. In those days everyone in the van talked to one another, ideas were exchanged, plans laid and revised. People got to know one another. Nowadays everyone in the van is on his or her cell phone, and the result is a half dozen cacophonous monologues, each department head yakking to some unseen underling.

There is a section of Oaxaca, just over the border from the province of Veracruz, that goes by the nickname "Little China," because of its strong resemblance to that part of the world. Indeed, when we later shipped down thirty Thai families to populate the Karen hill-tribe village we had created for them, they got off the bus utterly flabbergasted to find how much the place resembled home in the green, mountainous jungles near Chiang Mai. The site for our village even had a river, across which we would build the suspension bridge the Peace Corps volunteers must later blow up in order to thwart the intentions of Communists and drug warlords, who intend to exploit it for their own evil purposes. (The final structure would be the largest wood suspension bridge in the world.) Of course we were far from anything, including electricity. Whatever supplies we needed would have to be humped into the wilderness and later humped out again.

I had a strangely difficult time casting the role of Beth Wexsler, the fiery

Long Island Jewish Peace Corps volunteer with whom Hanks, playing a blue-blood Brahmin wastrel on the run from gambling debts, falls inconveniently in love. After a pair of films in which I had "discovered" first Mary Steenburgen and later Kirstie Alley, I was confused by my inability to settle on an actress for the part of Beth. Not being of an analytic turn of mind, I couldn't figure out what was preventing me from making a decision. I saw all the available "hot" actresses of the period on both coasts, some more than once. I finally realized that I had a "type" in mind, and for some reason I cannot now recall, that type was a blue-eyed brunette. Dick Shepherd and Walter Parkes, my two producers, were beginning to show signs of impatience. What was the problem? A sometime actress friend suggested a girlfriend of hers, so I brought her in. Rita Wilson was of Greek extraction and purely West Coast but she gave a terrific reading. I decided to take this one step further and give her a screen test, which was beautifully photographed by my old DP from *Time After Time*, Paul Lohman. Rita was great. I suggested, once she was cast, that she visit the famous Hollywood dialect coach, Bob Easton, to see if she could incorporate just the hint of a Lawn Gisland accent. Tom, I thought, should sound like George Plimpton, and then I had a slight epiphany: We would cast George Plimpton himself as Tom's father. The plan killed several birds with one stone. George was most amusing in the role, and after hanging out with him for three days, Tom mastered that lock-jawed New England drawl to perfection.

We made *Volunteers* in Mexico, and it was a happy experience—maybe too happy. The people were great, and my casting of Rita was validated when I realized my leading man had fallen in love with his leading lady; they would later marry. *Time After Time* redux. What could be bad?

Well, for one thing, our cinematographer, Ric Waite, whose doctor had assured him that he had the heart of an eighteen-year-old, suffered a heart attack. Ric had flown his own plane down to Mexico and on weekends had offered to fly me over the Oaxacan jungle to the picturesque ruins of Monte Albán. I am not an eager flier and had already had anxious times searching that selfsame jungle from the air for locations. I had sat dangling out of a helicopter with a camera, photographing establishing shots of our village, after

Ric had declined so I was sort of relieved when Dick Shepherd, as producer, forbade my going up with Ric as the movie's insurance didn't cover it. Later, I could only wonder what might have happened if Ric had had his heart attack when neither of us could've landed his plane.

Fortunately, the attack, when it came, was on the ground and while Ric was obliged to leave the picture, he is still very much alive as of this writing. I promoted our second cameraman, Jack Green, to cinematographer, and he's had a successful career working for Clint Eastwood, among others, ever since.

John Candy was a nervous flier, too. A sweet and amazingly funny man, it was all Hanks could do to keep a straight face when playing opposite him. Candy seemed startlingly provincial for someone who had enjoyed such success. He was still basically a boy from rural Canada. No Mexican food for him.

Filming on location is rewarding—there is no substitute for the reality captured on camera—but it is also hazardous, especially when you are as cut off from civilization as we were. And while you got used to and even thrived on the big privations, dumb things like bagels were sorely missed. And it was disquieting to see how easily, when things weren't going well, you could turn into the Ugly American, responding to a different world by which you were alternately disturbed and frustrated. When I caught myself veering into this unpleasant mode, I was shocked and disappointed. I picked up a sort of movie-Spanish. I could say "higher" or "lower" or "again" or "cut" or "action." Several years later, in India, I would master those same terms in Hindi . . . and in India, as well, I had to watch my incipient xenophobia.

There is another, more perplexing downside to some location filming. I always suggest people read Pauline Kael's perceptive review of Peter Weir's *The Year of Living Dangerously*, which she ingeniously compared to *Casablanca*: two people falling in love during a crisis in a third-world country and escaping by plane. Only in *Casablanca*, as Kael observed, the third-world natives were actually extras from Burbank, where the movie was shot. When filming ended, they went back to their homes, schools, Little League games—and the next movie, where they might be playing aristocrats at a ball. But the extras in *The Year of Living Dangerously* really *were* those deprived and desperate souls, hired for doubtless nonunion wages, who, when the film ended, could only return to their miserable, precarious existence. The fact that the white people made it out on the plane only trivialized their escape. In *Casablanca*, by contrast, you are undistracted by the sight of real poverty and so are able to concentrate on the fate of Rick and Ilsa.

Volunteers brought excitement and employment to this Mexican backwater. We worked harmoniously together as a team—but at the end, the white (and Thai) people would leave. . . .

After four months in the jungles of Mexico, we returned to LA, and I edited the film with my childhood best friend, Ron Roose, who had played Passepartout in our 8mm version of *Around the World in Eighty Days*. Maybe Ron hadn't wanted to wear a necktie, either, for he'd also gone into the movie business. He was an actor's editor, great at shaping performances. Editing was rhythm to Ron, constructed around what he referred to as the "moment": the look, the line, the close-up that seized a scene and directed all before and all after to its heart. He looked for those moments, sometimes viewing the film MOS—originally "*mit*-out sound" in the words of some transplanted European director—searching for the music in the images and faces and not just the words. Ron would find these "moments" where I had never noticed them, digging out the details and nuances in the scenes.

I would have done well to have been on my guard against all the conviviality during shooting. The film would have been better, though I count it a success overall, if I hadn't been having such a good time. My early successes had lulled me into imagining that I knew what I was doing and could therefore do it every time. There were things I learned from the experience, however. In no special order they are: (1) Just because something is funny doesn't mean it belongs in a comedy. There are different kinds of humor, different styles, and you don't just throw everything in the kitchen sink because it will get a laugh. (2) Be careful when you ask actors to do an "accent" that they are not imprisoned by said accent, that the accent doesn't become the performance. And (3) Henry James said that life is hot but art is cool. If you are the puppeteer you must toil behind the scenes, dry-eyed, and make sure the strings do not get tangled. If you're having too much fun, you're not thinking with the critical distance you need; you're not hearing the little voice inside your head that's supposed to be reminding you what the movie is supposed to be.

We flew to London when it was time to record the music for *Volunteers*, written by my other "discovery," James Horner.

Back in LA the film suffered a curious fate. Because Hanks and Candy had appeared together in the hit kid movie *Splash*, the studio wanted to market our film in the same fashion, so we previewed to a summer audience of teenagers in the San Fernando Valley.

There the film died on the screen. The events of the sixties and all the smart references went right over their heads. Jokes about Kennedy or Albert Speer were meaningless, since this audience had never heard of those people. Inside movie references to *The Bridge on the River Kwai* or *Lawrence of Arabia* were likewise wasted. I had been trying without success to warn management that this was the wrong crowd for our film. Now it was too late. We opened at the end of summer (I wanted Thanksgiving and hoped we'd play at colleges, not beaches), and predictably, despite rave reviews from such publications as *The New York Times*, our film found favor on the East Coast and among people who read, but, like many Woody Allen films, it was viewed as obscure elitist material everywhere else. A pity, but maybe its fate was embedded in its subject matter.

Or perhaps the film was simply not funny enough. It is always tempting to blame the ad campaign, the marketing strategy, or "the studio" for a film's failure. When your film gets good notices but doesn't do big businesses, the temptation is to blame marketing. In this case, a persuasive argument might be made but not necessarily a conclusive one. *Volunteers* was a quirky, grown-up comedy, aimed at baby boomers, not yuppies. (That would've been the *Splash* audience.) Looking for what Ted Ashley labeled the tom-tom factor, that magic frequency, the dog whistle that attracts everyone within earshot, is the crapshoot that movies have always been. Nowadays demographics and awareness surveys try to remove some of the guesswork but at the same time they also wean out the variety. Once bookstores begin stocking their shelves via computer calculations, esoterica is going to fall by the wayside, and soon we'll all be reading Nicholas Sparks.

Maybe Romeo and Juliet *should* have lived? Bookstores? What am I talking about?

Meantime, released in the fall of 1986, *Star Trek IV: The Voyage Home* was the franchise's biggest success to date. The film had what is known as "crossover appeal," meaning that Ned Tanen had been correct when he had said he would have made the film even without its *Star Trek* associations.

The film remains sprightly years later, the cast and crew clearly having a good time kicking up their heels in the service of an intelligent and worthwhile story. The film comes perilously close to being a spoof of the series, which may add to its appeal, especially for aficionados. Adding to the aura of good feeling was the score by the late Leonard Rosenman, a long-time friend of Nimoy's and one of the ablest composers ever to grace the medium of film. (His work on *Rebel Without a Cause* prefigured and greatly influenced Leonard Bernstein's score for *West Side Story*.) The fact that the film did not take place in outer space, that the crew was featured in real locations (including a nuclear powered aircraft carrier!), and that the comedy was broad throughout doubtless contributed in large measure to the crossover factor. *Star Trek* had been brought down to earth, where lots more people could relate to it.

The screen credits seemed quaint to me. The original writers were given screenplay credit, with Bennett and me in third and fourth place respectively. Evidently the WGA arbiters had had difficulty distinguishing between story and script. It was definitely the same (Nimoy and Bennett) story but couldn't possibly contain any of a screenplay I had never read. These results are not necessarily the result of ineptitude. When you agree to read an arbitration for the Guild, like as not a truck drives up to your place and drops off twenty drafts of a movie. You are (somehow!) expected to keep track of who wrote what in each. Inevitably, even the most conscientious reader's eyes glaze over and the most punctilious note-taking gets messed up. The credit, as I have noted elsewhere, mightn't be such a big deal if there weren't bonuses attached. Oh, well.

Subsequently I wasted several months (and two trips to Spain) at a company called Kings Road, where I tried to make a *Jules and Jim*–like romance, set during the Spanish Civil War. We had actually begun casting when the project fell to pieces, and I went into a serious depression, from which I was rescued when Dawn Steel told me and my partner, Steven-Charles Jaffe, to set up shop back at Paramount.

I became a fixture on the lot, staying there a total of fourteen years. I saw myself as the in-house mascot, housed (fittingly, I thought) in the Marx Brothers Building. I helped the studio on different scripts, ate lunch at the commissary, got my hair cut on the lot, and bought my blue cotton work shirts at the company store. Who needed to drive anyplace?

I'd fallen in love with a book called *Field of Blood* by the English journalist turned novelist Gerald Seymour. It was a shattering tale, set in Northern Ireland and chillingly reminiscent of one of my all-time favorite movies, *Odd Man Out*, with many of the same moral complexities organically intertwined in its plot. I knew exactly how to write and direct it.

"This studio is not making a movie about the IRA," said Ned Tanen when I broached the project to him. After I rolled around on the carpet of his office, foaming at the mouth, he offered Seymour's agent a generous option fee, but that gentleman, smelling Hollywood calling, was demanding something like ten times the amount.

"This is ridiculous," said Tanen. I rolled and foamed some more a week later, and he upped the offer—"all this for a movie we'll never make," he growled.

The London agent held firm. I asked my wife if we could kick in some of our money. She said yes; Paramount said no.

And that was the end of it.

For a time.

It must've been late 1986 when one of the producers of *Kramer vs. Kramer*, Stanley Jaffe (no relation to Steve), dropped into my office and asked me to give my opinion of a script called *Deception*. I had known and liked Stanley from the time when I'd been the office boy at Paramount in New York. He could be prickly, too, but funny, and I always looked forward to our encounters.

Deception was a really good script with a nifty, gut-twisting plot, well drawn characters—including one genuine original creation, a latter-day riff on Hedda Gabler named Alex Forrest. My only real problem with it was the ending, which didn't seem to quite go with the rest of the story. You have smart days and dumb days. This was one of my smarter days, and I punched out a four-page, single-spaced memo on how to fix the script. Over the next day or so, I got some more ideas and threw them in, too. I sent my revised letter off to Stanley and thought no more about it.

Some weeks later he invited me to lunch. As I walked to the commissary, I suddenly wondered if he was going to offer me the movie to direct, but this was not the case. At lunch I was introduced to Adrian Lyne, who had already been signed as director. We chatted, and I had another smart day, said some clever things I cannot now remember, and went home that night feeling pleased with myself.

Two days later I received a summons to Dawn Steel's office, toward which I headed with a slight case of dread. What indiscretion had I committed now? On her otherwise immaculate black basalt desk I spied, to my alarm, a copy of my memo.

"Listen, Nicky," she said without preamble. "Here's the straight dope. We're not making this movie unless you rewrite it according to what you put in this memo, and you can have anything you want, and yes, that means we'll even buy your stupid fucking IRA book."

Dawn never meant anything by these locutions; that's just the way she talked. Around this time *California* magazine ran an article about her entitled, "The Queen of Mean." I wrote a letter protesting the smarmy piece, pointing out that if Dawn had been a man, they never would have commissioned, let alone run it. They responded by revealing my screenwriting salary, as though that was the reason for my defense. Dawn's reaction was, "If I've done half those things (in the article) I'm goddamned ashamed of myself."

As for *Deception*, I thought it was silly on Paramount's part to spend all that money—first on my revisions of their script, then on purchasing the rights to *Field of Blood* at an extortionate price, then for my full freight to write a screenplay they never intended to film—but what did I know? In the event, it worked out for everyone. Paramount's movie, now titled *Fatal Attraction*, turned out to be a big hit, and I got to write *Field of Blood*, one my best scripts, even if they didn't film it.

(Until later. Live long enough and you'll see all your movies made.)

That same year I agreed to direct Michael Hirst's script of John Masters novel *The Deceivers* for Merchant Ivory, a task that would take me and my new family (which now included a daughter) to London and to India for a year.

It was in early '87 when I heard rumblings about the next *Star Trek* film. Taking a leaf from Nimoy's playbook, William Shatner's quid pro quo for participating in the new movie was directing it. I was again asked to write the screenplay. When I asked what the film was to be about, I was told, "the search for God."

This did not strike me as an especially promising premise. How could such a search possibly conclude? Fortunately, I had the multiple excuses of my *Fatal Attraction* chores and my imminent departure abroad.

TILTING AT WINDMILLS: A DIGRESSION

Movies get made not by accident, but because the planets align. Sometimes they do, sometimes they don't, and sometimes it takes a long time before they do. As *Don Quixote* falls into this category, it may be worth recounting the story thus far.

It was late 1986 and my producer friend David Foster (*McCabe & Mrs. Miller, The Getaway,* etc.) and I had always wanted to make a movie together. With typical perversity I asked if he'd ever read *Don Quixote,* and when he said he hadn't, I recommended the Samuel Putnam translation. After reading it David was hooked. "*Don Q! Don Q!* Gotta make *Don Q!*" became his mantra. Regretting my silly suggestion, I said it would never happen. There was a reason Hollywood had never tackled *Quixote,* that Orson Welles's fabled version was never completed, etc. The musical *Man of la Mancha,* inspired by an episode in the life of Cervantes, failed as a film. Still, Foster, nothing if not tenacious (a key virtue for producers), was not about to give up. We were lunching in the Paramount commissary when Ned Tanen walked by and said hello. "Never mind 'hello,'" Foster retorted. "This boy has done *Star Trek* for you, *Fatal Attraction* for you"—this was a gross exaggeration, to be sure, but exaggeration is the lingua franca of Hollywood—"what are you gonna do for him?"

"Anything he wants," Tanen blithely replied, moving off. David swung round to face me. "That's it," he stated. "We're taking him *Don Q.*"

"David," I protested, "it's a fool's errand."

"I'm making the appointment and I expect you to be there," he shot back with the satisfied mien of a man who has just accomplished something difficult and intends to accomplish more.

So it was that a week or so later we found ourselves in Tanen's office.

"Well, boys, what is this about?" he commenced, after the usual preliminaries.

David turned to me: *Your department*, his expression plainly stated.

Forcing myself to look Tanen directly in the eye, I said to him, "We want to make a movie of *Don Quixote*."

Tanen nodded, attentively. "And . . . ?"

I knew what that "and" meant. It meant, What's the gimmick? Is it Quixote in space? With music? Is he black? Does it have a video game tie-in?

"That's it," I said. "Just the no-frills, brown-bag *Quixote*."

He stared at me.

"Here's the thing," I continued, provoked by his gaze and breathing in the wrong places. "*Quixote*'s always played for sentiment." I mimed a violinist at this juncture. "Whereas, if you read it, it's baggy-pants funny, the first road comedy, the first buddy picture. It's Laurel and Hardy, complete with fart jokes and all kinds of physical gags . . . I even know the line on the poster," I concluded. "'You'll laugh . . . till you cry.'"

Tanen sat back and stared some more. On reflection it occurred to me that he must have been accustomed by this point to hearing all sorts of crazy ideas.

"That's crazy," he said as if reading my mind, and then amended hastily, "but that's not necessarily a criticism." He thought some more. It turned out that one of his daughters was currently reading and loving the novel.

"Okay," he said at last. "People will call me crazy." (People *had* called him crazy.)

I hardly dared glance at David. We were both holding still as hares in headlights. The planets were lining up . . . or starting to . . .

"Ned," I said, as he showed no signs of further speech but sat staring at the ceiling as if asking himself what he had just agreed to, "I think I'll need to go to Spain to do some research. . . ."

"Go, go . . . Don't break the bank."

We left him before he could change his mind and now, before heading to London and India, I had Spain on my itinerary. If it's not Mars, I always like to visit the places I am going to write about. With that experience you're not merely copying stuff from a book; you have some organic connection to the terrain, the culture. You don't exactly know what you're looking for but you find it anyway. It enters through your pores, and the script comes out better, somehow, as a result.

Lauren, baby Rachel, and I left for Europe, and Mari-Carmen Jaffe, Steve's wife, herself a Spaniard, took us to every place Cervantes had ever been on the Iberian peninsula and to some he hadn't but insisted Quixote had. I even went into the Cave of Montesinos, fabled and endless in the novel, a mere rocky indentation in reality. I doubt Cervantes would have written about it if he'd clambered into that damp, grubby space, as I did. We wandered around La Mancha, the arid province where most of the novel takes place, and visited El Toboso, a town of no particular distinction now transformed into something of a tourist mecca thanks to Quixote's alleged exploits there.

After Mari-Carmen returned to California, we stayed on in Spain, renting a house outside Marbella where a mountain outside my office window looked suspiciously like the Paramount logo and reminded me daily of what I was supposed to be doing there. It goes without saying that, other than the broad philosophical approach I had outlined to Tanen, I had no idea how to go about adapting a thousand-plus-page novel to the screen. All I knew for certain was that Los Angeles was not the place to try; the phone rang too often there. Here, away from all distractions, Rachel would learn to eat soft food, and I would fool around with *Quixote*, whose real subject, I realized on closer examination, was not the Don's monomania—chivalry—but Cervantes's: *words*.

One way you know that the Dark Ages have ended is each country's discovery—starting with Italy and working its way west—of its own vernacular for purposes of literature, hitherto the province of the classical tongues, Greek and Latin. But suddenly you have Dante writing *The Divine Comedy* in Italian; in France, Corneille, Racine, and Molière are discovering French; in England, first Chaucer, then Marlowe, Spenser, and Shakespeare are drunk on English;

and in Spain, in the same year *Macbeth* is written comes the first part of *Don Quixote*, composed in colloquial Spanish. The book is likewise high on the possibilities of language. There are big plots, little plots, poems, short stories, anecdotes, jokes, asides, puns, more poems, more tangents . . . every kind of language was grist for Cervantes's mill. (This was true for Shakespeare, too: his vocabulary—the vocabulary of someone linguistically intoxicated—was fifty thousand words. It's been shrinking ever since; I daresay we're down to about five thou?)

What do you do with all those damn words?

Quixote is also a book about nonconformity and the price nonconformists must pay. The foolish knight became my hero.

I decided that I would make an outline of the book. For every page I would summarize the action. In this way I would memorize the book, trick myself into believing I'd written it (like the man who copied out all of *War and Peace* so he could tell himself he'd written *War and Peace*), attaching a page number to each summation. Along the way, I'd be picking and choosing what to include and what to omit.

The outline took forever and came to 150 pages, but at least I now had a manageable précis of the novel with page references for all of it and could begin forming my attack on the Rubik's Cube d'España.

Being in Marbella helped. Marbella is a completely depraved place. Filled with drug smugglers, white slavers, and dissolute sheiks, it is Miami Beach with a cockney accent, has nothing to do with Spain, and is no place for a nice Jewish boy. Other than occasional forays into delicious eateries, we stayed at our little house, where I kept my nose to the grindstone, trying to remember lessons I'd learned from *Volunteers*. My job was to make others laugh, not indulge myself. Quixote, stripped of all Cervantes's literary experiments and digressions, is a fascinating, three-dimensional character. Far from being insane, he is a model of rationality on every subject but one, and Sancho's curious combination of savvy and gullibility makes him a poignant complement to his mentor. On some gut level Sancho *knows* better; on another, he finds the Don's beliefs superior to the reality he's experienced thus far. Nabokov may be right to dismiss Quixote as a novel, but he's wrong in the same breath to dismiss these two guys and their vaudeville antics.

Somehow the script got written (how? Can't say; I was in my usual trance), and before I left for London and India, I *sent* it off to Tanen. Word came back: he loved it and would see me upon my return.

To be continued . . .

THE DECEIVERS

My little family was now based in London and from there we went to India, where we had the time of our lives with Pierce Brosnan and company, filming *The Deceivers*. John Masters's novel chronicles in fictional form the true history of the notorious gangs of cult murderers known as thugs (the eponymous deceivers), roving bands of pseudo-travelers who attached themselves to itinerant merchant caravans only to strangle their victims by night with silken handkerchiefs before burying them in mass unmarked graves and making off with their goods. In 1825, when the novel is set, roads in India were so problematic that a man leaving on a journey might not be missed by his family for upward of a year. The cult was eventually broken by an enterprising English officer of the ruling East India Company (to be played by Brosnan), who penetrated the gang by successfully disguising himself as an Indian and becoming one of the killers, an action that in Masters's telling arguably causes him to lose his mind.

The film had been offered to me via my agent by Ismail Merchant of the famed Merchant Ivory filmmaking duo. They specialized in intelligent, literary adaptations but evidently were looking to branch out into more popular fare and widen their stable of directors, as well. I am certain Ismail, a charming man, originally from Mumbai, had no idea who I was, but once I was on his radar (being warm, if not hot, for the moment), he arranged to meet me in New York. Ismail originally had an American actor in mind for the role of the English officer but I demurred.

"Here's a story about an Englishman who disguises himself as an Indian," I reasoned. "If you cast this actor, you will have an American disguising himself as an Englishman, disguising himself as an Indian. We will be lost in the stunt, even if he pulls it off, and not pay attention to the story and the things we want to take for granted, i.e., that it concerns an Englishman."

In the end, Pierce Brosnan and I met in Los Angeles.

"Good grief, your eyes are blue," I exclaimed without preamble at the Beverly Hills Hotel. "You'll have to wear brown contact lenses." Brosnan blanched. He's a gent who takes things slowly, and we probably hadn't even sat down by then. Actors always start wary.

"I have a pathological fear of putting anything on my eyes," he objected.

"It's nothing," said I, staring to yank out one of my own lenses by way of helpful demonstration, causing him to turn very pale. Indians, excepting Pathans, do not have blue eyes, Amy Irving in *The Far Pavilions* notwithstanding.

One could write an entire book about making *The Deceivers*, and in fact there is one with Ismail Merchant's name on it, though I am not sure who the author really is and don't find it especially accurate. How could it be when neither Ismail nor his ghostwriter was there for most of the filming? (Commenting on music allegedly composed by Frederick the Great, Voltaire observed, "Never criticize music by a monarch; you may never know by whom it was written.")

The Deceivers was four months of backbreaking work, but I loved making an old-style, Alexander Korda–type movie. Once I discovered that there was a cavalry charge in the script, I was a goner. My wife felt the same way, provided she got to ride in the charge, which she did, swaddled in a hot, red, woolen uniform among India's crack 101st cavalry. People were alarmed at the prospect of our taking a nine-month-old child to India. "Why?" Lauren asked. "They have lots of kids there." I loved India, with all its color and contradictions, the staggering wealth, the appalling squalor—this is shorthand, I know, but if I start on India, I won't stop, and this isn't a travel book, it's a memoir. Besides, I am haunted by the suspicion that my travel writing may come out as hilariously as Robert Newton's Inspector Fix, bullshitting to Cantinflas's gullible Passepartout in *Around the World in 80 Days*. "India? Few know it as I do. The mosques! The minarets! Indian maidens! Statuesque! Barbaric! Ah, the Road to Mandalay . . ."

Despite our awkward early meeting Pierce Brosnan and I got on wonderfully. He responded to my exuberance, and I to his courtly hipness. He even mastered brown contacts, delivering a wonderfully self-effacing performance as the schizoid protagonist who goes searching for the worst thing in the world, only to discover he's carrying it in his pocket. In the hands of a lesser talent, the transformation of a white man into an Indian could have easily become a stunt, calling attention to itself as an act of empty virtuosity. In Brosnan's hands, it becomes part of this unlucky man's tragic descent into madness.

As I became friends with Brosnan, my wife became friends with his. Late at night, he would read Irish poetry aloud while we three sat and listened. Some of us were stoned. Beneath the suave, tuxedoed exterior for which he became known as James Bond, Brosnan is a Yeats-quoting beachcomber.

India was an adventure from start to finish. Ismail had promised to be on site for the entire shoot, guiding Tim Van Rellim, our producer, and me through the tricky intricacies of Indian culture, politics, and what have you. But in the end we were left much to our own devices until the last weeks of filming. It was the twenty-fifth anniversary of Merchant Ivory Films, and Ismail and James Ivory were busy taking bows at the Kennedy Center while Tim and I ran afoul of such characters as the head of the local Jaipur mafia, who, when we declined to deal with him, had to save face by making sure that our shooting was disrupted if not destroyed. Scores of hooligans stormed through our sets while we were rolling; equipment was sabotaged or stolen; "cultural" societies were founded for the sole purpose of suing us, alleging pornographic distortions of Indian culture.

But nothing could prevent the total exhilaration of our shoot, of India itself, where you can tack superlatives onto anything and be accurate. It was the most, the best, the worst; it was inspiring, dispiriting, colorful, irresistible—you name it. It was also a labyrinthine bureaucracy, whose economic models were India's long-time ally, the USSR, for whom economics (to paraphrase John McCain) was not a strong suit. This meant, among other things, that everything you brought into the country, you had to take out again when you left. A vacuum cleaner, for example, might deprive a sweeper of his job, so it had to go back with us. There was no Coca-Cola, only their poisonous approximation, and no cars except the ones they manufactured, called Ambassadors. (Driving in India makes you believe in karma.) The crew was great at improvising solutions to the endless problems that presented themselves. One day when we needed our tulip crane for a big shot, I was flummoxed to learn that four of its bolts had been stolen, incapacitating a vital piece of equipment. I don't deal well with last-minute alterations to The Plan, but my Indian crew managed to mill four new bolts by the time we were ready to roll.

Indian actors are terrific, and Indian people among the warmest, fastest (those superlatives again) friends you will ever make. One of our stars was Shashi Kapoor, the Paul Newman of India, so memorable in other Merchant Ivory films, notably opposite Greta Scacchi in *Heat and Dust*, where he was just about the handsomest (est!) man I'd ever seen. Now, even weighing in at about three hundred pounds, he drew thousands of enthralled observers wherever we set him before a camera.

The film was designed by the great Ken Adam, whom I'd met on *The Seven-Per-Cent Solution*, and shot by the eccentric Walter Lassally (*Tom Jones*, *Zorba the Greek*, etc.).

One of the paradoxical ironies of the movie business is that, if you do your job really well, your price goes up, and people can't afford you. Ken Adam, designer of *Barry Lyndon* and all those James Bond films, was thought to be too expensive to hire on anything less, by this point in his career—the irony being that as a production designer, it was his *responsibility* to make things look more expensive than they really were. Adam took the job at Ismail's bargain basement prices to prove that this was (still) what he was good at.

Ken was the film's artistic conscience, ready to lie down in front of the train if that's what it took to preserve its aesthetic integrity. We needed a Georgian church in which our hero marries at the start of the tale—essentially, Jane Austen's India. Find a Georgian church still extant in India, if you think you can. We drove hours on someone's recommendation and came upon what was self-evidently a Victorian church. "Let's go with this," I declared. "No one will ever know."

"*I* will know," said Ken Adam, with a glint behind his enormous, thick-lensed glasses, "and if you use this church, I take my name off the picture."

We kept looking and eventually discovered an exquisite Georgian church in Agra—and I learned something about what makes a great production designer, and how to keep your integrity.

Back in London, where the film was edited, there was good news and bad news. The good news was that my little family had fallen in love with the city, a passion that was to have far-reaching consequences.

The bad news was that I had picked the wrong editor. To be fair—to me—I had chosen him by default, over the phone from Mumbai, when my original choice had inexplicably bailed while I was hunting locations. Maybe his departure was not entirely inexplicable. I had learned only relatively late in the production of Ismail's reputation. He had his fans and his detractors, and like many independent producers was sometimes late with checks and low on salaries. In the beginning I was dismayed when the owner of our editing equipment would call, threatening to repossess same. I would call Paul Bradley, who ran the Merchant Ivory office in Soho, in a state of high alarm, relating these dire tidings. Paul always had the same answer: "Really? This is the first I heard of it" (i.e., the unpaid bill). Gradually, I became accustomed to this roller coaster, but Ismail's modus operandi was more than some people were prepared for. (Again, to be fair, the world of the independent producer is a precarious one. Checks are frequently late or go missing. Sam Spiegel, producer of four of the greatest films of all time, *The African Queen, On the Waterfront, The Bridge on the River Kwai* and *Lawrence of Arabia*, was notorious for being dilatory in the check department.)

My editor was a different problem altogether. With the loss of my original first choice, I panicked over there in India and chose a persistent substitute in whom I hadn't quite believed. Although Bill Dornisch ran a cutting room that resembled a madhouse, with torn, scratched workprint trims dangling everywhere, my editor on *The Deceivers*, by contrast, ran a surgically pristine editing room where nothing was out of place and the workprint didn't have a scratch. Unfortunately, he could not, to my way of thinking, cut film. Or, to make allowances, he couldn't cut *this* film, and I didn't do what I should have done in response. Why not? A good question. My congenital reluctance to confront? To make waves? My inability to find an available substitute? In the end my brother-in-law, Roger Spottiswoode, the director of such classics as *Under Fire* (and former editor for such as Sam Peckinpah) flew to London and made what sense he could of the footage, though by this time Ismail's funds had indeed run out. The film was not a commercial success but remains very watchable and gratifyingly dark, and Brosnan's performance remains a standout.

Following the completion of *The Deceivers* in the spring of 1988, my wife and I found ourselves driving down the M4 motorway outside London. "This road makes me sad," I declared abruptly. "Because this is the road to the airport," I explained when she asked me why, "and one day we'll be traveling it in only one direction."

She thought about this and then said, "I didn't realize you felt this way."

"Neither did I," I conceded, but I did. There was silence in the car as I realized we were both wondering the same thing. What if we didn't go back? Was it possible to earn a living out of Hollywood if you didn't live in Hollywood?

WINDMILLS REDUX

We decided a reality check was in order and returned to Los Angeles in July, still paying rent on our Soho house and me keeping the key and my passport in my pocket, telling myself that we could return at a moment's notice. In Los Angeles Tanen was still enthusiastic about *Don Q*, the script for which he found hilarious. The question now was, Who should play the Don? I suggested one actor and he scowled.

"I'd rather give the money to the American Cancer Society."

The question was answered by Ron, who had just seen John Lithgow on Broadway in New York in *M. Butterfly*.

"He's the Don," said Ron.

I had, as it happened, directed Lithgow in *The Day After*. Paramount sent me to New York to witness his astonishing performance in David Henry Hwang's play, and I went backstage to see him afterward.

"God no, not a starring role," he protested, when I explained why I was there. "I've never carried a picture. I couldn't carry a picture."

"Will you at least *read* it?" I begged. Lithgow was nothing if not polite. He promised to read the script, but I knew the planets were slipping out of alignment and phoned Lucchesi, trying not to sound desperate.

"He says he can't carry a picture," I reported. "How can we make him do it?"

Lucchesi thought and said, "We'll stage a reading of the screenplay on a night when his theater's dark. Get any actors he names to be in it with him and make a contribution to Actors Equity or something."

This ploy actually worked. On an insufferably hot, muggy August afternoon at the Minskoff Rehearsal studios in New York, with a roadshow company of *South Pacific* practicing next door and "Bloody Mary is the girl I love" thumping through the walls, I assembled my cast around a group of trestle tables, scripts in hand, and gave them the only stage directions for which there was time, all too aware of a clutch of Paramount executives who had flown in from LA and were watching the proceedings skeptically.

"Think *Wizard of Oz*," I told them. "And have fun."

With Lithgow as Don Quixote and Jerry Stiller as Sancho, along with Joe Morton and a host of other notables doing this out of the goodness of their hearts (and a substantial contribution by Paramount to an actors' charity), we launched into the Don's odyssey.

The script was a sensation. I sat there, no longer aware of *South Pacific*, in a state of pleasant astonishment. The small audience (also astonished) laughed heartily, the actors were clearly enjoying themselves, and at the end no one wanted to leave, a sure indication of success.

"I get it; I'll do it," said Lithgow, looking up, grinning and surprised.

The planets had aligned; we were home free.

Only we weren't, which is the moral of the story. You're not home until you're home.

Paramount was having having their worst summer in recent memory. Even their Sean Connery picture (*The Presidio*) had bombed, as did another film (*Distant Thunder*)—this one having the misfortune to include Lithgow in its cast.

And to top it off, Tanen's two-year contract was up, and he left to return to his beloved cacti. With him left Quixote's champion.

The script was later mounted on the radio by the BBC with Paul Scofield and Bob Hoskins in the principal roles, an interesting—interim—fate. Normally, when a play is produced with even a modicum of success, sooner or later the odds are good that it will be produced again. If it's a hit play, those odds grow in your favor. *Hamlet* is a good example, but *Sleuth* and *High School Musical* are, too.

Screenplays are different. Most never get made; they gather dust on shelves and with time, they become either dated or somehow less urgently plausible as properties than when they were new. And even if fortune smiles and your script *is* produced, the odds are that it will never be produced again. Even if your film is remade, the likelihood is that some version of the story will be filmed but not from the screenplay. If your lead actor was miscast, he will remain miscast forever, your screenplay, unlike its stage counterpart, dipped forever in cinematic amber. When Paramount decides to remake *The Manchurian Candidate*, they don't dream of using the same script. New is better. If there are reasons that screenwriters do not enjoy the same social or cultural or literary cachet as playwrights, this fact must be numbered among them.

Ten years later Lithgow called. I hadn't heard from him in some time.

"Please don't hate me," he began.

"Why should I hate you?" I asked.

"Because tomorrow you'll read in the trades that I'm going to play Quixote on TNT for Peter Yates from a script by John Mortimer. I wanted you to hear it from me first."

I drew a deep breath. What could I say? What was there to say?

"Promise me one thing," I begged, keeping my voice steady. "Promise it'll be funny."

It wasn't. But it succeeded in moving the goal posts for the feature I had written off the field to infinity.

Five years after that, Ian McKellan wanted to do the film, and Paul Giamatti was up for playing Sancho. Still no dice.

The planets had almost aligned—but, as the man says, there's many a slip 'twixt the cup and the lip. If Paramount had had a better summer, if Tanen had chosen to stay on . . .

But close is no cigar.

Does that mean never? Why should it? A period script, at least, stands a better chance of not dating. Terry Gilliam tried his Quixote, and that came to grief. Wait another fifty years and try again. . . . It takes only one yes to wipe out all the nos. . . .

One has only to point to John Huston's tenacious infatuation with Kipling's *The Man Who Would Be King*. He first sought to film it with Walter Huston and Bogart in the roles of Danny and Peachy; a generation later it was to have been Burton and O'Toole; finally, after another generation the roles were assumed by Sean Connery and Michael Caine and who's to say they weren't the best ones for it? Was it the same screenplay throughout all those attempts? Don't you believe it.

I tell this story glibly enough, but it fails to convey the feelings of heartache and despair that you can experience in this line of work when something into which you have poured years of effort and every fiber of your being because you love it so much comes to nothing. The sick feeling that overtakes you when you finally realize you've spent a substantial portion of your life on earth in pursuit of a goal that will likely never be reached is something that I, for one, have never really learned to process. Others may be more philosophical, but I didn't go into this line of work with any motive other than to see the movies I dream about. I don't worry about what is "commercial," because all too many examples have demonstrated that no one knows what that is, that the most unlikely material, if done correctly (whatever *that* means), can bring people to the theater. I carry my impotence around with me, cursing the fact that I don't have the wallet to make things happen that I know are wonderful.

Tolstoy (who later disowned the statement) famously said that the purpose of art is to teach us to love life and that to love life is to love God. I don't know about the second part but I'm pretty sure about the first. Books and movies have gotten me through some pretty tough times, and I'm fairly certain that this is the service they perform for most people, who could use a breather from reality and some inspiration every now and again, a time out before returning to the battle.

I don't give up on *Don Quixote*, just as I don't give up on *The Odyssey* or the story of the building of the Brooklyn Bridge or Arthur Conan Doyle's *The White Company*. Their scripts sit on my shelves, waiting to be read, waiting for another chance, for someone with imagination and money to see in them what I see.

SOMMERSBY

Arnon Milchan and Steve Reuther talked to me about making an American version of the story of Martin Guerre, recently the subject of a successful French film. I decided to base my script on the actual events, rather than the French movie, and researched the case, which is amply documented. In brief: the true events transpired in sixteenth-century France, in the Pyrenean village of Artigat, where sullen fifteen-year-old Martin Guerre married Bertrande de Rols and then, having impregnated her, ran off and was never heard from again, effectively condemning the woman to perpetual widowhood. (She could hardly remarry as her husband—so far as might be known—was still alive.) Eight years later, to her delight, Martin returned, filled out and matured. Where once he was surly and withdrawn, he was now gregarious and uxorious. He fathered a second child with Bertrande, and all seemed jake. Except for the growing suspicion on the part of first one and then another of the villagers that the Martin Guerre who left Artigat almost a decade earlier and the newly returned version might not be the same man. There were rumors that the genuine Martin Guerre had lost a leg at the battle of St. Quentin. Eventually the matter came to trial (the judge's book on the case is one of the sources that preserved it for us), with half the town swearing in one direction, the other half in the other. Suddenly, to the consternation of all, a one-legged man clumped into the court, instantly recognized as the real Martin Guerre (surly as ever). The imposter, one Amaud du Tilh, who had recognized their resemblance in the army, was hanged, drawn, and quartered.

The success of the story depends on the absence of certain technological developments—e.g., photography, fingerprinting, ready communications—that would have cleared up the mystery conclusively. What was the last moment in human history when such an event might plausibly have occurred? And where?

After mulling the matter for some time, I decided that the end of the Civil War might be just such an era. In Mark Twain's disturbing novel *Pudd'nhead Wilson*, set during this period, fingerprints are introduced for the first time, but their usage was clearly not commonplace. Telegraphic communication, especially in rural areas such as those in the decimated South, might plausibly be absent, and so might Mathew Brady and his camera. The conceit might just fly. I also liked the idea of doing a film in the Reconstruction era because I didn't know offhand of any other, with the exception of *Gone with the Wind* and *Bright Leaf,* an obscure Gary Cooper–Patricia Neal opus. The subject of tobacco—about which I knew next to nothing—would also, as I imagined it, constitute an intriguing part of the tale.

Milchan liked my idea, and I went off on a Southern tour, starting in Washington, D.C., and heading for nearby Richmond, Virginia, searching for a plausible locale and learning about tobacco growing. After Richmond and a tour of the Philip Morris factory ("PLEASE FEEL FREE TO SMOKE" read a sign in the reception area), various state film commissions assisted me as I poked into antebellum Southern mansions (the local of equivalent of French chateau country) in Virginia, North Carolina, Georgia, and Tennessee, where I finally found a milieu that satisfied me. I returned to Los Angeles and wrote what I called *Sommersby* and turned it in. Milchan and Reuther professed themselves delighted. They landed Richard Gere and Jodie Foster and they hired Jon Amiel, the English director of the spectacular British television series *The Singing Detective*, to helm the movie.

He told them he didn't want to change a word.

Sometime later I was puzzled to hear that another writer had been engaged to do the inevitable production rewrites on my script. My first reaction was possessive indignation. Why was someone else being hired to rewrite my original work—especially when that work had attracted all the talent? Then I thought about it for a while, and calmer feelings prevailed. After all, I told myself, he's the director, he can hire whomever he likes.

Then I thought about the matter some more and grew angry all over again. Surely there's a missing phone call here from my good buddies, the producers, I realized. The one that goes, *Nick, you're not going to like this but you know that crazy director we hired? Well, he wants to use his own blah blah blah*.

Working myself into a towering rage, I phoned Steve Reuther and told him what I thought of this behavior. He mumbled an apology but we never spoke again.

Later, when the new draft of the screenplay turned out to be an unholy mess, Richard Gere, who never quite understood why the first draft had been altered, wondered why they didn't simply go back to "the Meyer draft." According to Maggie Wilde, then Gere's manager, he was told by the producer that I was "unavailable." This led to a third writer being hired, whose job was somehow to put the thing back to where it was, which didn't happen. It would have been, I suppose, unthinkable to simply fish the original script out of a drawer.

COMPANY BUSINESS

In Los Angeles again and occupying square one, Lauren and I hung around until the advent of George Bush I in November, following eight years of Ronald Reagan, pushed me over the edge. We were back in London by Christmas, and I told myself I had escaped the pull of gravity. Lauren decided she wanted to purchase a home, and we did, in Holland Park. Paramount generously sustained my office on the lot in Los Angeles, and I was just about the first person to use e-mail. I could write a screenplay in London, hit SEND, and have it printed out in my office at Paramount by my assistant, Denny Martin Flinn.

Flinn, whom I had hired out of the Paramount personnel pool, had been with me for several years. Originally a Broadway dancer, he had starred in *A Chorus Line* and other notable hits before taking his bride west and settling in Los Angeles. Now the father of two, he took charge of my office, organized my life, and introduced me to computers, overcoming my lifelong technophobia. Not only was he a one-man living encyclopedia of the American musical theater (about which he subsequently wrote a number of informative books), he was also indefatigable, with several screenplays under his own belt and bursting with promising ideas for more. A lot of time in our office—even via e-mail when I lived I London—was spent in long, animated discussions and arguments over books, films, and ideas for same.

By this time Dawn Steel had also departed Paramount to head Columbia (where she would commission the restoration of *Lawrence of Arabia*). The musical executive chairs were empty only briefly. In 1987 Frank Mancuso named Gary Lucchesi, my former agent, head of motion picture production, and Sid Ganis, formerly head of Paramount marketing, was put in charge of the studio in 1988.

Around this time I decided to change agencies and was curious to know what it would be like at CAA, the powerhouse packaging plant where an old friend of mine, Rick Nicita, was a Big Deal. He suggested I write an original script for myself to direct, and so I tried my hand at something I called *Dinosaurs*. It involved two aging spies, a Russian and an American, who find themselves on the run together as the result of a spy swap gone wrong, in a world where they are technologically as well as ideologically obsolete. The whole point of the movie is more or less summed up when the American asks the Russian mole where he got his information, and the latter replies, "CNN."

Significantly, this line never made it into the finished film.

I showed Nicita my first draft to see if I was on the right track, and he became excited. I was nowhere near finished when another agent at CAA called and asked what I thought of Gene Hackman for the role of the American. I allowed he would be perfect—Hackman was arguably the preeminent film actor of this generation—and the agent said, "You've got him."

"I've got him?" I echoed.

"You've got him. Now what do you think about Baryshnikov as the Russian?"

I tried to think—this was happening very fast. "Well, he's not really old enough to be a dino—"

"He'll get the picture made," I was told on the other end of the line. I thought, *Well, this is why you came to CAA, isn't it?* And so I struck while the iron was hot—instead of finishing a decent script.

Dinosaurs (a name I couldn't use, as it turns out Disney had already registered it) was sped into production even as I tried to finish a screenplay that struggled to reflect fast-moving events in Eastern Europe, where the Berlin Wall was collapsing. I also tried to sit down with Hackman, but he was always busy. Gradually I learned that between the time he agreed to do my film and nine months later, when we were ready to roll in Berlin, he'd squeezed in three movies back-to-back: *Postcards from the Edge*, *Narrow Margin*, and *Class Action*. . . . This, I told myself, could not bode well.

That turned out to be an understatement. Two weeks before we started

Hackman wanted to be replaced. What comparable star he imagined would be available on such short notice was beyond me. Did he realize he would be leaving a lot of folks in the lurch? Did he care? MGM, the movie's financier, made it simple: if Hackman didn't show up in Berlin, MGM threatened to sue him.

So it wasn't a happy camper whom I finally got to meet, ten days before we were to start. He began by commenting on the script—the first time he'd addressed the material in the nine months since he'd agreed to perform in it—which he felt contained too much violence. (This from the man whose next film would win him an Oscar as the sadistic Little Bill Daggett in Clint Eastwood's *Unforgiven.*)

When I demurred at Hackman's critique and mumbled something about our film being a spy thriller in which such goings-on were typical, he glared at me. "You know, you and I don't get along."

"We don't?" I asked, in shock. "But we've only just met." In fact we hadn't been sitting together five minutes.

For me, used to getting people to do my bidding because they liked me, and because I liked them, this was not good.

The film, which came to be known as *Company Business*, was a catastrophe, and it was no one's fault but mine. Going forward without a finished script was suicide. And while on paper, the troika of Hackman, Baryshnikov, and Meyer might have appeared promising, in reality we were all pulling in different directions, and my bouts with Hackman just about wrecked me. Going toe-to-toe with talent is not my forte. I assume that people who get to make a film are (a) doggone lucky and (b) doing this job because they want to do it. The rest of the world may be struggling with god-awful tasks such as mining coal, but here the pay is good, you're seeing the world, and you're telling a story. What could there be to act up about? Of course this is a wild oversimplification, but it does contain some truth, and that made it hard for me to understand Hackman's attitude, though I understood that three pictures back-to-back before mine had exhausted him. The only result of our inability to work in harness was that I dropped twenty pounds and lived on Valium.

In truth, I didn't know what I was doing and I felt bad, especially for Barysh-nikov, who had shown up in good faith; bad, too, for MGM, who had jumped at the chance to finance a film with such promising "elements." At one point Hackman and I found ourselves sitting together in a jail cell in Maryland, wait-ing for the crew to show up and film a scene set there. "Well," he allowed, "I've behaved badly on a bunch of films but I've got to admit, this one takes the cake."

It was certainly memorable to be in Berlin during this period of convul-sive change. One week you had to go through the notorious Checkpoint Char-lie to get into bullet-pocked (from World War II!) East Berlin; the next week, you just sped past a bunch of broken windows where Checkpoint Charlie had stood. The world was changing.

There were a couple of sequences in *Company Business* of which I was proud, notably the tense spy swap sequence in the Berlin subway—but iso-lated sequences do not a good film make. A great movie is great from start to finish. *Company Business*, alas, did not come close.

Struggling with Ron in our cutting rooms outside London to make sense of virtually unusable footage, I welcomed the distraction of an invitation from Frank Mancuso and Martin Davis for lunch at Claridge's. The topic: *Star Trek VI*.

STAR TREK VI:
THE UNDISCOVERED COUNTRY

Over a suitably elegant repast and clanking, heavy cutlery, Mancuso and Davis asked if I would be interested in writing and directing the last *Star Trek* film to utilize the original cast. By this time the new television series, *Star Trek: The Next Generation*, was a hit, and Patrick Stewart and friends were waiting in the wings to make their *Star Trek* feature debuts. But the studio was, as Mancuso put it, disinclined "to go out with *Star Trek V*," a film in which they were frankly disappointed. As I understood him, it wasn't merely the film's economic performance about which he was speaking. I took him to mean it was a matter of pride to the studio to end the original cast's contribution on a more successful note critically as well as commercially.

Or perhaps that was the explanation calculated to appeal to a creative person. Perhaps they merely thought they could hedge their bets by squeezing one more film out of the surefire old hands before turning them out to pasture. Or am I being cynical?

"We're talking around thirty million dollars," Mancuso said.

I had no idea for another *Star Trek* movie but following my devastating experience on *Company Business*, I wished I did. The cozy familiarity of the *Star Trek* family seemed very appealing after what I'd just gone through.

I agreed that thirty million was feasible and further agreed to meet with Leonard Nimoy, who would function as executive producer, to see if we could cook up a story while I took a two-week summer breather on Cape Cod.

In my excitement at being thus wooed, I neglected to inquire where Harve Bennett fit into the plan. I would have been—as I subsequently was—distressed to learn that not only would he not be a participant but that he had left the Paramount lot under bitter circumstances, as he later recounted to me.

For the previous year, preoccupied as they were with internecine power struggles within the studio, Paramount encouraged Bennett to develop and revise his own proposal for a sixth *Star Trek* movie, one that featured young Kirk, young Spock, et al., during their early days at the Starfleet Academy.

Having strung Bennett along month after month, Paramount abruptly stipulated that he produce yet another film with the old cast first and then (maybe) they would move on to his young *Trek* story. Bennett was furious that the studio had thus unceremoniously abandoned his laboriously worked-out idea in favor of that last squeeze of the orange, as proposed to me at Claridge's. Feeling betrayed, Bennett left the studio. His complaint was not that Paramount had decided in favor of another approach but rather the amount of time they had allowed him to work under the delusion that they were seriously entertaining his. Someone observed that the chief problem in Hollywood is behavior. Paramount's treatment of the man who had saved the franchise for them over the course of five movies, making who knows how much money for the studio in the process, seemed graceless at best. (It is interesting to note that the 2009 *Star Trek* movie, directed by J. J. Abrams, deals with precisely Bennett's conceit: young Kirk and Spock.)

A month or so after my luncheon at Claridge's, Nimoy, a native of Boston and currently visiting his hometown, flew twenty minutes across Massachusetts Bay to spend the day with me in Provincetown. At low tide we ambled up and down the beach as Nimoy talked and I listened.

"*Star Trek* has always reflected current events," he began, pointing out that the alien Klingon race had always been *Trek*'s stand-in for the Russians, whose empire, even as we spoke, was crumbling like Alka-Seltzer. Reflecting on the collapse of the Berlin Wall and the Soviet Union, he mused: "What about a story where the wall comes down in outer space? What is the United States without the Soviet Union? Who am I if I have no enemy to define me?"

This was all I needed. I don't get ideas on my own, but typically with me all you need do is prime the pump.

"Right," I jumped in. "We start with a massive Chernobyl-type explosion in outer space. A Klingon moon has been destroyed, maybe ending their oxygen or energy supply—it's going to be like East Berliners streaming over the places where the Wall used to be unless there's a treaty. The Klingon Chancellor is coming to meet with the Federation to discuss the peace. It's a brave new world, and Kirk is assigned to escort the Klingon chief through Federation space to the conference. But Kirk hates Klingons because they killed his son (see *Star Trek III*) and he botches the job. The Chancellor is assassinated; Kirk takes the rap at a Klingon show trial (nifty alien courtroom scene here) and is exiled to a sand planet from which he must escape (think POW escape movie) and track down the real killers (Agatha Christie locked room mystery potential here) before more havoc occurs at the peace conference—or something like that. . . ."

Did it all come together that fast? Maybe not, but we did hammer out the basic story on the beach, after which Nimoy returned to California and I took my family back to London.

Things got weird shortly thereafter. Although Paramount approved our story idea, Nimoy called me in London a few weeks following our meeting to report that the studio had hired two other writers to write the screenplay of the story we had concocted.

Why on earth? I pondered this with him over the phone, but the one suspicion I had didn't make sense so I didn't say it aloud.

Maybe they were trying to save money? Over a *script*? It seemed penny-wise and pound-foolish. Were these writers less costly than Paramount knew me to be? (My fees as part of my on-the-lot contract were established and well known to Business Affairs.)

I was not unaware that the feature division of the studio was in trouble and had been hemorrhaging red ink for over a year, making films that lost money at forty million a pop. I knew this could not go on indefinitely and could almost hear the band tuning up for the next round of musical chairs.

In fact, the explanation was rather different. The executive in charge of *Star Trek VI* (as yet untitled) had two writers under contract to be paid for a picture—any picture—and he hadn't been able to find them one.

My deal called for me to be paid only *if* I worked, whereas these two would be owed money regardless.

No contest . . .

But Paramount's problems were small compared to those of my assistant. I got a strained phone call from Denny to tell me he had been diagnosed with cancer; a growth in his mouth, of all places. Denny, a health nut who exercised and had never smoked, would be in for the fight of his life.

And I couldn't think of a single way to be of help. The screenplay dilemma abruptly took a back place in my thoughts. In any case, there was seemingly nothing to be done except to sit tight and wait for the script I was supposed to direct and Nimoy to executive produce.

In the meantime, and from long distance, I kept track of Denny's progress and tried as well to stay in touch with his state of mind. The person next to you has just been struck by lightning. Your move. It is uniquely horrible to have someone you care deeply for in the fight of his life, and all you can do is hold his coat. If that.

A few weeks later there was more news on the screenplay front: "The boys are having a little trouble getting started," I was told, I can't remember by whom.

"Send them to London, and I'll talk them through it," I offered, eager to get on with things, and shortly one of them showed up, a pleasant enough fellow. He sat in my living room with a legal pad on his lap and took copious notes over three days while I led him step by step through the story, which had by now grown more detailed, as I'd had over a month to daydream about it.

When Nimoy learned that I had met the young man in London, he was furious that I had discussed "his" story without his knowledge or consent. I was surprised at his reaction because (a) I assumed that, as executive producer, he had been told of this plan (though given Paramount's convulsions at the time, it latterly made perfect sense that they hadn't bothered; see notes on behavior, above); (b) like Harve Bennett, I was now the one with an overall deal and an obligation to be helpful to the studio that had contracted me; and lastly (c) it had not occurred to me that Nimoy viewed the story as solely his.

While there could be no doubt that he had shown up on the Cape with the general thematic idea, we had (or at least it seemed to me)—walking up and down the beach—fleshed out the many if not most of the subsequent details jointly. But I learned none of this festering indignation until later.

In the end the script by the two prepaid authors went the way of *Star Trek IV*'s first draft, and I was asked to write the thing myself, again without consulting the discarded version.

By this point, I was mainly thinking about Denny. I now asked Paramount to hire us as a writing team for *Star Trek VI*, which I had already subtitled (once again!) *The Undiscovered Country*. I wasn't doing Denny a favor; he was a terrific writer, great with structure and witty dialogue. Why not?

By this point the studio was open to anything and didn't even blink at my request. They hired, as well, my long-time producing partner, Steven-Charles Jaffe, who had worked with me since *Time After Time*.

The question of postproduction (where the film was to be edited, the sound mixed, etc.) was left open. I wanted to finish the picture at home in London so as to be with my family. The studio tap-danced and said they would take this idea under advisement.

SCRIPT

Star Trek VI must have been the first screenplay written in collaboration using e-mail, with Denny and I bouncing drafts back and forth through cyberspace from LA to London. He was feeling wretched from the chemo and radiation he was forced to undergo but he had the constitution of an ox thanks to a life of dance, and the responsibility for delivering kept him from obsessing about his situation. It kept me from obsessing as well.

We showed the script to Paramount and to Nimoy, and Paramount sent me an enthusiastic memo along with some notes. I forwarded their enthusiasm to Nimoy but omitted their notes, preferring to let him reach his own independent conclusions. He later interpreted this as duplicity on my part—another black mark against me. I would have been wiser to tell him what I had done and why.

In the event, Nimoy didn't need any help from Paramount. He liked what he read but kept pushing us to make improvements. We were circling around a promising dramatic situation and then, in his view, failing to exploit it. In the story Spock has a new Vulcan protégée, Lieutenant Valeris. Originally we had hoped to lure Kirstie Alley back to reprise her character as Saavik—her backstory from the other films would have made this especially poignant—but once again she declined.

In our tale it turns out the Klingon Chancellor Gorkon (as close as Denny dared come to the name Gorbachev) is assassinated by a conspiracy consisting of Klingons and Federation members *working together* to preserve the eye-for-an-eye, cold war status quo. Better the devil you know than the "undiscovered country," which, in this instance was an uncertain future with no cold war or cold warriors left.

The newly introduced character of Valeris proves to be one of the chief conspirators. Nimoy wanted a scene where, if she's really true to her beliefs, she must shoot her mentor after she is unmasked by him. He chuckled as he described the "shoot, if you must, this old gray head" moment he was searching for. He was a keen and clever contributor to the final draft, never satisfied with what was facile or glib. In this as in other aspects of the script, Nimoy's experience as an actor, director, and producer prevented us from getting too pleased with ourselves and kept us on our toes, always searching to see if we had mined the material for all its potential, always probing and pushing to see if we had found all that was there.

It did not escape my notice that *The Undiscovered Country*, with its deliberate parallels to the collapsing Soviet Union and what conservative Harvard political philosopher Francis Fukuyama called "the end of history," was essentially another attempt (by me) to make a film about the demise of the USSR and the brave new post cold war world we were allegedly entering. *Company Business* had simply been a more literal version of the same movie. I could only hope the science fiction riff would turn out better than its earthbound (in every sense) predecessor.

Villains are always important in space operas, and in Khan we had created a tough act to follow. It was during this period that I spent a fair amount of recreational time listening to a new Chandos CD I had bought of Christopher Plummer declaiming passages from *Henry V*, accompanied by a fresh, stereophonic performance of William Walton's score for the Olivier film. Plummer's thrilling performance completely captivated me. For the first time that I can recall (other than for the members of the *Star Trek* cast), I tailored a role with a specific actor in mind. God knows what I would have done if we hadn't landed him. I dreamed of being around Plummer and hearing him spout Shakespeare with that trumpet voice. But how to get him to do it? All I could think of was using Shakespeare's words and sticking them in my villain's mouth. I found myself recalling the story of Nazis who claimed you had never heard Shakespeare until you had heard him in the "original (*sic*) German." (This isn't as kooky as it sounds; Shakespeare in German is a lot better than Shakespeare in French.) I thought: *You have never heard Shakespeare until you have heard him in the original Klingon.* Thus the jovial but deadly General Chang was born.

Another aspect of the story posed a really provocative problem: How do you assassinate somebody in space? There are a million pedestrian ways to do so—guns, poison, knives, bombs, etc.—but what form of dispatch would be unique to the context of space?

Where do creative ideas come from, anyway? A question more asked than answered, in all likelihood. It is easier to describe *where* ideas originate than *why* or *how*. My own ideas tend to come infrequently and when I'm not expecting them. They come, like sleep, when I let go. I don't fall asleep by clenching closed my eyes and insisting on unconsciousness; I fall asleep when I relax. Similarly, I get ideas when I let go, when I'm thinking of or doing something else, usually something manual like the laundry, rewiring a lamp, or building a model boat. I get ideas when I am falling asleep or when I'm waking up. I get them while driving miles of boring freeway with the radio turned off; I get them sitting in the tub and watching my toes turn into prunes. I know that I have a problem to solve—in this case, a writing problem revolving around an assassination in space. Whether I stay with this consciously, insisting on an answer (clenching my eyes to fall asleep), or whether I "forget" about it while doing the laundry, some part of my brain will continue to fiddle with the task at hand . . . and then the solution will "leak" out into my consciousness.

An assassination in space . . . I don't know what I was doing when I found myself wondering—not for the first time, as it happens—about footage I had seen of the space station and astronauts aboard various shuttles. They were always weightless, which looked like a lot of fun to me.

But in all space operas there is always gravity (pardon the expression) on those space vessels. How to account for this? Evidently, there is a centrifuge or some such device on board each vessel that simulates gravity. That being the case, how is it that in the battles between spaceships, this gravity device is never hit and put out of action?

What would happen if it were? Everything and everyone not secured would simply float. Haven't you ever wondered why no chair on the bridge of the *Enterprise* has seat belts? Because people wouldn't go flying around during explosions if they did. (Planets are another matter—there's simply no accounting for the fact that in these selfsame space movies, all planets have earth's gravity.)

This was starting to interest me. I posited a pair of assassins who, having shot out the gravity device aboard Gorkon's flagship, now beam aboard in magnetic boots and make their way through helpless, floating Klingon secret service details (imagine their ray guns levitating from their holsters, just out of reach!). The killers eventually make their way to the hapless, floating Chancellor Gorkon. When he's hit, his blood (what color, what color??) will float in the stillness as motionless *bubbles!*

I was giving myself goose bumps. Thus far, I was thinking in my role as screenwriter. Now I felt a tap on my shoulder from my alter ego, the director, demanding to know how the hell I thought an effect of floating blood bubbles (of *any* color) was going to be achieved.

I told the director to get lost. *It's the movies,* I comforted myself. *In movies, you can do anything. This isn't the moment to pull your punches.*

So I kept writing the most fanciful version of the sequence I could imagine and decided I would worry about how to execute it down the road. As it happened, recent technological advances of which I was then unaware would, in the end, make my floating blood simpler than I dreaded.

Eventually we had our draft, and the studio was pleased. David Kirkpatrick was now in the driver's seat (President of the Motion Picture Group of Paramount Pictures—these titles!), and his only comment was that he was tired of sand planets, so with the help of my trusty computer, the desert planet gulag where Kirk (and now Dr. McCoy as well) are exiled became an *ice* planet.

BATTLE OF THE BUDGET

The year 1990 was ending. My wife and I—now with a second daughter—took a six-month lease on a house in Beverly Hills. In January of 1991 we showed up in Los Angeles, and on January 4, my team, consisting of Nimoy, Ralph Winter, Steve Jaffe, and myself, sat down in Gary Lucchesi's office to "confab" with him, David Kirkpatrick, and John Goldwyn, the junior exec to whom the film had been assigned.

After the requisite smiles and glad-handing, Kirkpatrick began the meeting.

"Now, we're talking about twenty-five million dollars," he commenced, when my hand shot into the air.

"Excuse me, David, but we're talking about *thirty* million dollars. That is the figure Frank [Mancuso] mentioned at my lunch with him and that is the figure I agreed to. That is the figure that brought me to LA."

Kirkpatrick frowned and reiterated the figure was twenty-five million, that Frank had a "vision," which in turn was based on a formula, which derived from the calculation of how much money a *Star Trek* movie could make domestically and internationally (much less; *Star Trek* was a failure in France—the result of a penny-pinching decision years earlier to use the Canadian French Québécois dub of the original TV series, rendering it laughable in France, etc.).

"David," I interjected, knowing perfectly well that it was the feature division's continued wretched performance in the months between my lunch at Claridge's and this present meeting that was responsible for lowering the budget on our film, "let me explain why the film cannot be made for twenty-five million dollars.

"You have fourteen million dollars *above the line,* for starters. ['Above the line' refers to costs of starring cast, writer, director, producer, etc.] You have to pay for Shatner, Nimoy, and all the rest of the *Enterprise* crew, and this comes to fourteen million dollars. You have four and a half million dollars in special effects. This is the same effects budget as *Star Trek V,* two years ago, but I'll live with it. That brings us to eighteen and a half million dollars."

Their faces were clouding over.

"Then," I concluded, "you have two and a half million dollars in postproduction [editing, music, etc.], which brings us to a grand total of twenty-one million dollars, leaving only four million dollars to make an outer space sci-fi extravaganza. Where's the movie going to come from?"

Dead silence greeted this calculation. I could sense the execs wanting to trade looks but not quite daring to.

Finally Kirkpatrick spoke. "Would you please excuse us for a few minutes?" His team withdrew into his office across the hall, leaving us to twiddle our thumbs. Ten minutes passed. Then twenty. Eventually they returned, their faces as expressionless as jurors reentering the courtroom with a murder verdict.

"Twenty-seven million," Kirkpatrick stated without preamble or embellishment.

"David," I responded, trying to keep the panic out of my voice (how could I have been so foolish as to move bag and baggage to LA for six months without having an agreed-upon budget?), "you are under a misapprehension. I am not negotiating. I am giving you reality."

I now spread out the top sheets (budget totals) of every *Star Trek* movie for their perusal. I was mightily annoyed; numbers was supposed to be their department. I was supposed to be the "creative" person; why was I having to take them through figures they should have researched long before this meeting?

"Please note: *Star Trek: The Motion Picture*, 1979, cost forty-five million dollars. *Star Trek II: The Wrath of Khan*, 1982, cost eleven point two million. From then on, each successive *Star Trek* film—numbers three, four, and five—cost forty-one percent more than its predecessor.

"The only exceptions were *The Wrath of Khan*, made by me, which cost only twenty-five percent of the first film's budget, and the one I am now proposing to direct for you, which will cost exactly the same as its predecessor, *Star Trek V*, namely thirty million dollars. Allowing for inflation over two years' time, it will actually cost less than *V*, but the figure will remain thirty million. You cannot get blood from a stone."

But you can get stony silence. Then came the hurt accusations. I was not being a team player, I was inflexible, I was noncooperative, etc. I listened to this until I lost my temper.

"This is pointless and graceless," I said, standing. "I will meet with Frank Mancuso and give him the same facts and figures I've given you. Let him make up his own mind."

Which is what I did. Frank, courteous, even courtly, heard me out in respectful silence some days later in his office. I produced all the numbers and took him slowly, carefully through the process, explaining the nuts and bolts of making a *Star Trek* movie in 1990.

"Obviously," I concluded, pleased with my performance, "this is entirely your decision. I just wanted you to have all the facts from the horse's mouth."

He shook my hand in a most civil manner and thanked me for my comprehensive explanation. I left, feeling I had made the situation perfectly clear.

He then canceled the film.

I can't remember who gave me the news, but it came at the end of a day, and I only recall being stunned. While I had recognized intellectually that this decision was a distinct possibility, once the boom had actually been lowered, it sucked the wind right out of my sails. I subsided into my chair and tried to think.

But nothing came. I would have to drive to Beverly Hills and explain to

Lauren that we were stranded high and dry in Los Angeles, tethered to our house lease with no earnings in sight.

I wandered over to Gary Lucchesi's office in the administration building and sat on the floor in his office, my eyes filled with tears, my back literally to the wall. Gary looked at me not unkindly. He's an old and dear friend, but he's a realist. I had taken a gamble and lost. "If you want love, go home," he advised me. So in the end, I did.

It was a melancholy evening, made palatable by only the cheerful un-awareness of our daughters, whose smiles and laughter took away some of the sting, though not all.

The next day I returned to my office to pack my things, after which I strolled around the lot in a kind of daze. I cannot now remember when or from whom I heard the improbable rumor floating across the lot that Frank Mancuso had lost his job, but I do recall vividly what happened next: I was standing in the middle of Stage 5, which we were to have used, taking a last, silent look, when the stage phone rang. Bizarre, I thought. Seeing no one else to answer it, I picked up.

On the other end of the line I heard Stanley Jaffe tell me that he and his producing partner, Sherry Lansing, were now running the studio.

"Kid"—it was always "kid"—"I hear you have problems," Stanley said, after giving me the chance to digest his news.

"I need two and a half million dollars," I explained.

"You got it," was his answer, and *Star Trek VI* was back on again. I don't know how long I stayed on that empty stage before I began to move, slowly at first, then breaking into a run back to my office, still located in the Marx Brothers Building.

I started calling people, beginning with my wife, and relating the improb-able deus ex machina that had rescued the film, shaking my head in disbe-lief every time I delivered my news. Stanley Jaffe, my friend and supporter since my work on *Fatal Attraction*. He was bold and decisive. Sometimes pro, sometimes con. Today was pro. Like Tanen, an experienced hand at running a studio (Jaffe had headed Paramount when he was in his twenties, his father having run Columbia), Stanley knew what the feature division needed: a hit. *Star Trek* had been halfway backed out of the starting gate when he pushed the buzzer and we were back in again, running forward, full tilt out the other side.

I've since heard it said that we got the money because Stanley's son, Steven-Charles Jaffe, was my producing partner.

As I mentioned earlier, Steven-Charles Jaffe is no relation to Stanley Jaffe.

PREP–CASTING

There were other obstacles to overcome, among them the fact of our film's being the sixth in a series that was generally perceived to be played out. The critical drubbing received by its predecessor seemed to epitomize the conventional wisdom. *Star Trek VI* had a credibility problem; no one was taking us seriously. No one was going to be in a great hurry to take part in the flaccid continuation of a moribund *Enterprise*.

The possibility of this perception and the accompanying resistance to participation in the film had not occurred to me. I thought the script Denny and I had written was terrific: complicated and ambitious, managing to deliver the *Star Trek* goods (it featured an assassination in weightless space, for heaven's sake), as well as examining the post-Soviet world and its effects on inhabitants who had lived eye to unblinking eye for over half a century. Denny, who had by now thankfully almost completely recovered from his bout with cancer, was of the same sanguine view. There was, at the same time, something niggling at my brain connected with all this doom and gloom. Where had I heard all this before? Of course: when I had first reported for work on *Star Trek II*. It was funny how I always seemed to come up in the same position in the batting order.

I learned around this time that my floating blood would be a relatively simple effect to produce, thanks to advances in computer-generated imagery or, more familiarly, CGI. The more I studied this new phenomenon, visiting once more with the magicians of San Mateo, the more intrigued I became with its possibilities. The technique had come a long way from its stylized use in Carol Marcus's Genesis Planet proposal from *Star Trek II.* Used properly, the images it produced could easily pass for reality.

One person who believed utterly in the movie from the get-go was our casting director, Mary Jo Slater. She never treated it like the hand-me-down or leftover others saw. The script worked and this was a movie she wanted to see. By happy coincidence, her son, Christian, was an avid Trekker and desperate to be in the film, which we took to be a good sign. Comedian and actress Whoopi Goldberg was equally enthusiastic, and I met with her to discuss the possibility of her playing a Klingon princess. This idea, however, was vetoed by Nimoy, who felt—perhaps rightly—that a supporting cast of stars might detract from the farewell appearance of the *Enterprise* crew. (Later, Goldberg showed up as a regular on *Star Trek: The Next Generation.*)

Nimoy understood, however, that our villain needed to be top drawer. For the Shakespeare-spouting General Chang, there was only one actor possible, and I begged Mary Jo not to come back without Christopher Plummer, the actor for whom I had written the role. Mary Jo took off for Plummer like a pedigreed foxhound and returned almost bearing the prize in gleaming teeth. "Just don't bury me under a ton of makeup so I can't act," was his only request.

Nimoy also saw the logic of a name actor of talent and presence to play Gorkon, our Gorbachev/Lincolnesque Klingon Chancellor, who foresees a brave, new, and peaceful world and who is assassinated for his vision. Parallels with the real world abounded—not only was Lincoln murdered after espousing a policy of reconciliation with the defeated South but, more recently, the Irish patriot Michael Collins had been killed by his own men for failing to obtain sufficient territory from Northern Ireland for the new republic, and Gandhi had been shot by his Hindu followers for agreeing to Partition and the creation of Pakistan. Anwar Sadat was slain by his own troops for recognizing and visiting Israel; Israeli Prime Minister Yitzhak Rabin was killed by an extremist Israeli for signing the Oslo accords and shaking hands with Arafat.

David Warner, the famous postwar *Hamlet* and oleaginous Mr. Blifil of *Tom Jones*, had played Jack the Ripper in *Time After Time*. He seemed perfect for Gorkon, and I cast him, failing to remember—or never knowing—that he had appeared in *Star Trek V* (in a very different role), thus making Warner the only actor to play two different parts in the original *Star Trek* feature series.

A more difficult role was that of the treacherous but oddly sympathetic Vulcan lieutenant, Valeris, who would betray Spock and the Federation. Valeris would later, at her court-martial, quote Kirk's own words regarding Klingons ("They're animals! Don't trust them! Don't believe them!") in support of her actions. Regarding her complicity in Gorkon's murder, she would, like Brünnhilde pleading with her father Wotan in *Die Walküre*, demand of Kirk, "Did I misinterpret you?" (Coming from Valeris, admittedly, her plea is more an ironic taunt.)

As I have noted, in an ideal world Valeris should have been the stalwart Saavik, a character we had already come to love. And trust. This would have sharpened the pain of her betrayal, but absent Kirstie Alley, we decided it would be better to introduce a new character. We read a lot of actresses searching for that elusive quality that was at once alien, opaque, funny in its humorlessness, and yet touching because of its vulnerability. Valeris doesn't know how to express her misgivings about the peace conference to her mentor, Spock. She can't give voice to her own fears about the coming rapprochement with the Federation's lifelong enemies, and Spock, sounding a bit like Polonious, shuts her down. "You must have faith, lieutenant," he admonishes. "Faith?" echoes the bewildered Vulcan. "That the universe will unfold as it should," Spock concludes, sententiously, leaving her to her expanding terror of an unknown future in the wake of disarmament.

Kim Cattrall nailed the part and understood it so perfectly that any regrets over the loss of Saavik in the story were forgotten.

But I remained intrigued by the idea of a character from previous *Star Trek* adventures, someone we had come to trust, turning out to be one of the conspirators. I settled on Admiral Cartwright, already portrayed by the intensely sympathetic Brock Peters in *Star Trek IV*. Peters, also an accomplished singer, had played villains before, notably in *The Pawnbroker*, but as far as *Star Trek* audiences were concerned, he was Federation true blue. His racist denunciation of Klingons—akin to Kirk's own views—would be especially unnerving as Peters was an African American, and all the slurs against Klingons that he lays out at the Starfleet briefing are queasily akin to anti-black epithets from planet Earth centuries earlier. (In fact Peters's big racist speech was so repugnant to him that he experienced great difficulty memorizing it; I had to film it in sections.)

RODDENBERRY

There was one other party who took the gravest possible exception to Cartwright's sentiments, and that was *Star Trek*'s creator, Gene Roddenberry. Roddenberry's deal on the *Star Trek* movies called for him to receive a credit ("Based on *Star Trek* created by Gene Roddenberry") and, I assume, a salary and profit participation, but it did not include actual involvement in making the movies after *Star Trek: The Motion Picture*.

Nonetheless, there had evolved the tradition of kissing the ring, obtaining Roddenberry's blessing for each of the successive films and giving ear to his opinions. I didn't recall doing so on *Star Trek II*, when our contact was limited to a brief meeting at which we shook hands; but now, a decade and five features later, an audience had become part of the process.

In the case of *The Undiscovered Country*, Roddenberry's opinions were many and heated. He was pained and angered by the script, which depicted bigotry not only among Starfleet brass like Cartwright but also among the *Enterprise* crew, not merely Kirk (whose prejudice might be excused as being related to the death of his son at the hands of Klingons), but even ordinary Able Seamen aboard the ship complained of how Klingons "all look alike" and alluded to the aliens' distinctive odor.

I could advance explanations for what followed. I had been through the ringer on this film from the moment we had sat down in Kirkpatrick's office in early January. We hadn't even called *Action!* and I was already stressed and exhausted trying to make thirty million dollars into thirty-three. For monetary reasons we'd had to junk Denny's nifty prologue, in which the crew of the *Enterprise*, now retired, had gone their myriad post-Starfleet ways, only to be summoned back into harness for one last mission. (Uhura, I seem to remember, had her own intergalactic radio call-in show.) Salary cuts, FX cuts, wardrobe cuts (I had asked for Starfleet uniforms with pants pockets, but no)—all had taken their toll. Instead of making the film, I had been spending far too much time trying to figure out how it would be *possible* to make the film.

Nonetheless explanations are not excuses. There was no excuse for my tactless and impatient handling of Gene Roddenberry when I finally sat down to meet with this big, tired man in his offices, our respective henchmen hovering silently on the sidelines as the conversation degenerated into barely disguised acrimony. I suppose underneath it all was a conviction on my part that Roddenberry's was a specious utopian vision for which there was no historical evidence. Did he really believe in the perfectibility of man, or (as I suspected) was this just some sort of pose? I was cynical, maybe because somewhere along the line, I'd learned that Frank Capra was a Republican. I found myself straining against the shape of the *Star Trek* bottle, rewriting the words of the Mass, not merely altering the music. These were big no-nos, but I mulishly persisted, straying off the Federation reservation and not caring whether I ever found my way back to the Neutral Zone. Against Roddenberry's complaints, I dug in my heels. Where was there any evidence, I wanted to know, that bigotry had disappeared—or would disappear—in human affairs? Was racism still not a powerful force in America? Were the Serbs and Croats not intent on "ethnic cleansing"? Were not Muslims still fighting Christians? Had it not always been thus since the beginnings of man? What, I demanded, was the justification for Roddenberry's optimism? The evidence of millennia was on my side. In the meantime, I insisted, in my movie people would continue to act like human beings.

It was not, as I say, my finest hour. Roddenberry was old and in ill health, soon to die. The fact that I was tired and unwilling to revisit the screenplay when it was almost time to start shooting was of less moment than my conviction that what was in the script was correct. I left the meeting and returned to work, leaving others to mop up the damage I had done. I like to think of myself as a decent, straight-shooting person but as I write these lines, I have to admit that I am not always the person I like to believe I am.

FILMING

Shortly before we started shooting, shooting of a different character began. The first Gulf War (we didn't realize then that there would be more than one) broke out and distracted us with events "back on earth." Iraq had invaded Kuwait, Saddam Hussein having been convinced that the United States would not interfere. It was a sobering time; wars, as every generation seems fated to relearn, are easier to start than to stop. Who knew where this one would lead? But there was little to do except watch the news and continue with our work.

At any rate, that's what I told myself at the time. The odd thing about making a movie is that events beyond the film suddenly seem relevant only to the degree that they can affect the film, rendering it irrelevant or suddenly conferring it with additional resonance. As the director, you develop tunnel vision, distilling outside information through the obsessive prism of what's good or bad for the movie never mind about the world. When I made *Company Business*, rapidly unfolding international events constantly caused me to revise the script in an effort to stay au courant. I realized that with *Star Trek VI* we faced potentially the same task. After all, there had been no coup or assassination as yet in the Soviet Union, but what if there were . . . ? The Three Mile Island nuclear accident had been "good" for *The China Syndrome* as, before too long, events in the Soviet Union would be perceived as "good" for *Star Trek VI*.

Meantime, as was usual with my underfunded *Star Trek* movies, I continued to exhaust myself trying to find ways to skin the cat. I could not afford Jerry Goldsmith to write our score; I couldn't even afford James Horner, who had risen in prominence (and price) in the years since *The Wrath of Khan*. With what we had for music in our budget, perhaps I ought to play the kazoo.

I was back to listening to demo tapes and, as so many times before, disheartened by what I heard. I wondered whether there wasn't some existing piece I knew that depicted stars or the heavens. I sat up when I remembered Holst's *The Planets*. Now here, I told myself, was a very classy idea: Get someone to arrange Holst for *Star Trek VI*. I began listening to *The Planets* and fell in love with my idea: The granddaddy of all outer space music would finally be used where it belonged, in a space opera. (I knew that Holst's music was intended as illustrative of astrological rather than planetary symbols, but who cared?) The music department at Paramount, when I explained my idea and played them some selections, had no objections. Had they ever heard of Holst?

Throughout the making of *Star Trek VI* the Paramount front office continued its state of seismic convulsions, which had at least one happy effect: The players were so concentrated on their jobs that our film was more or less left to its own devices. The movie was in the nominal charge of a capable, young executive, John Goldwyn, who, I gathered, had more important things on his mind.

At any rate we gave him scant cause for alarm. The people making this film were old hands, a team that had done this kind of thing before. True, Harve Bennett was not around, and I, for one, missed his warmth and analytic intelligence, but there was Denny and my long-time editor, Ron Roose, as well as Marty Hornstein, who would go on to become a regular *Star Trek* feature film producer.

The weightless space assassination was storyboarded and largely filmed by Steven-Charles Jaffe, working the second unit. Corridors in the Klingon vessel, originally built on the horizontal, had been designed by production designer Herman Zimmerman (now also a *Star Trek* vet from the series *Next Generation* and *Deep Space Nine*), in such a fashion that they would be lifted, like towers, into vertical configurations. Then we could dangle helpless Klingons at the ends of long ropes within the towers, "floating" helplessly as the assassins in their magnetic boots blew them away. Later, CGI techniques would be employed by ILM to erase the ropes.

There was a debate over the color of blood, which I wanted to be different than human blood. I wound up choosing a pink shade that seemed suitably weird, only to regret my choice down the road when I realized it reminded me of Pepto-Bismol.

The ice planet presented a different set of problems. Having no time in our ridiculously tight schedule to travel to the glaciers of Alaska for our exteriors, we dispatched Steve Jaffe and his second unit there, with stunt doubles for Kirk and McCoy, again to cover material specific to my carefully worked-out storyboards. The rest of the ice gulag would be filmed on soundstages.

I found many differences between shooting *Star Trek II* in 1981 and *Star Trek VI* ten years later. And while many of these differences were of a technological character—primarily, conspicuous advances in special effects, as I have noted—others were more unnerving. Security on sets had become progressively tighter. Because of the high incidents of theft—props and entire sets had been known to vanish—all members of the cast and crew were now required to wear identifying badges, complete with the wearer's photo, in what proved a largely futile effort to stem the flow of contraband from the Paramount lot. (Piracy had also become endemic to films themselves, which were frequently released abroad before they'd even been finished at home. Illegal video and DVD reproduction has caused horrific economic damage to studios and filmmakers alike.)

Star Trek VI was always short of everything. I had asked for knee-high snow for the soundstage version of the ice planet; there was barely enough to cover anyone's feet, so that shots had to be redesigned to make the stuff look deeper than it was. Sets had curtains where there were no walls. Art, as I have suggested, thrives on restrictions but it can't thrive on nothing. When the costumes never turned up for the murder of Cassio in Orson Welles's *Othello*, he brilliantly staged the sequence in a Turkish bath, but I could hardly stage all of *Star Trek VI* in a similar location.

Some sequences worked out amazingly. The weightless assassination pleased me very much, as did the gulag mines where prisoners were forced into hard labor with light-emitting helmets far below ground on railroad cars. It looked like hell, it sounded like hell, but it was only Bronson Canyon, just up the street from Paramount where they used to film episodes of *Highway Patrol* and, for all I know, *The Lone Ranger*. We could have traveled halfway around the world, and the result would have been no better.

Goldwyn was nervous nonetheless. His characteristic mantra was, "I think we have a problem," to which my auto-reply always was, "No, we don't."

Sometimes, he was right. On the day we filmed the scene where Kirk's crew sits down to a formal banquet for the Klingon delegation in the officers' mess aboard the *Enterprise* ("Guess who's coming to dinner," in Denny's clever line), we had visitors from the Holst estate. As part of their meeting with the Paramount legal department, we invited them to visit the set, where I went out of my way to treat them like royalty.

We were in the middle of an enjoyable though complicated sequence. I have always had a weakness for blue food, probably because—aside from blueberries—very little exists. So I had decreed that all the food served for the occasion (including the infamous, forbidden Romulan ale) be blue. The actors were understandably reluctant to eat any blue seafood or pasta, so the Holst delegation was treated to the spectacle of the director pulling out his wallet and offering ten bucks a bite to Kirk & Co. And of course, being actors, they chowed down for bucks, to the amusement of Gustav's representatives. There must have been close to twenty diners in the sequence, so we had to keep photographing the scene over and over to cover all the participants.

This was also the scene wherein Chang recites part of Hamlet's soliloquy "in the original Klingon." Some may be surprised to learn that Klingon is an actual language, concocted by Marc Okrand, a linguist hired by Paramount to develop the Vulcan and Klingon languages, and it comes complete with its own dictionary. However, "To be or not to be" in Klingon posed a problem not only for the redoubtable Chris Plummer but for Okrand himself, who, in creating the language, had long ago decided there would be no verb for "being"; hence, "to be" would be impossible to utter in Klingon (just as

I am told that there is, for example, no word for "foot" in Russian). More recently, on the Internet, it is possible to watch excerpts of *Hamlet,* performed in Klingon.

But in the end, as I understood it, the Paramount legal department wanted all rights to *The Planets* in something like perpetuity with permission—I wouldn't put it past them—to reorchestrate and use the music for whatever else they liked. *The Planets* is the cash cow of the Holst estate (there must be at least forty different recordings of the piece), and there was no way that it was ever going to agree to give away its crown jewel.

So much for my Holst idea. It was back to the drawing board— and those tedious demo tapes. To speed the process along I gave a bunch of them to my editor, Ron Roose, who had a musical background.

The actual shooting of the film proceeded smoothly, with only the usual hiccups. The celebrated Somali supermodel, Iman, who played a yellow-eyed shape-shifter in the gulag, had the flu and bravely soldiered through her scenes, deep kissing the imprisoned Kirk (who did not, thankfully, succumb to the illness); Plummer's Klingon makeup did get wearying for him as the day went on; Nimoy felt I was missing close-ups of him. I was, and had to go back for them.

With Plummer the problem was that no movie screen could contain him. He was truly a theater actor, larger than life before any camera ever rolled. He was well aware of this propensity and always at pains to make his performance as "small" as possible. Still, this was hard to do when he had to deliver a line like, "Cry, 'havoc!' and let slip the dogs of war!" Nonetheless, he forged his own version of a *Star Trek* villain. Instead of a wild-eyed raver like most of the *Star Trek* rogues' gallery, Chang didn't even boast two eyes (one had a steel patch bolted over it), and he rarely raised his voice above a dry chuckle. If Khan's appeal and strength lay in the personal origins of his rage, Chang's terror and fascination originated from the polar opposite source: the impersonal considerations of realpolitik. ("Tell Mike it was only business," pleads Tessio in *The Godfather.*) In pursuit of his goals, Chang would crush his enemies with mildly sadistic indifference. "As flies to wanton boys," he'd kill them for their sport. A smiling villain with a heart of lead, Chang become Plummer's most popular role after Captain Von Trapp in *The Sound of Music*.

Christian Slater, the movie-star son of my indefatigable casting director, was a *Star Trek* devotee and made a one-day appearance aboard Sulu's ship as a bewildered communications officer. I tried to shoot him in such a way that audiences might be pleasantly confused. "Was that . . . ?"

Overall, it was fun to shoot the film. For one thing, I wasn't stuck on the *Enterprise* bridge all the time, as had been the case on *Star Trek II*. Ice planets, Klingon show trials (a riff on the Nuremberg war crimes tribunals), alien boxing matches, and alien guard dogs—as well as revealing parts of the *Enterprise* not heretofore shown (crew quarters, the galley, etc.)—made each day something to look forward to.

The music was still an ongoing concern, until one day Ronnie met me in the cutting room, a cassette in his hand. "Listen to this one," he suggested, so I put it in my car's tape deck as I drove back to Beverly Hills following wrap. The composer was one Cliff Eidelman, and the music was surprising in its originality. Moreover, his attached résumé specified Eidelman had done his senior thesis on *The Planets*. I listened again and had my assistant, Mike (Denny having long since been promoted to writer status), locate young Eidelman and invite him for a chat on the lot.

Between takes, in shuffled the Jewish Jimmy Stewart. Tall, lanky, with blue-gray eyes and an aw-shucks delivery, Eidelman was eight when he began violin lessons. He continued his musical education at Santa Monica College and USC. By this time, a new thought had begun percolating in my head. Rather than imitate Holst, I was now fixated on Stravinsky, specifically the opening of his ballet *The Firebird* (1919) with its uneasy, quietly brooding sounds. While *The Planets* might be described as "generic" space music, *Firebird*'s opening sounded Klingon all the way—an alien, mysterious, and dangerous culture.

Directors talking to composers about music is a tricky business. Typically you have two parties who tend not to speak each other's language. For directors that language tends to be visual; for the composer, it is likely aural. The lingua franca relies on reference points known to both (whether recordings of other music, previous film scores, or rock, marches, or madrigals), specifically music the director likes and wishes he could hear in his film. Some composers find these "temp" scores very helpful; others can't bear to listen to them.

I usually tried to split the difference by citing scores rather than actually playing them. Eidelman was, of course, familiar with *The Firebird* and didn't need me to play it for him to know what I was on about. I screened some film for him, minus any temp track, and we chatted for another fifteen minutes or so, after which he left to think over what he'd seen and what I'd described.

"He's the man," Ron predicted.

In this he was correct.

A day or so later Eidelman returned with another synthesizer-generated tape, this time a composition *à la manière de Firebird,* which amply demonstrated his understanding of what I was after. Good film composers must be quick-change artists, and directors must have some idea of what role music is to play in their film. If they don't, the results are likely to be generic, undistinguished, or redundant. Is the music intended to emphasize what is already going on? To provide emotion where there is none? To foreshadow things to come? To tell us things are not what they seem? ("I hate you," the actor says, while throbbing violins insist he's actually in love.) Or, as I suggested earlier, discussing James Horner, will the music give the movie a voice? Surely no one who is familiar with Anton Karas's haunting zither in *The Third Man*, Jerry Goldsmith's eerie electronic pan pipes in *Under Fire*, or John Williams's Strauss-Korngold bombast in *Star Wars* can hear this music without immediately thinking of the films for which they were written. Bette Davis complained that Max Steiner's scores for her movies always tipped what was coming, and she may have had a point, but Steiner's score for *Gone with the Wind* undoubtedly gave that film its voice, just as his pioneering score for *King Kong* made that ape bigger and more threatening than it would have been without those earth-shaking footsteps in the orchestra. Nowadays the fashion is for music to be songs and for their words to direct the audience's feelings and tell them more intellectually what the director wishes them to understand. Not to my taste, but I concede its effectiveness.

In addition to Bronson Canyon and Alaska, the company went into deepest Simi Valley, where we filmed the climatic peace conference at a Jewish community center with what we hoped would register as futuristic architecture. I had planned an elaborate ceremonial introduction to the peace conference (different alien nations marching in under different banners) prior to a second assassination attempt by the conspirators, but in the end it played too long, and much of it was dropped. The influence for the actual assassination attempt was the finale of *The Manchurian Candidate* in Madison Square Garden, and that part thankfully did work.

I knew how ridiculous our budget was when I shot a scene in which Scotty breaks through a door to reach the assassin before he can squeeze off a second round. When I asked for another take I was told there would be a twenty-five minute caesura. The reason: the effects department had to rebuild the one door we had.

Later, when he realized that the film was going to be something more than merely the sixth installment in a spent franchise, Goldwyn said, "We should have given you enough money to do it properly." He was referring to the mundane office furniture chairs so in evidence in our peace conference finale. It did occur to me that it would one day be fun to make a film like this when I wasn't relief pitching.

The last scene was a touchy affair because it was not merely the end of the picture (which, like Spock's death in *Star Trek II*, had tactfully been scheduled at the conclusion of shooting), but because it was also the end of *Star Trek* for the original cast. Whatever ambivalent feelings the actors had about this lifelong, enforced association now manifested themselves as that association neared its end. They were edgy, irritable, suddenly dissatisfied with lines of dialogue, bits of business, reluctant to do this or that, caviling over the ninth particle of a hair. The result was a scene that started well but whose focus and shape were dissipated beneath a welter of last-minute, ad lib adjustments and alterations. As a result, I felt the movie lacked the satisfying climactic feel of Spock's death and funeral in *The Wrath of Khan*.

Star Trek audiences were suitably moved nonetheless—in this respect and given that it was the final film with the original cast, the material was essentially bulletproof. Someone had the idea that the cast should literally "sign off" with their handwritten signatures on appearing (in contractual order) on the screen. I thought the notion hokey but felt that in light of my disappointment with the final scene, I might have need of hokey and so lodged no objection.

And, bringing the series up to date with political correctness, Kirk's sign-off was now amended to: "to boldly go where no man—where no ONE—has gone before . . ."

After we wrapped the last scene, a party was held on the soundstage, something between a funeral and a wake, with no one quite sure how he felt or exactly what had happened. There was sentiment and sorrow, tears of happiness and of grief, a sense of confusion overall. Only time would distill the significance of this journey's end, and that significance would vary for each of the participants, who would now be facing life without *Star Trek*, though it could be argued they had already done so. After all, when the television series had been canceled, these same actors had gone almost ten years without playing their roles and with no expectation of ever revisiting them. As Spock says in the last film, "I've been dead before."

FINAL CUT

And now I was back in the cutting room, where strange things happened. For starters Paramount decided that they didn't have the money to let me finish the film in London, the result of which was that I was separated from my family, who returned to England following the shoot, leaving me to live by my lonesome in a hotel, flying home periodically to see them.

The real shocker, however, turned out to be a genuine coup d'état in the Soviet Union, which we learned had occurred while we were in the midst of assembling our version of the coup in the cutting room. Mikhail Gorbachev had been overthrown, disappeared, and had very possibly been assassinated—just as in our film. There was a flurry of bewildered phone calls among the filmmakers ("Can you believe this?") followed by excited calls from the studio, Goldwyn wanting to know how soon we could get the movie in theaters. This last was an absurd consideration, as not only was my cut incomplete but most of the FX shots had yet to be delivered from ILM. To give him credit, Goldwyn knew this perfectly well but he had to ask. . . . In the stupefaction and glee of our film's prediction coming true, the fate of poor Gorbachev and of Russia generally, was, I blush to say, of only theoretical concern. *Was it good or bad for the film?* (To our credit, we were genuinely relieved when we finally learned Gorbachev was unharmed.)

It was certainly strange to contemplate. Denny and I had tried to imagine our own brave new world in the absence of the Soviet Union. We had created Gorkon and then, in effect, extrapolating from what we read in the newspapers or saw on television, imagined his likely fate. And then it had seemingly come to pass.

Of the movers behind the coup I shall have more to say presently.

Nimoy saw my first cut and was pleased. We continued working and showed it to him again, substantially improved. But this time his reaction was oddly subdued, which was puzzling. I had known Nimoy for several years and several films by this point, but knowing someone long is not the same as knowing him deep. I couldn't quite figure (and never did) what was really going on. I was certainly unaware of the rage he had apparently been stockpiling.

He asked me if he could fiddle with the last reel, and I didn't see why not (he was, after all, the executive producer), so he took it home and sat down with an editor before giving it back a day or so later. He had improved the reel and in doing so had sparked more ideas for Ron and me, so we went to work and built on the structure introduced by Nimoy.

When we showed him our efforts, he exploded and screamed bloody murder. By what right had I altered his cut? I was in complete shock. *His* cut? At no time had Nimoy suggested that what he had given back to me was sacrosanct. *By what right?* I was the director as well as the cowriter. What more right was I supposed to need? I became equally enraged and remembered shouting back at him (this was, I recollect, over the phone), "I am not your secretary! I am not a stenographer!" Or words to that effect.

Eventually we cooled off, but from then on I kept myself at an emotional remove.

Scott Farrar's effects shots dribbled in from ILM, and Gorkon's floating blood was every bit as spectacular as I'd imagined. We also had a character who "morphed" (then a new term, which I infer was short for "metamorphosed"), again thanks to the brave new world of CGI, and there was a lively scene in which Kirk battled a version of himself. Shooting "effects" scenes is usually tedious beyond belief, but the results are eye-popping when all the pieces come together. Kirk fighting himself was enormous fun to watch, especially the quips he tossed in both directions. "I can't believe I kissed you!" "must've been your lifelong ambition." And so forth. (There is a whole geekian subliterature of snappy dialogue during fight scenes and duels. Check out the exchanges between Errol Flynn and Basil Rathbone in *The Adventures of Robin Hood;* also in the clinches between Ronald Colman and Douglas Fairbanks, Jr., in *The Prisoner of Zenda.*)

The studio's notes were, as I recall, minimal. They were still involved with palace putsches: David Kirkpatrick was out, and Brandon Tartikoff, the *wunderkind* from NBC, was in.

We recorded the music with Eidelman conducting a large ensemble and chorus (Was this the first musical setting of "To be or not to be"? Not if you include the 1868 *Hamlet* of Ambrose Thomas, but it it may safely be said it was the first setting of the words in Klingon) on a scoring stage at 20th Century Fox, where it quickly became apparent that something remarkable was taking place. Visitors to the session as well as those connected with the film came into the booth and listened with mounting excitement to what everyone recognized was a great score and one that would define and elevate the film. Once again I got a particular charge out of the presence of my sister, Constance, in the violin section.

THE WOOL

At the end of the shoot it is customary to offer the director some souvenir of the experience. I was given the heavy, iron steering wheel from the Klingon Bird of Prey (always useful) but, asked if there was anything I might prefer, I asked for one of the attractive blankets from the *Enterprise*'s crew's quarters. The prop man said fine but regretfully informed me that the colorful *Enterprise* logo was merely a temporary stencil. I was disappointed to learn this and began turning over the blanket idea in my mind, finally calling up Paramount merchandising.

"If I suggest something for you guys to sell and you go for it, what do I get out of it?" I asked the lady. She asked what I thought I should get.

"Ten percent?"

She said yes so quickly I knew at once I should have asked for more. I then proceeded to describe my idea. "What are the two problems with most souvenirs?" I began. "The first is that they are cheaply made items that will gather dust on a bookshelf or go into a garage sale within two years. The second drawback is that they tend to have no organic relationship to their actual subject. I used the example of a *Star Trek* mouse pad. "On the other hand," I continued triumphantly, "wouldn't you sleep better knowing you were underneath the same blankets that covered the crew of the greatest starship of all?" I then went on to detail the blankets. She listened in unenthusiastic silence. The blanket, I was given to understand, would be a headache to create and sell for more money than they believed fans would be willing to pay.

Nonetheless, in the grip of my own enthusiasm, I pushed for the product that was finally authorized *on the condition that I sign a certificate of authenticity to accompany each blanket.*

This time it was my turn not to hesitate: "Fine." It took months and many phone calls—and many signatures—to nudge the blankets into being but they were splendid when finished and Paramount brought them to a *Star Trek* convention where the entire lot sold out before the convention even opened. One would have thought this was sufficient inducement to produce more blankets but Paramount merchandising evidently still thought they were more trouble than they were worth. And I got tired of signing my name—though I did enjoy telling my wife that if we ever fell on hard times, all we had to do was buy several hundred blankets and bank those 10 percent royalties. She'd looked at me strangely when I offered this logic.

ENDINGS

When the mix was complete, the finished movie was screened for Gene Roddenberry, who was by now very ill. Word came back that he liked the film, which was a load off my mind. I was still feeling guilty about my behavior when we'd met before shooting began. Three days after viewing the movie, Roddenberry died, a loss that sent shock waves through the studio. It was a foregone decision that the film be dedicated to him. (Later an entire new building on the lot was named for him.) I wanted the wording of our dedication to be simple—*For Gene Roddenberry*—but Brandon Tartikoff had other ideas. Various longer, more flowery versions were considered ("For Gene Roddenberry and his enduring vision") but I argued strenuously against them, insisting that less was more. I felt the sentiment required no embellishment and I was irked that Tartikoff, who hadn't been around for any of the film's making (or involved with any of the previous *Star Trek*s, for that matter) should take it upon himself to decide *corporately* how the dedication should read. Tartikoff, who loved the movie and was nothing if not good-humored, allowed himself to be persuaded to employ the simpler wording.

(Tragically, Tartikoff succumbed to Hodgkin's disease in August of 1997 at the age of forty-eight.)

There followed the usual credit arbitration, during which Nimoy was understandably outraged to learn that the original screenwriters were to share story credit without him or, for that matter, Denny and me. It certainly struck me as absurd; I still had vivid memories of taking one of these gentlemen through the story scene by scene in London ("the boys are having a little trouble getting started") while he dutifully copied all I told him on a legal pad. The story had definitely originated with Nimoy; the problem from the Guild's point of view was that he had not literally *written* any of it down. There was no paperwork— only what "the boys" had transcribed from conversations between Nimoy and them and, later, between one of them and me. Nimoy cut through this Gordian knot by threatening to sue the WGA. The credits were duly altered to reflect his prime contribution; Denny and I received screenwriting credit.

During the postproduction period I was informed by Art Cohen and Barry London, heads of PR and marketing, that they would like to meet regarding the title of the movie. It was déjà vu all over again. After we'd sat down and sipped our coffees, they told me they felt that *The Undiscovered Country* as a title was "soft."

But I was in a different position now than I'd been in ten years earlier, when no one except my assistant, Janna Wong, had even troubled to inform me that my title was being discarded.

"Listen," I responded, "you've exhausted all the superlatives. We've had the 'final,' the 'last,' the 'ultimate'—no one is paying any attention. Put aside for the moment the fact that no one cares what the subtitle of a *Star Trek* movie is, you might do well to throw people a curveball this time, something oblique like, well . . . 'The Undiscovered Country.'" I put up my hands before they could respond and went on amicably: "However, let me make this easy for you. If anyone comes up with a better title, I will be happy to relinquish mine."

In the good old days of real studios (before they became subsidiaries of conglomerates and bean counters) titles were often decided via a contest. The secretary who named the movie got a bonus. Nowadays the matter is turned over to a computer, which will take a word and do mechanical riffs on it. Take, for example, the word, *escape*. The computer will spew forth, ESCAPE TO THE FUTURE, ESCAPE FROM TOMORROW, ESCAPE TO YESTERDAY, BIG ESCAPE, GREAT ESCAPE, etc. Or try the word *bridge* and you will get BRIDGE TO THE FUTURE, BRIDGE ACROSS TOMORROW, BRIDGE FROM THE PAST, and so forth, before proceeding to the next word. Love? Hate? Death? Balloons?

When we reconvened I found myself in a huge room populated by over thirty men and women whose job it was to help sell *Star Trek VI*. Reams of computer printouts confronted me. I picked up the first title—I forget what it was—read it slowly and then asked what the assembly thought of it. No one seemed very taken so I went with deliberation onto the second name, *Bridge to Tomorrow*. "Any takers?" I inquired. Silence. As I prepared to go on to *Bridge* number three of what looked to be ten thousand possibilities, Barry London interrupted.

"You win," he smiled. And so did I.

The film opened on December 6, 1991, to excellent notices and a huge box office. (One reviewer was so enthusiastic he wondered why the original cast didn't simply keep going.) I think we broke another opening weekend record, and among Monday's congratulations was a call from Lucia Ludovico in marketing. "Thank God we didn't change your title!" she exclaimed. I had to smile at the thought the title had made any difference one way or the other.

Some months later, while I was getting my teeth cleaned, my dentist told me how much he enjoyed the movie. In acknowledging his kind remarks through all the instruments jammed into my mouth, I marveled yet again at how we had managed to predict the Soviet coup.

"Come again?" said Dr. Brown.

"Well," I pointed out, "you know that this was basically a movie about the Wall coming down. The Klingons were stand-ins for the Russians. We called Gorbachev 'Gorkon' and so on and basically staged the coup before the one that actually happened in the USSR. . . ."

He regarded me with a puzzled demeanor.

"Huh," he conceded at length, "I guess I'll have to look at the movie again."

And we had worried about being too obvious.

I made a few subsequent alterations for the VHS and DVD release, mainly to improve a sequence that I felt I had bungled in the cutting (the scene where Scotty stumbles on an important clue in the empty officers' mess) and adding some quick cutaways to the conspirators' faces for clarity when Valeris reveals their names under compulsion in the Vulcan mind meld. It is a curious reality of film that audiences frequently have difficulty learning the names of characters. They may have no problems with Indiana Jones or Lawrence of Arabia, but subsidiary names tend to mean little. (When we describe *North by Northwest,* we invariably refer to Cary Grant, not Roger Thornhill.) When Valeris reluctantly identifies her coconspirators, I realized—belatedly—that it would help the audience if they could *see* the faces belonging to those names. Surely Admiral Cartwright, when you saw him as embodied by Brock Peters, would pack more of a wallop for viewers than a conspirator whose name rang no bells. I hadn't made Cartwright part of the conspiracy by chance, either; I loved the idea of going against the stereotype movies had embraced of African Americans as flawless heroes in the Sidney Poitier mold and thought it would be stingingly politically incorrect to include Cartwright among the traitors, a decorated Starfleet officer, one we knew and trusted from an earlier movie.

No wonder Gene Roddenberry had been so dismayed by the script.

But aside from these minor improvements, I resisted the temptation to fiddle and I refused to let the DVD promoters title the slightly altered movie the "director's cut," as I felt the changes were so minimal that such a label would amount to deceptive advertising.

Postmortem

The passage of time has, however, altered my perceptions of the film itself. While I am still pleased to find it entertaining, there can be no doubt that part of what we intended has dated in melancholy and chilling fashion. At the end of *The Undiscovered Country*, we learn that the conspirators were in fact a cabal comprised of Federation members and Klingons acting in concert to preserve a cold war status quo. "People can be very frightened of change," Kirk sums up, and we cut to the stricken expression on Valeris before she is led off, under guard. Our point at the time certainly anticipated a wonderful new chapter in human history once the cold war was over. According to our view, people frightened of change were just scaredy-cats.

THE VIEW FROM THE BRIDGE

In fact, however, a wonderful new chapter in human history is not what has occurred. Instead, we got 9/11 and a resurgent form of human horror, terrorism, in which incalculable destruction is visited upon us not by dictators and armies but rather by crazies with box cutters and primitive but lethally destructive capabilities. The age of the suicide bomber was at hand. How long before that bomb would prove to be a nuclear one? Was this any improvement on the cold war era or is it not, in fact, much worse? As awful as MAD (Mutual Assured Destruction) was, no one was actually destroyed. But as of 2001, the world became an infinitely more dangerous place—all of which now leads me to wonder if the conspirators of *Star Trek VI* were not more justified than we gave them credit for being. Knowing what I now know (in the famous formulation of Senator Clinton), would I still maintain that Valeris, Cartwright, and their Klingon counterparts were misguided in their attempts to thwart détente between the Federation and the Klingon Empire?

I also confess to being troubled by the Vulcan mind meld, clearly a form of torture, wherein Spock attempts to forcibly extract vital information from the traitor, Valeris. In light of the Bush administration's treatment of "enemy combatants," I blush.

PART 3

POST *TREK*

FIFTEEN YEARS

By 2009, when this book is published, almost twenty years will have elapsed since the release of *Star Trek VI*. Much has happened since then—to the world; to *Star Trek*. And to me. I have worked on multiple scripts, some of which, like *Sommersby, Voices, The Informant* (aka *Field of Blood*), *The Human Stain*, and *Elegy*, were eventually filmed, for better or worse. Behind each of these titles lies tales of hard work, high hopes, dreary frustrations, and memorable people. I once saw a slip of paper on which were written the five stages of movie production: (1) Wild Enthusiasm; (2) Total Confusion; (3) Utter Despair; (4) Hunt for the Guilty; (5) Punishment of the Innocent. I wrote many screenplays—some I consider equal to if not superior to those that were filmed—that never saw the cinematic light of day. Just a lot of chopped-down trees. This is not unusual. In the '90s movies themselves were undergoing a transition whose momentum was gathering steam. At first, competition from such venues as television was offset by the bonanza that was DVD, but as time passed, it became clear that the monopoly movies had once enjoyed with the general public was being steadily eroded by competing and insistent claims on its attention, including hundred-channel television, video games, and latterly, the Internet. Also, as big corporations swallowed up the studios and burdened them with their huge corporate debt, the choices about which movies to make became increasingly conservative, driven by market demographics rather than instinct or guts or passion or taste. Once upon a time, before Eve gave Adam a bite of the Apple and there was Knowledge, film studios would make movies out of all kinds of stories. "Hey, this tale of sheep drovers in Australia seems cool," etc. But as the bean counters, those descendents of Eve, applied their—alleged—Knowledge, films now must fit into genres: the gross-out teen comedy, the slasher flick, the comic book translation, etc. Quirky was starting to look like polar bears on melting ice seeking solid ground. Older filmgoers were alienated by louder, more bombastic soundtracks, unrelenting special effects, and puerile scripts. For a while the independent market provided these moviegoers with an alternative, but with Pay-Per-View and Netflix, many preferred to simply stay home. Movie criticism languished in the absence of films worth writing about, and soon newspapers, struggling themselves, cut costs by sacking voices to which—they argued—no one was paying any heed.

Watching movies at home, on a screen however large and a sound system however noisy, is simply not the same thing as seeing them in a theater. My dad used to say that watching movies on TV was like getting kissed over the telephone. What's missing in seeing a film on television is a central component of what it means to be human—the assembly. Whether it's at a church, at a play, or at the movies, the idea of losing your identity at a gathering of others—known or unknown to you—while sharing a common experience, a journey, an event, is uniquely human, and in my opinion we abandon such practices at our peril. Gatherings are important, and certainly better than going through life with ear buds. Never mind the theology or medium in question, concentrate on the part where you rub shoulders with strangers. Cities are places you walk or ride the subway, places where you look at people, they look at you; you don't pass them on the freeway at seventy miles an hour. At the end of a performance of Beethoven's Third, you and the audience have shared an adventure, at once individual and collective. The experience makes you a better person. Don't ask me how or why, but it does. There isn't any movie shown on televsion that wouldn't be better in a movie theater. Art is fragile—it can be interrupted by crying kids, the telephone, the neighbors, what have you. Gatherings, whether for music, church, plays, films, or ballets, are experiences to which you must make a commitment and in making that commitment, in leaving your home to devote yourself to that communal experience, you reaffirm your humanity.

Speaking for myself, the career artery in which I work has narrowed. I am still absorbed by stories, which I thought would never go out of fashion, dating as they do back to Homer. But lately narrative has been replaced by rides. Endless action sequences, unrelated to character or plot, are just a different kind of pornography, one in which standalone episodes of violence are substituted for standalone episodes of sex. The stories that nominally link these episodes are of little interest because—at least to me—they are unconnected or unrelated to life, which is what appeals to me. I am interested in heroes, not superheroes. Caped crusaders and movies that end with the word "Man" strike me as rather pathetic attempts to dial out an encroaching reality that most Americans appear unwilling to confront. The movies I am interested in making—and watching—are all attempts to confront reality, however quirky, peculiar, hilarious, or unpleasant. Even in (my) *Star Trek*s, as Kirk remarks, everyone is human. Tell me a story.

Of course franchise films have endured, and that includes *Star Trek*. After *VI* came *VII*, *VIII*, *IX*, *X*, none of which I saw on their release, partially because I was afraid I would like them better than my own, and I was petty enough to be frightened by this possibility. Eventually I did find myself watching them— for a segment on *Star Trek* villains for yet another DVD repackaging in which I had agreed to participate—and at first my worst fears were confirmed. I thought the other films looked better, in many cases were better acted, with superior effects, etc. Later, I gained some perspective and decided mine were just as good and my actors had a certain esprit de corps that struck me as pretty much inimitable.

DEATH

I have said that this is not a travel book; nonetheless it is the account of a journey and every life journey throws you IEDs.

Shortly after we returned from India in 1987, Pierce Brosnan's wife, Cassie, was diagnosed with cancer, from which she later died.

In January of 1992 my own wife was also diagnosed with breast cancer and died a year and a half later, aged thirty-six, leaving me the widowed father of two daughters, aged three and six. Directing a film during that period was out of the question; I wasn't sure I could even frame a sentence. Some have marveled at my bad luck at losing my mother and then wife to cancer, but this isn't how I found myself feeling about it. However sorry I felt for myself, I felt worse for Lauren and our children, so prematurely and horribly separated.

There followed several years of which I have only the haziest recollection, and during which I am sure I made little sense. Brushing my hair or teeth seemed weirdly unimportant, and writing was a financial necessity, nothing more. At the beginning I thought about killing myself but quickly realized that even if I'd had the nerve, I couldn't really entertain the idea: I had two children for whom I was responsible. I was annoyed with them at the time, failing to recognize their gallantry and the example they set until later. I can never repay my debt to them for teaching me how to endure. But here I can at least acknowledge it.

The only project that resonated with me was the first one I was offered following Lauren's death: HBO commissioned me to write and direct an adaptation of *The Odyssey*, a tale that had been my favorite since the age of five when an uncle of mine had told it to me as an ongoing bedtime story. I knew this material inside out, and it wrote itself. In the process I realized I was also writing my autobiography, the story of a man trying to get back to his wife; more, it was the tale of a man punished for his inability to distinguish between cleverness and wisdom. Yes, it wrote itself.

Brosnan and I would lunch in Westwood on a regular basis and compare widowers' notes. Occasionally we'd include other guys whose wives had died, but mainly it was just the two of us, taking each other's pulse. At one of these lunches he started to talk about Cassie and soon tears were rolling down his cheeks. I brought up Lauren and shortly I was weeping, too. At this point, while sobbing into our gazpachos, a lovely girl with a great bosom walked by and we both instinctively turned to admire her. Then we looked at each other, caught in the act, and began to laugh while still crying.

In the event there was no way I could leave my kids to direct *The Odyssey* or anything else. Eventually the film was taken over by Andrei Konchalovsky (HBO left it when I did). He hired his own screenwriter and over at

NBC threw out my script; together they concocted *The Odyssey According to Danielle Steele*. The trashing of Homer seemed of a piece with everything else that had happened.

Then one day I met a beautiful woman named Stephanie, and everything changed. It takes a large heart for someone to come into a family in place of a beloved wife and mother. Stephanie made it look easy and saved the lot of us. I am not a profound person and I've never been able to sort out the metaphysics here, but I certainly know love when I feel it. I know other people in similar circumstances who have not been so lucky as to get a second chance at life.

Many years ago I read an article in the Science section of *The New York Times* that has stayed with me. It had to do with the genetic component of happiness. What side of the bed did you wake up on the morning you were born? The article pointed out that people seem born with an innate level of happiness that appears to exist independently of outward circumstances. You get a raise, win the Oscar, fall in love—and your level of happiness rises in response to good news. But eventually it resettles at its standard level. Similarly, you can get fired, have your house burn down, and so forth. Your happiness declines appropriately—but by and by it tends to slide upward to where it was before. This idea seems very relevant my own experience of life. I've gone through some horrendous stuff. I haven't recovered from Lauren's death; a part of me doesn't want to recover from it. But I have learned to ingest it, to coexist with the fact of it, to incorporate it into a life that includes my love for Stephanie, a love that measures no less. My glass always goes back to looking more than half full.

VENDETTA

And as long as you're alive, life doesn't stop. More things happen. In 1997 HBO offered me the chance to direct a film called *Vendetta*. By now I was happily married to Stephanie (with a third daughter to show for it), and finally in a position where things were stable enough for me to spend time behind the camera again, and so I was delighted to accept. The script by Timothy Prager was based on a nonfiction account by Professor Richard Gambino of events surrounding the biggest lynching in American history. The victims were not—as I had anticipated—African Americans, but rather Sicilians in New Orleans in 1891. They had been accused and acquitted of having murdered the city's very popular—and very corrupt—chief of police, David Hennessy, who had been gunned down in a heavy fog on his way home from work the previous October by persons unknown. The city's white oligarchy saw in Hennessy's murder an opportunity to throw a monkey wrench into the power of the growing Sicilian population. It was a compelling tale, the more shocking as it was so little known. When the Sicilians were acquitted, the judge nonetheless refused to release them, holding them overnight on a bizarre technicality, "lying in wait" (for a murder of which they'd just been found not guilty!), long enough for a mob of twenty thousand to be rallied by an advertisement in the next morning's newspaper: COME PREPARED FOR ACTION TO ADDRESS THE DEFECTS OF JUSTICE IN THE HENNESSY CASE! The mob stormed the parish prison and shot, stabbed, and used for target practice, *while* hanging, these unfortunate wretches, before going home, satisfied that they had, in one newspaper's editorial, done the jury's work for them.

The script was an ensemble piece, a cutaway view of New Orleans as an anthill with several different strata, including—just above the blacks—the

Sicilians, most of whom spoke no English. It seemed crucial to me that their scenes be filmed in Sicilian. John Matoian, then head of HBO Films, agreed, though he did feel that the film needed a star—HBO traditionally hooked their films to stars—even though there wasn't a starring role in the script. In the end Christopher Walken undertook to play the chief white oligarch, who might or might not have been the real culprit behind the chief's murder. (The theory being that it was pinned on the Sicilians to allow the whites to take over their businesses when they were executed—which they did.)

I visited New Orleans (which then existed), only to find that the French Quarter had become a sort of Disneyland and bore little resemblance to the New Orleans of 1891. HBO wanted me to film in Canada, which I thought ridiculous until I visited Kingston, midway between Montreal and Toronto. The city was situated on Lake Ontario, and with its period architecture parts of it could—with a little help—pass for Louisiana and the Mississippi and/ or Lake Pontchartrain. With the help of my ingenious production designer, David Chapman, Kingston soon became the very vanished New Orleans of our story.

I had labored under the common delusion that Sicilian was merely a variant of Italian, only to learn that it had about as much relationship to that tongue as Yiddish does to German. All my Italian actors had to learn their lines in an alien tongue. I might as well have cast Americans; the linguistic chore would have been essentially the same.

Like *The Day After*, *Vendetta* depended on the goodwill of an entire town to provide size and scope to the story. What Lawrence had done for nuclear war, Kingston did for lynching. Folks came out by the thousand to go through makeup and wear period clothes (and mustaches for the men) in order to get paid a pittance and a sandwich for their infinite pains. They were wonderful.

In my admittedly subjective opinion, I think *Vendetta* is my best work. I had mysteriously improved as the result of my hiatus from the camera. My coverage was more efficient and more imaginative than before, my work with actors, shaping performances, increasingly subtle.

My only explanation for my improvement has to do with watching my oldest daughter learn to ride a bicycle, a process that took five days. On the first day, wearing helmet and knee and shoulder pads in an empty parking lot before a closed restaurant in Provincetown, she lasted about ten minutes before crying that she'd had enough. On the second day she went about fifteen minutes before giving up—but there had been some improvement. By day three, fifteen minutes had become twenty, and Rachel was actually pedaling. *Something had happened in the night.* Simply put, she hadn't woken up where she'd left off the day before. Her brain and then her muscles had processed something she had experienced or learned. By day four she was almost there, and by day five, she was riding a bike—but the major part of the work had somehow occurred when she wasn't on the parking lot. So it was with my other two daughters, and so it was with me when I resumed directing after the time following Lauren's death.

It was harder, after so much time had passed, to return to features. I tried the independent route, spending a couple of years attempting to put together a film Ronnie and I had cowritten entitled *Spoils*, a film noirish piece, set during the waning days of World War II and involving two officers of the German occupation—male and female—who discover the German crown jewels in the basement of the castle where they've been billeted and decide to steal them. Bruce Greenwood and Linda Fiorentino were to have been our leads. A wild, true story, our script came heartbreakingly close to filming (we were ten days out) when the money disappeared, and I was obliged to fly home from Germany on air miles. The world of independent cinema is rough. Ismail may have been tardy with his checks but enough of them went through to make his movies.

THE HUMAN STAIN

When I was in Belgium, trying to hold together my production of *Spoils*, I got a phone call from Gary Lucchesi, asking if I'd read Philip Roth's novel *The Human Stain*. Gary, having done the executive shuffle from Tri-Star to Paramount, was now heading production at a company called Lakeshore Entertainment. I had not read Roth's novel but determining by this point that I would shortly be home (and unemployed), I agreed to have a look at the book and meet with Gary and his boss, Tom Rosenberg.

Tom, who hailed from Chicago, had attended Berkeley and gone on to work as a civil rights lawyer in Kentucky before becoming an Illinois real estate mogul. He ran Lakeshore as a mini-major studio, making the films that pleased him. Like a salmon swimming upstream, Tom was still interested in movies about people. By 1999 this was already becoming a rarity, but under Tom and Gary's stewardship, plucky Lakeshore was doing okay.

I devoured Roth's novel and was deeply affected by what I read. Roth's in-your-face hyperarticulateness sometimes works and sometimes doesn't, but it matters not to Philip Roth. He just keeps writing. To use a baseball analogy, some of Roth's books are singles, others strikeouts, still others home runs, while some are out and out grand slams. What you learn about art (and possibly life) from Philip Roth (and maybe also from Woody Allen) is that the name of the game is showing up and swinging for the fences.

In the case of *The Human Stain*, there was no question that Roth had written a grand slam. The story of a black man passing as white and succeeding wildly in his deception, only to lose tenure at the college he has created for an allegedly racist remark, was provoking and disturbing, let alone ironic. Coleman Silk's subsequent love affair with an illiterate custodial worker, leading to their tragic destruction, was, I felt, the work of a genius operating at the height of his powers. Roth's snapshot of America during the Clinton impeachment proceedings was dead on, as savagely accurate as it was heartbreaking.

I had no idea how to make a movie out of the novel, but I had six weeks in which to figure it out. Six weeks became five and before I knew it, three. I was back in Los Angeles, recuperating from the *Spoils* debacle but no closer to cracking *The Human Stain*. Finally, with three days to go, Stephanie advised me to give it up. I was just making myself—and everyone else—crazy. Tell them the truth, she urged. No point bullshitting.

Her advice came as a great relief to me, and I was instantly reconciled to it. Unknowingly this served to do what was really needed, namely to take my conscious mind off the problem. As I have indicated earlier, my best creative work takes place when I am able to let go. In the present instance I remember I was sitting in the bath, staring at my toes and wondering—not for the first time—why long immersion in water causes the skin to wrinkle like prunes.

Suddenly, unbidden, like safe tumblers falling into place—*click, click, click*—came acts one, two, and three of *The Human Stain*.

I sat completely motionless, letting the water get cold around me, afraid that if I moved, my elegant solution to the film would vanish like a dream following a morning cup of coffee.

But it remained, and I became convinced it was the right way to adapt Roth's novel. Adapting novels or short stories or plays is a tricky process, and one that varies with the piece being adapted. Let's confine ourselves for the moment to novels. The better a work of art, i.e., the more successful it is in the medium for which it was originally created, the more difficult its successful translation into another form is likely to prove. Something—much?—will likely be lost in translation to another venue. Novels are a flexible form—they can be long, they can be short, they can be written in the third person, the first person, etc. But films—or plays, or operas for that matter—must obey certain dramatic conventions. They must, for instance, be digestible at a sitting, two hours, three if you must and five if you're Wagner, but that's pushing it. Descriptions, interior monologues (think Molly Bloom's forty-page soliloquy), multiple narrators or points of view—these present problems for the filmmaker that the novelist need not think twice about.

I was determined to preserve as much of Roth as possible and found a structure that seemingly allowed me to do this gracefully, faithfully, and economically. Once those tumblers had fallen into place and Tom had given me the go-ahead, the script was not that hard to write. Both Tom and Gary were delighted with the result, and Anthony Hopkins and Nicole Kidman agreed to make the film before a director was in place, another flattering testament to the script's success. That director was not, I realized, going to be me. I had simply been away too long, and there was not enough heat under my name. Pity, as I felt I knew how to do it. The director search proved unexpectedly tough. Here was another way in which movies had changed since the early '90s when I had last directed a commercial feature: While I was agreeably surprised to get calls from agents all over town congratulating me on the script and saying how moved they were by it (these were *agents*, mind you), directors were reluctant to sign on for anything so serious and "uncommercial."

I heard Robert Benton was interested and I eagerly supported this idea, as I had always regarded him as enormously gifted. He was the right age to appreciate the dilemmas of Coleman Silk's era and he was wonderful with actors, including Miss Kidman, with whom he had worked before. I argued vociferously on his behalf and met with him in New York, thumbing through the script, page by page, explaining why I had done this or that.

Tom hired him, and I flew again to New York to a script meeting with Benton, Tom, and Gary, which took place September 9th of 2001. Before leaving for the city I got a call from a friend telling me startling and distressing news that was apparently unknown to his friends: Herb Ross was dying in New York.

As soon as I reached Manhattan I went to visit Herb, who was in an attractive room at the Lennox Hill Hospital. He was dying and he was alone. I was amazed to find him in this condition. Herb Ross, a man who had moved so glamorously in the public eye for so long, who had directed Barbra Streisand, had been friends with so many glitterati and married to the extraordinary ballerina Nora Kaye (at whose funeral I had spoken some years earlier), was now inexplicably facing death without a soul to gaze comfortingly into his eyes. For whatever reason, he had not wanted anyone to know about his condition. What *was* going on? When I tried to ask him, he looked at me and merely shrugged. His eyes were clear; he understood my question. Perhaps he simply didn't know the answer, but he didn't seem reconciled to his isolated hospital room. Or perhaps he was entirely reconciled, concentrating on his imminent journey to the undiscovered country. I held his hand. I kissed his unresisting cheek. Only at the last minute did other people realize where he was and what was going down. On my way out of his hospital room, I met Dick Benjamin and Paula Prentiss arriving to see him. I couldn't—and still cannot—understand a life that ends on such a bizarre note. Granted, we are born alone and die in the same way, but surely this last, heroic rite of passage might have been eased by the comfort of friends or family. Alas, Herb seemed to want neither. He had seemingly chosen to go through this final transit without witnesses or companions. On *his* deathbed, Leonard Bernstein's last words had been, "What is this?" When I utter those syllables, I'm sure I want to be holding someone's hand.

Herb's melancholy final days preyed on me as I attended my script meeting on *The Human Stain*. New York was beautiful in those early September days. None of us had a clue everything was about to change.

I had gone into the meeting expecting it to be three against one—with me being the lone defender of what I had written. The balance turned out to be quite different, with Tom, Gary, and me shooting down suggestions for changes from Benton. I was pleased and moved to find myself among allies.

Later, after Herb's death and the calamity of 9/11, *The Human Stain* was shot—where else?—in Canada, and I was mysteriously frozen out of the shooting. I was allowed up for a very circumscribed visit. (Although the Writers Guild negotiates such privileges, the writer, that necessary evil, is typically eagerly dispensed with by filmmakers at the earliest possible opportunity.) I was treated with every courtesy, introduced to all and sundry by the director as the author of this "brilliant" screenplay, but after watching one scene, I called

Stephanie and said I was coming home. It wasn't my script and, more to the point, it didn't seem to have much to do with Roth's novel.

Later, sharing drinks at the Old King Cole bar at the St. Regis, I asked Benton, "Bob, why'd you shut me out of the movie?" and he answered, "Because you wanted to make a different film, Nick, and I couldn't fight you and do my job at the same time. I made the only film I knew how to make."

This, I have to admit, was an honest answer from a decent man. I just couldn't for the life of me figure out why he'd wanted my script to begin with if he couldn't come to terms with Roth.

ELEGY

My relations with Lakeshore, however, remained cordial, and a good thing, too, as they were still interested in films about people. I wrote an adaptation of Richard Russo's novel *Straight Man* for them and adapted another Roth work, a novella called *The Dying Animal*. It usually takes forever to get movies made, so I was pleasantly astonished five years after writing it to learn that my second Roth script was going to be filmed. In the interim, Al Pacino had toyed with it and us. We'd spent years trying to land him for the role of New York intellectual David Kepesh. We'd argued with the Italian director Pacino had envisioned directing the film—I felt he wanted to domesticate or sentimentalize Roth—before getting lucky with Spanish director Isabel Coixet, and a cast that included Penélope Cruz, Ben Kingsley, Patricia Clarkson, and Dennis Hopper.

I've noted elsewhere my skepticism about the importance of movie titles, but I concede that some are more off-putting than others. *Forrest Gump* may not sound terribly inviting, but *The Human Stain* or *The Dying Animal*, while plausible book monikers, are not, in my view, enticing names for movies. I try to picture a couple planning their Saturday night—*Hey, honey, how about taking in* The Dying Animal *tonight?*

When I wrote *The Human Stain*, I suggested that we change the title. I wanted to call the movie *American Skin*, which I thought fit like a glove, given the subject of the book. Lakeshore demurred, counting, I imagine, on the novel's readership to constitute its core audience. When it came time to turn in *The Dying Animal*, I chose to take matters into my own hands and simply wrote *Elegy* on the title page. Lakeshore, however, wasn't 100 percent sure about that, and while they agreed that Roth's title would probably not sell tickets they worried that no one would know what "elegy" meant. I argued that the audience for this film probably would but offered to change the title if we could come up with something better.

In the end no one could and the movie was released to lovely reviews and enough business to justify Lakeshore's herculean efforts in getting it made.

I've since written another film for Lakeshore, this one something I brought to them, based on William Doyle's riveting minute-by-minute account of James Meredith's enrolling at the University of Mississippi in the fall of 1962, *American Insurrection*, a title, I suspect, we'll keep.

I've also spent five years trying to get my screenplay of *The Rise of Theodore Roosevelt*, based on Edmund Morris's Pulitzer Prize–winning biography, before the cameras. More recently, I've adapted the nonfiction book *Patient Number One* for HBO and written a biographical movie about Bangladeshi 2006 Nobel Peace Prize winner Muhammad Yunus, known as *Banker to the Poor*.

Will any of them get filmed?

If I live long enough. Meantime, like Eliza, I hop from ice floe to ice floe. . . .

EPILOGUE

I always dreamed of writing and directing movies and have been lucky enough to realize that dream. Nonetheless, I remain a transplanted Easterner, still a stranger to the world of Hollywood and filmmaking. I used to be amazed at parties at the response I got when I said I loved such and such a film.

"What do you *mean,* you loved it—it didn't do a dime." If I've heard this logic once I've heard it a million times. And the converse: "You hated it? It did two hundred million, how could you hate it?"

How can I complain or cavil with this standard of measurement? It is called "show *business.*" Am I maintaining that films are art? And if I am, how can they not also be business, any less than Shakespeare's Globe Theatre was a moneymaking operation? If a play didn't please, it didn't make money, and if it didn't make money, you can bet it wasn't revived.

Well, not until years later. The world of art is full of posthumous success stories. For every Mozart, buried anonymously in a pauper's grave, Hollywood can point to films that flopped—*It's a Wonderful Life, Citizen Kane, Bringing Up Baby*—but are today revered as classics of the medium.

Such ruminations are part of my attempt to figure out just what I feel about the *Star Trek* series, which I once dismissed as the one about the man with pointy ears. While its scientific trappings and much of its premise may be absurd, is that absurdity any greater than, say, the Greek myths with their half-man, half-bull monsters, flying horses, and all-too-human Gods? Are Spock's ears any more improbable than wings on the ankles of Hermes? For that matter, is the content of *Star Trek* any more improbable than Moses parting the Red Sea or Christ rising from the dead? Are Homer's bickering gods and goddesses more plausible than Mickey and Minnie? Are the only valid legends *old* legends? Do the *Star Trek* tales perform no useful purpose other than as a reassuring gloss on an America-first, gunboat diplomacy view of America's place in the world/universe?

I know the answers to none of these questions, and certainly, having contributed to some of these "legends," I am too close to be in any way objective regarding their value.

But I suspect that in the long run it is the long run itself that counts. *Star Trek*'s importance—or lack of same—will not be determined by how much money the films have made; it will not be determined by critical appraisals in varying venues. No, Time is the ultimate arbiter of Art. When Nixon visited China he banqueted with that wily courtier, Zhou Enlai, and asked him during the meal what he thought of the French Revolution.

"It's too early to tell," was Zhou's answer.

So I think it is with all manner of art. There is a kind of aesthetic Darwinism at work in art: The fittest survive but oftentimes works initially celebrated pass quickly into oblivion while those dismissed at the time stubbornly defy internment. There seems to be no logic or formula by which survival or extinction can be predicted. Sometimes art intended as highbrow (what Hollywood refers to as "prestige pictures"—made to win awards) disappears without a trace while "programmers" (also known as B pictures) turn out to be the real thing. It is certainly not without meaning that George Lucas's *Star Wars* films, as well as his Indiana Jones series, were made as homages to Saturday morning serials, quickie productions that didn't "count." Films on which Hollywood lavished extraordinary care and ambition, such as Darryl Zanuck's *Wilson,* don't seem to wear as well. Is *Ben-Hur* a film worth watching aside from its justly celebrated chariot race? I'm only asking. Were the folks turning out what we celebrate today as film noir really believing that what they were doing was art? Was *The Curse of the Cat People* supposed to be art?

And yet it is often these films, relegated to the bottom half of the double bill, that seem to endure. (One could go a step further and wonder whether movies themselves were ever thought of by their creators as art, or was art conferred upon them, and their makers, with the passage of time?)

On the other hand, one can always point to ambitious enterprises that have indeed fulfilled the lofty ambitions of their creators. *Citizen Kane* and the original Broadway production of *West Side Story* were both self-consciously conceived as Art and (so far) have been embraced as masterpieces. Artists do tend to be ahead of the curve, and what is dismissed at the time often goes on to conquer. Stravinsky's *Rite of Spring*, booed at its premiere (a woman stood up in the balcony and shrieked, "I've never been so insulted in my life!") was only twenty-five years later adopted by Disney (Disney!) as the soundtrack to fighting dinosaurs, and no one bats an eye. Au contraire: audiences have belatedly caught up with Stravinsky.

So far. *Star Wars* may have entered the pantheon, but will its residence be permanent? Check it out in another fifty years. There is an ebb and flow to art, as well. Films, music, and painters drift in and out of fashion. Remember the words of Zhou Enlai.

And so with *Star Trek*. I cannot gauge its value or understand its meaning except subjectively. While the films are not ones I would have deliberately chosen as a vehicle for self-expression (I did begin this book by acknowledging the happenstance paths of life and their unlooked-for consequences), I cannot deny that my life has been changed—enriched—as a result of my association with the series, and perhaps the lives of others have been affected as well. Who's to say if I had got to make my film version of Robertson Davies's novel *Fifth Business* that as many people would've been affected by the result? How many scientists and astronauts at NASA were first inspired by the silliness that was *Star Trek* to reach for the stars? Answer? A lot.

Sir Arthur Conan Doyle lavished a great deal of time, effort, and research on his historical novels, among them *Micah Clarke* and *The White Company*, but it is for the "programmer" Sherlock Holmes stories that he is best remembered. Does it mean Holmes is "better" than *The White Company*? Arguably not, but Holmes's popularity cannot be without meaning, for either Doyle himself or the rest of us. Interestingly Doyle remained willfully obtuse on the subject of Holmes: He could do it but he didn't "get it."

In some ways, as this memoir has shown, I have had similar feelings about *Star Trek*. I could evidently "do it" while at the same time I told myself for long periods that I simply didn't get it.

That can no longer be said to be entirely true. And by this point it would also seem graceless of me to insist that it is. Enough time has passed so that, though I may not be able to assess the lasting merit of *Star Trek*, I can certainly give some consideration to how *Star Trek* has changed me.

Or for that matter, movies generally. It has long been traditional to knock Hollywood as a place where talented people lose their souls, prostitute themselves for—what else?—money and fame, and generally forfeit their integrity. There are books and indeed movies that reinforce the stereotype of the sellout, the Faustian bargain, etc. The self-pitying writer has become his own stock character, marinating in lacerating self-hatred, wallowing in capitulation to the seamy forces of darkness and commerce.

I don't believe I fall into this category. I love movies and try to make good ones; I recognize that show business (like America itself) has its tawdry and vulgar side. But it also has its splendid aspects, and if I continue to be seduced by those, I plead guilty. I think storytelling is a worthwhile profession, and you try to tell the best stories you can in the best way you know how and you try to steer clear of the crap. I suppose I am not a mainstream Hollywood creation but merely a peripheral character, working in a narrowing artery that I hope is not my own. Granted, most movies are worthless, but the ones that aren't are as meaningful—to me, anyway—as any other form of art.

Someone once said that work is doing something you don't like in order to earn a living. I am fortunate that that has not been the case for my own career. I have been blessed to struggle with what I love, *for* what I love. And whatever heartaches, disappointments, flops, setbacks, occasional betrayals, and bad behavior (including, on occasion, I fear, my own) I've had to face, I am still of Walter Mirisch's opinion. I don't think I would have lasted this long had I not found this strange place and strange occupation to be as full of the most wonderful, loyal, creative people and friends as I could hope to find anywhere. While telling stories may not be rocket science, it's arguably less lethal. And given that it's the world's second oldest profession, I'd like to keep doing it for as long as people are willing to listen.

ACKNOWLEDGMENTS

This book began with an anecdote in which Walter Mirisch declared he would not have lasted in this business had it not been for the support, encouragement, and love of the many splendid people in it.

Similarly, there are a great many friends and coworkers who have stood by me, put up with my nonsense, or held my hand, in a word hung in there and helped sustain me in my life as I hope I have helped them in theirs.

I can't possibly name them all, but as regards the creation of this book, I must acknowledge Alan Gasmer, who suggested I write it; Charlotte Sheedy, who thought she could sell it; Rick Kot, my diligent editor, who sought to spare me my worst excesses; John McNamara, who encouraged me to keep them in; and my assistant, Wendy Kush, for staying unfazed throughout.

I must also thank Karen Moore for introducing me to my shipmate Harve Bennett and the world of *Star Trek*.

I owc thanks as well to the cast of the original show, who generously put up with my new ideas and graciously let a stranger among them.

And to my *Star Trek VI* writing partner, Denny Martin Flinn, now sadly departed, as well as my able editor and comrade-in-arms on *Star Trek II* and *The Day After*, the late William Dornisch.

Also, the late Ned Tanen, who was "crazy" enough to green-light the film version of *The Seven-Per-Cent Solution*, let me try my hand at *Don Quixote*, and generally stayed more amused than angry when I tried his patience.

Acknowledgments

Thanks as well to Ron Roose, film editor par excellence and the best friend a man could ask for.

And also Tony Bill, Craig Fisher, Michael Phillips, Michael Lerner, Herb Jaffe, Steven-Charles Jaffe, Bob Papazian, John Pomfret, Shep Faison, Siobhan Darrow, Eric Young, Alex Young, Jeff Kleeman, Mark Edmundson, Stanley Jaffe, Gary Lucchesi, Holly Palance, Tom Rosenberg, Max Kennedy, Roger Spottiswoode, Juris Jurjevics, David Foster, Marty and Sandy Davidson, William Kinsolving, Harry and Mary Jane Ufland, Pierce Brosnan, Tim Van Rellim, Mary Jo Slater, Jerry Leider, David Chapman, Bob Shapiro, David Dierks, and Aaron Zidenberg.

And finally, a special thanks to my family, to Rachel, Madeline, and Roxanne, whose unflagging enthusiasm for movies and for life has helped inspire my own—

And to Stephanie, to whom I owe everything.

INDEX

INDEX

INDEX